MY CHINA

In loving memory of Maurice Kwong (1936–2006)

Kylie Kwong

MY CHINA

A Feast for All the Senses

Photography by Simon Griffiths

VIKING
STUDIO
an imprint of
PENGUIN BOOKS

CONTENTS

Introduction

Writing this book has been such a life-enhancing project. In the course of its creation, I have been able to explore subjects I am fascinated by – food, of course, but also family, geography, people, art, jewellery, textiles, markets, landscape, literature, religion and spirituality.

My previous books were essentially food books. While *My China* contains plenty about food, along with eighty new recipes, it also explores the many rich and varied aspects of Chinese and Tibetan culture. As I travelled through ten different cities and provinces, I recorded my impressions and experiences, researched history, and tracked down facts and figures. I sampled extraordinary meals in glamorous Shanghai restaurants and humble bowls of noodles and pickles at the wooden stalls that line the gritty, cobbled walkways of Lhasa. With a cook's love of undiscovered flavours and curiosity about different techniques, I sourced authentic regional recipes, then re-worked and adapted them for cooking at home, inevitably putting a personal spin on them. Much of my cooking style has evolved from living in Australia, where we have access to some of the world's finest, freshest produce, including seafood from pristine waters, a bountiful range of Asian fruits, vegetables and herbs, free-range poultry and organically raised beef.

During my travels in China, I met some intriguing characters, many of whom generously shared their life stories. Although I don't speak Cantonese or Mandarin, I was warmly welcomed everywhere. In fact, my sign language was often greeted with much smiling and laughter, which helped to break the ice. And, in some instances, my very foreignness seemed to free people to open up in a way they wouldn't otherwise have done.

Having been lucky enough to visit China several times now, leading culinary tours with World Expeditions, as well as spending many months researching and filming for my television series, I know I will always return. It is such a vast and diverse country, and there are so many places and peoples I have yet to encounter. I long to visit the extraordinary Hakka settlements of Fujian, in southern China, where whole villages live communally within a single fortified citadel; I also want to see the birthplace of Confucius and to climb the Daoist holy mountain of Tai Shan, both in the northeastern province of Shandong.

From a personal point of view, I am keen to return to cement the bonds forged with the people of the Kwong ancestral village in southern China. This is the birthplace of my great-grandfather, Kwong Sue Duk, who came to Australia during the gold rush, acquiring along the way four Chinese wives, with whom he produced twenty-four children, thus creating the largest Chinese family in Australian immigration history – my family. In my ancestral village there grows a magnificent tree that is several hundred years old. It has an almighty thick trunk, which is firmly embedded in the earth through a network of gnarly roots, and branches that extend far into the sky, reaching proudly and fiercely in all directions. I am one of the branches of this family tree.

My father's parents were born in Australia, while my mother's parents migrated from China to Australia in the mid-1930s, initially settling in Darwin, where my mum was born. My dad was born in Sydney and first met my mum when he was 14 and she was 9, after her family moved there. Each Sunday her parents would play cards and mah-jong in the city, near Chinatown and Surry Hills. It was always a family outing and, while the adults were occupied, the children would play in the streets with other children from the neighbourhood, my dad among them. Mum's family then moved to a suburb further away, so she and Dad did not meet again until some five years later, when their paths crossed at the monthly Chinese dance evenings in the city that my mum went to with her older sisters. As they got to know each other again, they soon became inseparable.

My two brothers and I were born in Sydney, and our everyday life was outwardly very Australian. However, in keeping with the extended family concept that is so central to Chinese culture, both grandmothers lived with us at different times during our childhoods. Their presence reinforced our links with our Chinese heritage, and we followed many traditional customs at home, including ancestor worship to show respect for those who preceded us.

Having finally located the ancestral village on my father's side, we were stunned to learn subsequently that my mother's ancestral village, Chao Xi Cun, was less than 20 kilometres away. Given that my parents had met in Australia and never even been to China, at first we thought this was an amazing coincidence, but we later discovered that many Chinese migrated from this same part of Guangdong province in search of better prospects overseas.

I have since visited my mum's ancestral village three times. Unlike in my dad's ancestral village, none of her descendants lives there any more, but paying my respects to our ancestors is always central to my visits. The haunting yet enchanting brick house built by my goong goong (my mother's father) still stands in the village, and is well cared for by one of the neighbours. Uninhabited and virtually untouched since he left, the house feels like a museum: his modestly furnished bedroom contains a small wooden-framed four-poster bed, and there are incense holders and family altars throughout. Ranged against a wall are rows of rustic claypots that I like to think may once have been used for storing Goong Goong's famous pickled vegetables. In the kitchen, the old-fashioned wood-fired stove with two holes for wok cooking is in excellent condition, and a wooden tray holds a selection of beautiful deep-red, black and brown chopsticks, burnished by many years of use. According to the neighbour who looks after the house, these chopsticks belonged to my grandfather, and on my first visit, she sweetly offered them to me, so that I could present my mother with her father's chopsticks upon my return home.

Like my great-grandfather, Kwong Sue Duk, I was born hungry for opportunity and adventure. I am Australian–Chinese: born and raised in Sydney, but shaped by Chinese culture and sensibilities. Throughout my life I have always asked the question, 'Am I really Australian or am I more Chinese?'

While I was researching and writing this book, my search for the answer to this question assumed greater significance and became more poignant when my family received some devastating news: my father was dying of cancer.

Typically, he insisted that we all got on with our lives. So, while spending as much time as I could with the family, I continued to visit China and to write this book – but my journey became as much an emotional one as a physical one. In a strange sort of way, re-establishing the connections with my father's ancestral village, the very source of his being, made me feel able to cope with his terminal illness more adequately and calmly. In Tibet, this ancient culture's enlightened views on life and death subtly prepared me for the difficult times which lay ahead. Through learning about the traditional Tibetan sky-burial ceremony, I came to accept the plight of my father's physical body and began to look forward to helping him prepare emotionally and spiritually for his ultimate journey – into the afterlife. My father died in July 2006, and my perspective on everything shifted in a profound way.

So, as much as this is a book about the experience of travelling – the contemplation of cities that are vast in scale and villages that are as remote and strange as anything Westerners are ever likely to encounter – it is also a book that tries to describe another kind of journey, one that unknots the complex mesh of heritage, family, identity, culture, memory and connection, the sort of journey that enriches lives, regardless of where we came from, or where we now find ourselves.

With its rich collection of stories, recipes and photographs, *My China* will, I hope, inspire dreamers to travel, and travellers to experience China and Tibet with a greater depth of appreciation.

TIBETAN PLATEAU
Yellow River
Yangtze River
LHASA
Sera Monastery
Drepung Monastery
Ganden Monastery
Yamdrok-Tso
Panda Breeding Center
CHENGDU
Le Shan Buddha
Tiger Leaping Gorge
Lijiang
N
100 KM

MY CHINA
Great Wall
BEIJING
Yellow River
XI'AN
Terracotta Army
Big Goose Pagoda
Yangtze River
SHANGHAI
Wuzhen
HANGZHOU
Dragon Well tea plantations
Guilin
Yangshuo
Li River
GUANGZHOU
HONG KONG
Toishan
Kwong ancestral village

Guangdong: Going Home

GUANGDONG: GOING HOME

Today represents the culmination of a dream: I am returning to the clan village, the first family member to visit our ancestral home in ninety years.

As a 29th-generation Kwong, I have long dreamt of visiting the Kwong ancestral village in China, where my great-grandfather was born in 1853. A dedicated practitioner of Traditional Chinese Medicine, Kwong Sue Duk was lured to Australia in 1875 by the promise of gold. Over the years he travelled many times between China and Australia as he forged business connections and secured a future for his family. His descendants now number around 1200 and span five generations, and I am honoured to be a part of what is possibly the largest Chinese family tree in Australia. I've always felt inspired by the story of his life, and have often wondered whether I owe my drive and sense of adventure to him.

Thanks to my uncle and aunt, who started researching our family history more than thirty years ago, and months of effort from World Expeditions liaising with local authorities, Wong Nai Hang, Kwong Sue Duk's home village, is finally found. It lies in the countryside outside Toishan, a big and modern city in Guangdong province, about three hours' drive southwest from Guangzhou (Canton). *Wong Nai Hang* translates as 'Yellow Mud Ditch', a reflection of the village's fertile soil, but it's also known a little more auspiciously as 'The Good Luck and Peace Village'.

And now, after all this planning and preparing, here I am being driven down a dirt road through the fields towards Wong Nai Hang, a scattered group of elderly, square-sided houses shaded by huge old trees. I get out and begin walking along the white-pebbled track leading to the Kwong family's ancestral village – the feeling is primal. I find out later that the path was pebbled in my honour.

As I make my way through the village, it buzzes with life: mottled chickens peck at the ground, twitchy-eared dogs sniff the air and stare at us; farmers steer water buffalo through the lush, green rice paddies; worn and weathered wooden wheelbarrows lie by the sides of the fields; ducks glide through the murky waters, and waddle in and out of their coops; and pigs run wild and generally make a nuisance of themselves. Some of the villagers, clad in thin polyester floral-patterned shirts and knee-length pants, stand in the doorways of their houses, looking on and wondering what all the commotion is about. I notice one tiny little boy who looks about five or so – he seems shy and withdrawn, but is unbearably sweet . . . a little angel. All the women look out for him, protect him, fuss over him. It makes me remember how shy I used to be when I was little.

When I finally arrive at the top of a small hill, there stands Kwong Sue Duk's home – I can't believe it! Over 130 years old, infused with tradition and ritual, the house is built of mud bricks and wooden beams, and earthy, musty smells permeate the air. The building comes from a China I have only ever before seen on the television screen

An ancient, spreading tree and a red-painted sign mark the entrance to the Kwong ancestral village

PREVIOUS PAGE: Fields surrounding the village

or in books. A patina of dark brownish-black and deep sea-green mould covers the narrow, densely layered bricks – I run my fingers over the walls, hoping to 'feel' a little bit of my great-grandfather's spirit. Old wooden lids and baskets sit in what must once have been the living room but is now a safe haven for chickens. On the wall is the Kwong family seal – I am overwhelmed by the feeling that I really belong somewhere. I am thrilled; my heart is pounding with emotion, and I cannot recall the last time I smiled this much.

Warned of my visit in advance, a group of villagers is waiting for me and within a few moments we are talking through an interpreter as if we have known each other for ever – they treat me like I am their child, their sister, their aunt. With their high-pitched vocal tone and rather blunt, down-to-earth manner, Chinese people can be quite a noisy bunch . . . and at this moment I don't know who is louder, the chooks or the villagers! I'm surrounded by a lot of squawking as I am affectionately dragged toward the porch of my great-grandfather's house, in preparation for the ritual of thanks to my ancestors.

Posing for a family photo

OPPOSITE: The kitchen in Kwong Sue Duk's house

Qing Ming

A Chinese tradition firmly upheld by the Kwong family is 'The Essence of Qing Ming' – that is, the celebration of the spirit of love and respect within a family, and this extends to a special remembrance of our ancestors. For those of us still living, this tradition gives a reassuring sense of where we came from and who we are in the world, and binds the family together. Buddhist beliefs and Confucian teachings hold that when the ancestral spirits are happy and know that their descendants are thinking well of them, they will continue to be close to the family and work for its good fortune. The associated rituals usually consist of offerings to ancestors to provide for their welfare in the afterlife. Necessities and luxuries, such as favourite foods, wine, paper notes of 'spirit money', and even models of houses and cars, are placed on the family altar in bowls or burned in front of the altar.

Two important festivals of the lunar calendar revolve around ancestor worship: Qing Ming, in the third month (around April); and the Souls' Month, which spans the seventh lunar month (about August). I have vivid childhood memories of the trips we would make to Sydney's Rookwood Cemetery at these times, to pay our respects to my mother's father and mother. Dad would switch the radio off, we three children would cease our bickering and Mum would stop chatting to Dad. Before we even got out of the car, wafts of Chinese joss sticks consumed the air; ornate altars adorned many graves, and on them were placed offerings to the spirits of the dead – flickering candles, smoking incense, bowls of oranges and apples, even the odd chicken. I remember dancing in and out of the rows of gravestones with my cousins, legs and shins tickled by tall flowers and stray weeds. I was always moved by the sight of my mother with her sisters and brothers, conscientiously weeding, sweeping and dusting their parents' graves. These days would always end with everyone sharing food at an enormous and chaotic family meal.

賜福

The ancestor shrine is inside Kwong Sue Duk's house.

A wobbly old card table holds bowls filled with food: a white-cooked chicken, still with head, neck and feet; one unpeeled orange; a juicy, fat strip of roasted pork, complete with crackling (I suspect Kwong Sue Duk would have loved that!); and small bowls variously filled with tomatoes, stir-fried potatoes and some cauliflower cooked with salted radish. It occurs to me that, even in the context of ceremonies, the Chinese are *always* thinking of balance and harmony of flavour, texture and ingredient. One of my relatives is saying something to me in Chinese, and is becoming more and more insistent. After a lot of kerfuffle, I work out that tradition demands I add a sweet to the table for good luck – and to impart sweetness to the afterlife. I look around desperately at my friends and we all rummage in our bags until, finally, a mint is retrieved . . . phew!

Three tiny plastic red cups, similar to ones you might find in a doll's house, are placed in a row in front of the food, along with three sets of matching chopsticks. Another relative pours wine into the three cups and then lights a wad of joss sticks, which area wonderful magenta colour with camel-coloured tips – exactly the same as the ones our family used to light at Rookwood Cemetery in Sydney. Following instructions, I hold the incense between my palms and bow forward three times. I then hand back the joss sticks and proceed to pour the wine, one cup at a time, onto the ground in front of the table; the cups are promptly refilled and repositioned, before the ritual is repeated. Next I light a wad of paper money, which is left to burn itself out on the ground, and bow a final three times.

To complete the ritual, we all stand back as a box of red firecrackers is lit, and everyone shrieks and runs for cover as they let off an almighty bang and a blinding cloud of smoke. For me, these firecrackers unleash a flood of memories of Chinese New Year celebrations marked by captivating lion dances and the distinct beat of the drums. The Chinese enjoyment of noise, fuss, big crowds, bright lights and loud colours is all to do with driving away bad luck and evil spirits; silence, gloom and white are always associated with loneliness and death.

Stir-Fried Potato with Lup Cheong and Green Chilli

2 large potatoes, peeled
1 medium carrot, peeled
2 tablespoons peanut oil
5 cm (2 in) piece ginger, cut into thin strips
1 teaspoon sea salt
2 lup cheong (Chinese dried sausage) or rindless
bacon rashers, finely sliced
2 tablespoons shao hsing wine
1 teaspoon brown sugar
2 tablespoons brown rice vinegar
2 tablespoons light soy sauce
1 large green chilli, finely sliced lengthways
1 teaspoon sesame oil
¼ cup water

Cut potatoes lengthways into 5 mm (¼ in) slices, then into 7 cm (2¾ in) strips. Use a vegetable peeler to shave carrot into ribbons, then cut into fine strips.

Heat peanut oil in a hot wok until surface seems to shimmer slightly. Add potatoes, ginger and salt and stir-fry for about 2 minutes, or until the potatoes are lightly browned. Add sausage or bacon and stir-fry for 2 minutes.

Add shao hsing wine and sugar and stir-fry for a further 2 minutes. Stir in carrot and remaining ingredients and stir-fry for about 6 minutes or until potatoes are just tender. Serve immediately.

Serves 4–6 as part of a shared meal

Stir-Fried Cauliflower with Salted Radish

1 small cauliflower – about 1 kg (2 lb)
2 tablespoons peanut oil
5 cm (2 in) piece ginger, cut into thin strips
100 g (3½ oz) lup yook (Chinese dried pork)
or rindless bacon rashers, finely sliced
75 g (2½ oz) salted radish, finely sliced
¼ cup shao hsing wine
2 tablespoons light soy sauce
½ cup water
1 tablespoon brown rice vinegar
1 teaspoon sesame oil
1 tablespoon coriander (cilantro) leaves

Cut cauliflower into florets – you should have about 500 g (1 lb).

Heat peanut oil in a hot wok until surface seems to shimmer slightly. Add ginger, lup yook or bacon and salted radish and stir-fry for 2 minutes. Add cauliflower and stir-fry for 2 minutes.

Pour in shao hsing wine and soy sauce and simmer, covered, for 2 minutes. Add water and simmer, covered, for 3 minutes. Stir in vinegar and sesame oil and simmer, covered, for a further minute. Sprinkle with coriander and serve immediately.

Serves 4–6 as part of a shared meal

Yanrou
HONDA
迅恒 电话:5611008
车行
粤J
TL079
AAA

文明经营户
中国电信

The ritual is over and it's time to move outside of Kwong Sue Duk's home to a perch overlooking the fields, where I'm going to cook lunch for the crowd of villagers and relatives around me. There could be no better spot to do it than here, in the middle of a rice paddy in rural China. My translator tells me that, in fact, few Kwongs still live in the village today, but one of them – who I immediately think of as an 'uncle' – stokes the fire for me, and I have to do a double-take because he looks so much like my eldest brother, Paul.

We had scoured the local markets that morning for the freshest vegetables, including yellow garlic chives, wonderfully crunchy lotus roots and shiny purple eggplants; live baby fish and snappy little crabs; large red chillies and small green chillies . . . As usual, I was in a food frenzy and, as usual, I bought far too much.

I make up the recipes as I go along. I am on such a high, I am talking very quickly and I feel as if my mind is about to explode with ideas – I don't know who to smile at next. As the flames roar into life under what seems like the world's biggest and hottest wok, and with the temperature climbing as the sun rises in the sky, it is sultry, sweaty and smoky. In the background are timeless scenes of paddy fields tended by workers wearing traditional bamboo hats, while closer to me old men sit around the fire flashing gold-toothed smiles and smoking rather interesting-looking cigarettes.

The village women are enchanting. Although we first met just hours ago, I feel as if we have known each other for years, and we easily slip into a harmonious and efficient 'working bee'. Squatting on their haunches, three of the women wash and wipe dishes, while the fourth goes up and down the path to the well, filling and carrying two pails on each trip. I am struck by the women's energy and zest for life. These villagers are very fit: they live simply, eat only fresh food and, as farmers, work very hard in tune with the seasons. Despite having so few of those essentials we take for granted (there's no piped gas, running water or electricity in the village), they have such spirit – their eyes dance, they laugh all the time, they are responsive and seem to live in the moment . . . I say to myself, *This is what living is all about.*

I look around once again at my ancestral village, taking in just how genuine and untouched it all is. Even my well-travelled friend Kathy can't believe how 'pure' this village feels. During our two-hour walk, we see no signs of tourism and few intrusions of the modern world – another reason the experience is so uplifting.

I think we should all experience such places, to help us understand the true nature of life, and to put things in perspective. Being here, and seeing people with so little living obviously fulfilling lives, is a humbling experience when so much of our time is spent unhappily striving for the next thing, rather than enjoying what we have and living in the present.

Shopping at the markets in Toishan

PREVIOUS PAGE: At the local corner shop

As I cook over an open flame in this remote village, I feel so at home.

My mind begins to wander. *So this is where the old man came from, this is what his family life was all about. What incredible courage on his part, firstly to want for more than this simple existence and, secondly, to venture out of this corner of the world and sail to faraway Australia.*

A million questions come to mind – how I wish that Kwong Sue Duk was here right now to answer them. I would ask him what prompted him to embark on such a momentous journey; what was going through his mind and what lay in his soul at the time; I want to know where he got his pioneering spirit from, and I wonder whether my sense of adventure can be traced back to him.

Imagine what it would have been like for him . . . What inspired a 25-year-old man to leave all he had ever known: did he see Australia in a newspaper, did he hear about it in the local township, did he dream about distant lands, did he talk with his friends about opportunities overseas? What was his experience like growing up in this tiny, simple village? Was it a happy one? What were his parents like? Did he have a good relationship with them? What was their reaction when he announced his departure? What were his parents' dreams, what made them tick, what made them happy? Where was he educated – where did his intelligence, entrepreneurial spirit and business sense come from? Where, what, how, why, when?

I would give almost anything to have had just one conversation with my great-grandfather about his thoughts, his feelings, his views . . . I feel he and I would have had a great rapport. I never even got the chance to meet my grandfathers: by the time I was born, both had already passed on. I always felt sad about this when I was growing up as I had heard so much about them: their crazy characters, their passions, their particular ways – my maternal grandfather Goong Goong's famous homemade pickles, my paternal grandfather's excellent musical talent.

By returning to Kwong Sue Duk's ancestral village, this gap is somehow filled for me, even though a thousand questions race through my mind, and my thirst for knowledge about the patriarchs of our family is eased. I am very interested in understanding the 'male consciousness' in my family, and in learning more about the character and personality traits of my ancestors. I come away from the village with an inner peace I have not known before. I feel as though I have a deeper understanding of myself – I have gained more insight into why I am the person I am, and why I do the thingsI do. I feel sure that Kwong Sue Duk would be thrilled to see all of us connecting and living our lives in the same enthusiastic fashion as he lived his own. I guess he is here in spirit . . .

Cooking lunch outdoors

OPPOSITE & PREVIOUS PAGE: Timeless scenes of everyday life in Kwong Sue Duk's ancestral village

18厘米
广东

I have promised to take everyone out for dinner tonight.

We leave the village late in the afternoon and drive to our hotel in Toishan. Virtually the whole village is turning up at the hotel restaurant at 6 p.m., and before we know what has hit us, two busloads of people arrive, all racing over to greet me. What a welcome – there is just so much chattering, giggling and good cheer that, once again, I feel bowled over by the generosity of spirit and sheer vitality of these people. One elderly woman comes up and stands very close to my face and, as she tightly grasps my hands, she speaks in quick-fire Cantonese. My translator tells me she is recounting anecdotes about the great 'old man', and I yearn to be able to talk to her directly and share her spontaneous excitement.

We spend a great evening together: there are speeches; children running around everywhere; people of all ages, appearances, sizes and shapes. I sit back, shaking my head in amazement and disbelief. What an extraordinary family to belong to – so diverse, layered and textured and so, so loving.

Among my newly discovered relatives is Kwan Miao Juan, a beautiful, serene woman whose grandfather was Kwong Sue Duk's brother. Kwan and I develop an instant rapport and over the course of two days, she becomes my new best friend. She and I do not leave each other's side: we walk though the village holding hands like two young girls, we sit near each other when eating and, like a mother with a newborn child, she can't take her eyes off me. Her steady gaze follows me everywhere: she laughs at everything I say, gives me the 'thumbs up' every time I dish up a new creation from that brilliant wok my uncle has fired up for me, and watches me take my last mouthful of food at the dinner table, just so she can quickly fill my bowl again!

The strange thing is that Kwan does not speak English, and I certainly can't speak Cantonese, yet we communicate our feelings and thoughts to each other so clearly and deeply. It's amazing how much information can be transferred through touch, by smiling and all our other facial expressions, and through the aura that surrounds us. I am almost pleased that we are forced to exchange on this level, for its intensity and purity.

Meeting and greeting relatives

OPPOSITE: Sharing lunch

OVERLEAF: Kwong family banquet in Toishan

囍

The next day, back in the village, we chomp, cook and cackle our way through the day – I laugh until my face and belly ache.

Drawing inspiration from the produce, the land, the country and the life of these people, I surrender to the flow and conjure up several new recipes based on China's great reserve of hearty, unpretentious peasant cooking. I take enormous pleasure in cooking my versions of various traditional dishes: stir-fried eggplant with red chillies; fresh rice noodles with bean sprouts and ginger; stir-fried mushrooms with ginger and garlic; a pickled vegetable salad that I like to think of as a Chinese coleslaw (see page 429); and, of course, some of the fantastic hot and sour cucumber salad (see page 361) that seems to be everywhere in China. The villagers clearly enjoy them – and go wild when I serve up an enormous bowl of squid cooked in oyster sauce and vinegar.

A few of the women also teach me some wonderful new dishes. We had bought a pumpkin at the market that morning, thinking it would look good in some photos. Well, not for long – one of the women has other ideas! She takes the pumpkin from me, deftly removes the skin with a small sharp knife, finely chops it up, then motions me to throw it into the hot wok, along with a dash of peanut oil, some ginger, a splash of shao hsing wine, a sprinkle of sugar and then, the star of the show, salted black beans. YUM! I now proudly have a version of this dish on my restaurant menu back in Sydney – 'Billy Kwong's Stir-fried Organic Pumpkin with Ginger and Black Beans'.

We'd also noticed a basket of tiny silvery sardine-like fish glinting in the market and just had to buy some. One of the villagers notices me looking at them with a bemused expression: *What will I do with these?* But no sooner has this thought entered my mind than the women are motioning me toward the wok. They fill it with plenty of oil for deep-frying, watching and waiting for the tell-tale shimmer to indicate that the oil is ready before gently lowering in the fish. They let the fish sizzle and swirl in the hot oil until they are brown and crunchy, then carefully remove them and drain off the oil. Into the wok go some sugar, a dash of vinegar and generous splashes of both dark and light soy sauce to infuse and caramelise for a few moments before being poured onto the fish. Needless to say, it is all swiftly devoured.

Stir-Fried Eggplant with Red Chillies

400 g (13 oz) Japanese eggplants (aubergines)
3 tablespoons peanut oil
5 cm (2 in) piece ginger, finely sliced
3 garlic cloves, roughly crushed
¼ cup shao hsing wine
1 tablespoon brown sugar
2 tablespoons brown rice vinegar
1 tablespoon oyster sauce
1 teaspoon sesame oil
1 large red chilli, finely sliced lengthways

Remove stems from eggplants and cut into 1 cm (½ in) slices on the diagonal.

Heat 2 tablespoons of the peanut oil in a hot wok until surface seems to shimmer slightly. Add eggplant and stir-fry for about 2½ minutes, being careful not to let it burn.

Add remaining peanut oil to wok with ginger and garlic and stir-fry for 1 minute. Add shao hsing wine and sugar and stir-fry for 1 minute. Add remaining ingredients and stir-fry for a further minute. Serve immediately.

Serves 4–6 as part of a shared meal

Stir-Fried Rice Noodles with Bean Sprouts and Ginger

500 g (1 lb) fresh rice noodle sheets
2 tablespoons peanut oil
3 tablespoons light soy sauce
1 teaspoon brown sugar
1 cup fresh bean sprouts
1 teaspoon sesame oil
1 large red chilli, finely sliced – optional

Cut the noodles into 2.5 cm (1 in) strips and carefully separate them.

Heat peanut oil in a hot wok until surface seems to shimmer slightly. Add soy sauce and sugar and simmer for 10 seconds. Add noodles and stir-fry for 1 minute.

Stir in bean sprouts and sesame oil and stir-fry a further 2–3 minutes or until noodles are hot and just cooked through. Serve immediately, garnished with chilli if desired.

Serves 4–6 as part of a shared meal

Stir-Fried Squid with Oyster Sauce and Vinegar

300 g (10 oz) cleaned squid, including tentacles
2 tablespoons peanut oil
5 cm (2 in) piece ginger, cut into thin strips
2 spring onions (scallions), trimmed and cut into 5 cm (2 in) lengths
2 tablespoons shao hsing wine
1 tablespoon oyster sauce
1 teaspoon brown rice vinegar
1 teaspoon brown sugar
½ teaspoon sesame oil

Cut squid bodies down the centre so they will open out flat, then cut into strips about 7 cm (2¾ in) × 2 cm (1 in).

Heat peanut oil in a hot wok until surface seems to shimmer slightly, then add ginger, squid strips and tentacles and stir-fry for 2 minutes. Add remaining ingredients and stir-fry for a further minute. Serve immediately.

Serves 4–6 as part of a shared meal

Stir-Fried Pumpkin with Black Beans and Ginger

500 g (1 lb) pumpkin, peeled, quartered and de-seeded
2 tablespoons peanut oil
5 cm (2 in) piece ginger, finely chopped
1 tablespoon salted black beans
¼ cup shao hsing wine
2 teaspoons brown sugar
¼ cup water
1 tablespoon brown rice vinegar
1 tablespoon light soy sauce
1 teaspoon sesame oil

Cut pumpkin into slices about 7 cm (2¾ in) long and 5 mm (¼ in) thick. Heat peanut oil in a hot wok until surface seems to shimmer slightly, then add pumpkin and ginger and stir-fry for about 2 minutes or until pumpkin is lightly browned.

Add black beans and stir-fry for 1 minute. Add shao hsing wine and sugar and stir-fry for 1 minute. Pour in water and stir-fry for 2 minutes. Add remaining ingredients and stir-fry for a further 2 minutes. Serve immediately.

Serves 4–6 as part of a shared meal

Deep-Fried Whole Sardines Caramelised in Soy Sauce and Sugar

300 g (10 oz) whole sardines, gutted and scaled
2 tablespoons plain (all-purpose) flour
2 cups vegetable oil for deep-frying
¼ cup shao hsing wine
1 tablespoon dark soy sauce
1 tablespoon light soy sauce
2 teaspoons brown sugar
½ teaspoon brown rice vinegar

Toss sardines in flour to coat lightly, shaking off any excess. Heat oil in a hot wok until surface seems to shimmer slightly, then carefully add half the sardines and deep-fry for 2 minutes. Using a slotted spoon, gently remove fish from wok and drain on kitchen paper. Repeat process with remaining sardines. Carefully pour oil out of wok and wipe clean with kitchen paper.

Place remaining ingredients in cleaned wok and cook over medium heat for about 3 minutes or until slightly caramelised. Return fish to wok, gently spooning sauce over sardines. Serve immediately.

Serves 4–6 as part of a shared meal

ENMIN YINHANG

Stir-Fried Asian Mushrooms with Ginger and Garlic

3 tablespoons peanut oil
2.5 cm (1 in) piece ginger, finely sliced
3 garlic cloves, crushed
1 teaspoon sea salt
100 g (3½ oz) fresh shiitake mushrooms, stems discarded and caps halved
150 g (5 oz) oyster mushrooms, stems trimmed
½ cup shao hsing wine
2 teaspoons brown sugar
2 teaspoons light soy sauce
1 teaspoon brown rice vinegar
½ teaspoon sesame oil
100 g (3½ oz) enoki mushrooms
1 tablespoon water

Heat peanut oil in a hot wok until surface seems to shimmer slightly. Add ginger, garlic and salt and stir-fry for 10 seconds. Add shiitake and oyster mushrooms and stir-fry for 30 seconds.

Add shao hsing wine and stir-fry for 20 seconds. Add sugar, soy sauce, vinegar and sesame oil and stir-fry for 1 minute. Add enoki mushrooms and water and stir-fry for a further minute or until mushrooms are just tender. Serve immediately.

Serves 4–6 as part of a shared meal

Stir-Fried Choy Sum with Garlic

1 bunch choy sum
2 tablespoons peanut oil
1 teaspoon sea salt
3 garlic cloves, roughly crushed
2 tablespoons shao hsing wine
2 tablespoons water
½ teaspoon sesame oil

Trim choy sum and wash thoroughly.

Heat peanut oil in a hot wok until surface seems to shimmer slightly. Add salt and garlic and stir-fry for 10 seconds. Add bok choy and stir-fry for 1½ minutes.

Add shao hsing wine and stir-fry for 30 seconds. Add water and stir-fry for a further 30 seconds or until leaves are just tender. Stir in sesame oil and serve immediately.

Serves 4–6 as part of a shared meal

Any other Chinese greens, such as bok choy or gai lan, would also work well in this simple stir-fry.

生抽王
SOY

Sadly, the time comes to pack up and leave.

Our farewells are accompanied by much hugging, and Kwan and her son help me carry all my bits and pieces to the bus. As we walk down the track, one of the villagers roars up beside me on his motorbike. Looking at me with a cheeky smile, he points to me and then back to his bike. The next thing I know I am perched on the back of his Suzuki, charging through the village at quite a speed. I laugh helplessly as we pass a blur of houses, chook pens, pig pens and duck ponds, with the rest of the villagers waving and cheering us on. As our bus pulls out, we wave the family goodbye and drive at a snail's pace over my beloved white-pebbled track. I fall back in my seat, smiling and speechless. I can't wait to call my family in Australia and tell them of my experiences – of the path freshly pebbled for my visit, of my uncle's wok and, especially, I can't wait to tell them how deliriously happy I feel to be a part of this enchanting, extraordinary and energetic village family.

Farewelling the villagers

PREVIOUS PAGE: The stove in a village house

Yangshuo and the Li River

YANGSHUO AND THE LI RIVER

电
肉
行
26日

知
招 标
28日交
一楼

We leave Guangzhou and fly on to the province of Guangxi for the next part of our Chinese odyssey.

Situated to the west of Guangdong province, Guangxi is in China's humid, subtropical southwest. One of its main cities is Guilin, famous throughout China for its astoundingly beautiful landscape of weathered limestone (karst) pinnacles that everywhere spear skywards out of the surrounding pancake-flat countryside. Add an appealing patchwork of bright-green rice fields, muddy country roads and tiny villages, not to mention a languid 65-kilometre cruise down the Li River through the idyllic scenery between Guilin and the market town of Yangshuo, and this really is one of those rare 'see it to believe it' places.

Our two-hour flight from Guangzhou takes us to ultra-modern Liangjiang international airport, some 30 kilometres west of Guilin. The airport building is designed to resemble the head of a ram, a highly revered beast in China, with the left and right wings of the airport representing the two horns. I am fascinated by the symbolism that runs through Chinese culture: the ram symbolises all that is strong, virile and male, and the Chinese word for ram – *yang* – sounds exactly like the 'yang' in yin and yang, which represents the male principle of the universe. Chinese symbolism makes much use of this kind of word-play: for instance, because 'fish' and 'surplus' are pronounced the same way, you often see fish decorations on houses, intended to encourage a surplus of good things for the family within. It also explains why goldfish (which sounds like 'gold surplus' in Chinese) are so popular here, both in paintings and as pets – some pet markets in China sell nothing else.

Outside the airport, we hop into a waiting bus and speed all the way to the small but vibrant highway town of Yangshuo, passing roadside vendors perched alongside massive baskets of oranges. As the landscape becomes more dramatic, we stare out of the bus window at the sheer pinnacles rising some 300 metres above the plain – here squeezed together like a forest of tall grey spires, over there a solitary, humpbacked outcrop standing alone in the fields, its sides dotted with vegetation.

One hour into our trip, the rocky towers fade to distant silhouettes, replaced by not nearly as attractive, man-made buildings. As more and more signs of human civilisation become apparent, we find ourselves in a completely different world. Unlike the buzzing metropolis of Guangzhou, Yangshuo is a small rural municipality, a popular backpacker destination crowded with overseas travellers; there are street vendors everywhere and market stalls on every corner. A sort of carnival atmosphere prevails – one never-ending celebration, or so it seems. For many travellers, Yangshuo makes a great pit stop, a place to catch their breath after many months on the road, somewhere that encourages relaxation.

Our bus, struggling with the weight of our luggage, comes to an abrupt halt just before the main street of Yangshuo, where our hotel is situated. Some hasty words are exchanged with our driver and a road official (there are a lot of 'officials' in China, or at least people dressed in uniform), then the bus screeches loudly as the driver executes an

PREVIOUS PAGE: The distinctive scenery around Yangshuo

林饭店
BAMBOO HOUSE
INN 竹林饭店
CAFE
住宿
NO. 23GUI HUA ROAD
WEST STREET
桂花路23号 TEL: (86) 773-8823222
B.B.Q
烧吧 中餐厅
庆玲旅馆
有房
阳朔县旅游咨询服务中心
蟠桃商店

impatient and anger-fuelled U-turn. Scratching our heads, we wonder what all the commotion is about. Our guide, Scott, explains: because he is not a local guide from Yangshuo but comes from a different province, we are emphatically *not* allowed to enter the street – instead, we must lug our heavy bags ourselves. All through the trip we come across incidents like this, when China's hidden but all-pervasive bureaucracy unexpectedly rears its head – though, to be fair, this time the locals are only trying to protect their own livelihoods.

Begrudgingly hopping off the bus, we stand like rabbits caught in the headlights, in what feels like one of the world's most dangerous streets – bikes, cars, scooters, trucks and lorries all seem to be heading straight for us. If there are road rules, very little heed is paid to them – it just seems as if the biggest vehicle has priority, and everything else has to do its best to get out of the way. What's more, car horns sound incessantly.

Our quarters for the night are meant to be in the Paradise Hotel, famed for hosting political leaders on official tours, Bill Clinton included. However, due to a bungle, our first night sees us residing in the New Centre Hotel, a rather quaint place in a back street. Replete with traditional dark-wood panelling, whirring ceiling fans and marble floors, it feels comfortable enough, and we unpack our bags and take stock. Our introduction to Yangshuo has been accompanied by a measure of unease and disillusionment. But over the coming days and weeks, as we venture deeper into China, we realise that the only thing to do is just 'let it all go'. Little mishaps and stuff-ups are quite the norm for foreigners travelling through China: first, there is the language barrier; second, the Chinese sometimes have different priorities and standards; and third, in a small town like Yangshuo, life just does as it does, there is no hurry and no rush. All quite refreshing, actually. We resign ourselves to the situation and shrug our shoulders. Our mantra becomes, *Oh well, that's China for you* . . . The gift of travel – new experiences.

Unpacked, hungry and eager, we hit the cobblestone pavement.

Our first stop is at Linda's restaurant, Cloud 9. Linda is a local, born and bred in Yangshuo, and as our stay progresses, I realise we have really fallen on our feet in finding her. She is ever so smart and cluey, 'in' with all the locals, and is forever pointing us in the right direction and introducing us to the best people.

Yangshuo is justly famous for its breathtaking landscape, but not especially for its food. It was, after all, just a small market town in a notoriously poor, rural area of China before the tourists arrived. As many of the tourists are Western backpackers, it's not surprising that Yangshuo's bustling main thoroughfare of West Street (Xi Jie) is packed with rather ordinary restaurants serving dreadful, MSG-laden imitations of Chinese cuisine and bad versions of Italian and German dishes. But even so, with its lush fields and rivers, Yangshuo is a good place to enjoy hearty, rustic southern Chinese home cooking, if you know

The tranquil backstreets of Yangshuo

母儀天下

where to look. Some of West Street's restaurants prove to be real gems, and we also find fresh, authentic and flavoursome food – steamed bread buns, brisket stock-based soup and sticky-rice parcels – sold on the street from 6 a.m.: all part of the staple breakfast for this part of China.

Against this backdrop, Linda's restaurant is clearly one of these gems, and fast becomes our sanctuary. One of the first things she serves us is a spicy cucumber salad, and I soon become obsessed with this dish, a version of which seems to be offered in almost every restaurant in China. In response to my enthusiasm, Linda tells me how it's made: 'Take a fresh cucumber and slice it in half lengthways. Deseed the cucumber with a small spoon, so you are left with cucumber "canoes". Slice these into irregular shapes, salt and sugar them. Allow to stand for 30 minutes, then drain off water. Add soy sauce, vinegar and fresh chillies. Serve sprinkled with Sichuan pepper and salt.' Apparently, in China, the whole cucumber is generally given a whack with the flat of a cleaver before it is roughly chopped – this shattering allows the flavours to penetrate.

Next a local speciality, beer-braised carp, arrives at our table. Hmmm, I think to myself, this will be interesting . . . Yangshuo is adjacent to the Li River, where much of the local fish is caught. The sheer volume of traffic carried by the river, all day every day, means that sightseeing cruises downstream from Guilin can take up to six hours, the boats jammed together like a parody of some inner-city main road, churning up the river bed. I struggle with the thought that the fish in front of us is most likely taken from this same river. Coming from Australia, I am naturally influenced by my upbringing and have been spoilt by the wonderfully fresh and wholesome ingredients so easily available there. Here in China, I am learning and observing so much about my food heritage, but – despite my Chinese background – I can't help seeing many things through my 'Australian eyes'.

I find the river carp has a dirty, muddy flavour and, irritatingly, is filled with many bones. (However, when I make the dish back in Australia, with a fish sourced from sparkling, unpolluted waters, it is an absolute winner, a fine example of the balancing of diverse flavours, textures and ingredients so characteristic of Chinese cuisine.) Soon forgetting my initial disappointment with this dish, I suddenly realise how interesting I am finding this trip: contrasting and comparing the whole time, all part of the beauty and fascination of travelling.

A spicy aroma snaps my awareness back to lunch, and I marvel at a sizzling plate of stir-fried eggplant bathed in Linda's homemade chilli sauce. Prepared like this, eggplant is exquisite – its silky, purple skin enclosing velvety, piping-hot flesh, and with that unmistakable, smoky wok-seared quality. The secret ingredient, though, is Linda's lip-smackingly luscious homemade chilli sauce – note to self: must get *that* recipe from my new friend! I persuade her to part with a bottle, which I stash in my day-pack alongside my wallet and camera and, throughout our stay in Yangshuo, we find ourselves smothering everything with Linda's heavenly creation.

Preparing and sharing a meal at Cloud 9 restaurant in Yangshuo

Stir-Fried Eggplant with Linda's Homemade Chilli Sauce

6 Japanese eggplants (aubergines)
1 teaspoon sea salt
2 tablespoons peanut oil
½ teaspoon Sichuan pepper and salt

Linda's chilli sauce
½ cup peanut oil
6 large red chillies, roughly chopped
10 garlic cloves, roughly chopped
7 cm (2¾ in) piece ginger, roughly chopped
1 tablespoon light soy sauce
1 tablespoon chopped coriander (cilantro) leaves and stems

First, make the chilli sauce. Heat oil in a wok until surface seems to shimmer slightly. Add chillies, garlic and ginger and stir constantly over medium heat for 5 minutes. Reduce heat to low and cook, still stirring, for a further 5 minutes. Stir through soy sauce and coriander. The chilli sauce can be used straightaway, or allowed to cool and then stored in an airtight container in the fridge for up to 1 week.

Cut eggplant into 2.5 cm (1 in) slices on the diagonal, then sprinkle both sides with salt and spread on a tray in one layer. Set aside for 1 hour.

Rinse eggplant in a colander under cold running water. Drain and pat dry with kitchen paper.

Heat peanut oil in a wok until surface seems to shimmer slightly. Add eggplant and stir-fry over high heat for 3 minutes. Reduce heat to low and stir-fry for a further 3 minutes.

Add 2 tablespoons chilli sauce and stir-fry for 1 minute. Serve immediately, sprinkled with Sichuan pepper and salt.

Serves 4–6 as part of a shared meal

You only need a couple of tablespoons of Linda's homemade chilli sauce in this recipe, but the rest will keep for at least a week in the refrigerator, and is great for adding a kick to stir-fries.

Beer-Braised Whole Fish

1 × 750 g (1 lb 8 oz) whole fish, scaled, cleaned and gutted
4 cups vegetable oil for deep-frying
¼ cup plain (all-purpose) flour
2 tablespoons peanut oil
5 cm (2 in) piece ginger, finely sliced
3 garlic cloves, finely sliced
1 large green chilli, deseeded and sliced
1 large red chilli, deseeded and sliced
3 spring onions (scallions), trimmed and cut into 5 cm (2 in) lengths
1 medium tomato, roughly chopped
2 tablespoons brown sugar
3 tablespoons light soy sauce
1 cup beer
3 tablespoons brown rice vinegar

Pat fish dry with kitchen paper and place on a chopping board. With a sharp knife, make three diagonal slits into one side of the fish, then turn over and repeat on the other side.

Heat vegetable oil in a hot wok until surface seems to shimmer slightly. Lightly coat fish with flour, shaking off any excess. Carefully lower fish into wok so it is completely covered by the oil and fry for 1 minute, then turn fish and fry for a further minute. Using a spatula, gently remove fish from wok and drain on kitchen paper. Carefully pour oil out of wok and wipe clean with kitchen paper.

Heat peanut oil in cleaned wok until surface seems to shimmer slightly. Add ginger, garlic, chillies and spring onions and stir-fry for 1 minute. Add tomato and stir-fry for 1 minute. Add sugar and allow to caramelise for 1 minute, then add soy sauce and cook for 30 seconds. Add beer and vinegar, bring to the boil, then reduce heat and simmer for 1 minute. Gently lower fish into the beer sauce and braise gently, ladling the sauce over the fish, for 3 minutes. Carefully remove fish and place on serving platter. Pour over the sauce and serve immediately.

Serves 4–6 as part of a shared meal

Suitable fish for this recipe include snapper, bream, halibut, ocean perch or sea bass.

I decide to walk off lunch by exploring West Street, which is lined with shops stocking a range of arts and crafts from all over China.

My eye is caught by intensely rich and electric tones of orange, lime green and burnt dusty red. Among the hundreds of market stalls lining West Street is an inviting place overflowing with ornate, hand-dyed and embroidered tablecloths and serviettes. I scamper over and purchase one in every colour – I have a penchant for fabrics and textures and layers, and this stall has my name written all over it. Too late, I remember my friend Helena Pan's advice: 'Remember, KK, travel light, my dear.' Hmmm, my version of 'light' is rapidly becoming heavy and abundant.

Feeling refreshed and ready for another adventure, later in the afternoon we are escorted by Linda to the eye-opening Farmers' Market – not recommended for the weak-stomached! I am first struck by the beautiful shafts of sunlight filtering into the vast central area of the market hall. I am transfixed, as if viewing some great work of art.

But the moment passes. As our eyes adjust, we see live chickens, ducks and pigeons squawking, squealing and screeching hysterically – I guess I might do the same if I were confined to a tiny cage with twenty or so members of my family!

Oblivious to us odd-looking foreigners with our cameras and backpacks, local Chinese obsessively sort through the cages, prodding and poking, seeking the prize bird. Other stallholders go about their daily business: some are squatting on the dirt floor chopping up animal gizzards and guts; one man is diligently picking over a bucket filled with snails, while another tries his hardest to sell us fresh pig's intestines. 'Ahhh . . . errrr . . . not today, thank you,' I blurt out.

Before we can gather our senses, we find ourselves in what appears to be a 'dead poultry' section of the market. A sickly smell permeates the air, and I hold my hand up to my nose and mouth as we pass freshly slain birds arranged neatly in rows, their feet sticking straight up in the air, their necks hanging lifelessly over table edges . . . I remind myself that this isn't a part of the world where people have their food presented neatly at the supermarket or butcher, but one where they raise their own livestock and live alongside it. Their attitude towards their animals wholly lacks our romanticism; here it's all just food – though this can of course be unsettling to Westerners.

We are hugely relieved to walk into the fruit and vegetable section of the market. More familiar, and less confronting sights settle our nerves and our bellies: amazing thick plaits of fresh lotus root; bright orange, elongated pumpkins; flourishing clumps of oyster mushrooms pulled straight out of the earth; plump bundles of what initially appears to be white asparagus, but is actually fresh, finger-shaped 'water bamboo' shoots. As in every market in Asia, there are mountains of chillies of all descriptions – fresh red, fresh green, dried large and medium, fiery hot small ones and pounded chilli pastes. I caress the velvety black cloud ear fungus, so called for its ear-like shape. Never before have I seen it so wild-looking and abundant; you could almost use it as a soft, comforting pillow.

Yangshuo Farmers' Market

净 含 量: 50kg
级 别: 一级
通过ISO9002

My attention is caught by huge hessian sacks of different types of sugar. They make a stunning display: caramel-coloured sugar granules, mounds of refined white and dark brown sugar, cascades of yellow rock sugar crystals, and blocks of brown sugar resembling candy bars. I cook dishes in my head while running my fingers through each sack: I would use the rock sugar in my red-braising stock, the caramel sugar when making dressings, the white sugar for sprinkling over steamed snapper with ginger and spring onions, I would, I would, I would . . . *This* is what I treasure about fresh food markets – the range of ingredients on offer each day. That moment creates the menu for you; the produce dictates, you do not. It's all just so stimulating.

I am in raptures over the extensive display of dried spices and dried everything. A mound of alluring star anise intoxicates the air, and reams of cassia bark teeter precariously. There are dried lily buds ('golden needles'), every type of dried mushroom imaginable, sun-dried sheets of beancurd reminiscent of a bundle of musical scores, and transparent strips of mung bean noodles ready to be plunged into boiling water and drowned in soy sauce and sesame oil.

Linda dutifully follows me. I point, I purchase, she haggles, she pays; I point, I purchase, she haggles, she pays. This dance goes on for about 45 minutes, as I excitedly plan the evening's meal. Linda has a generous space above her restaurant, an open area with those astonishing limestone pinnacles as a backdrop. She holds Chinese cooking classes there, and so the kitchen is fully equipped with gas burners, running water and plenty of bench space. I am in my element: in an exotic foreign country, in the middle of a truly amazing market, with a local who knows her stuff and knows everyone in town, and I'm scheming about what to eat next!

Strolling through the streets back to Linda's, laden with overflowing bags and with our tummies rumbling in anticipation, we take great interest in the life around us. Everything happens on the streets in China, at ground level: men and women, children and grandparents are squatting in the streets, on the pavements, in the shops, at the restaurants – washing, cleaning, slicing, dicing, pounding, carving, fashioning, singing, selling, massaging, smoking.

We encounter three Chinese women engrossed in a game of cards huddled around a table that somewhat incongruously bears the Coca-Cola logo. Next we chance upon an elderly woman busily tending to her claypot shop, arranging the brown, lidded bowls over the cooker and playing them like a percussionist. Her sweet bobbed hair, the shape of her face and her slight frame all remind me of my dear pau pau (my mother's mother), who lived with us for seven years during my adolescence. Cheekily I lift a lid to have a peek inside one of the pots, only to discover steaming sticky rice topped with lup cheong (Chinese dried sausage) and pickled mustard greens – my pau pau's favourite.

Back at Linda's restaurant, we dump our market treasures and slump in cane chairs to admire the fading Oriental sun and down a few bottles of icy-cold Tsingtao beer.

702小猪膨化料

阳
龙颈河漂流

The sun here really is red in hue – a spectacular but unnerving consequence of the widespread industrial pollution created as China's colossal modernisation program pulls a nation of 1.3 billion people into the twenty-first century.

The cooking frenzy begins. I have several of Linda's charming cooking and waiting staff busy washing, trimming, picking and peeling. I am desperate to cook those amazing white water bamboo shoots – I've never dealt with them before, but after a nibble of a raw one and a squeeze to gauge their texture, and therefore cooking time and method, I settle on stir-frying them with a little peanut oil, soy sauce, sugar, sesame oil and a splash of shao hsing wine. A roast duck is deftly chopped up and I envelop it in red-braising sauce, eliciting wafts of the unbelievable anise and cassia bark aroma that permeates the streets of Yangshuo.

Linda generously provides a live river carp for the meal. I am grateful, yet cautious: my last river carp experience was less than satisfying. But this time we're in for a shock, as Linda proudly fillets the stunned but still live fish in front of us. Realising that this is a sign of her esteem for her honoured guests, done so that we can see for ourselves how fresh the fish for our meal really is, I try to keep the horror off my face. Instead, I pick up a sharp knife, and show her my technique of dispatching fish quickly and painlessly with a quick stab behind the eyes (based on the traditional Japanese method of ikijime spiking). This isn't just sentiment: the method of killing a fish – or any animal, for that matter – directly affects the texture and flavour of its flesh, and a humanely slain fish has a firmer, silkier texture. If a fish suffers trauma when it is killed, not only is its flesh bruised but the stress it endures causes enzymes to be released, giving its flesh a mushy texture.

I long for the day when Linda can visit me in Sydney, and she can explore my culture as I am exploring hers.

Although we have only spent one day and night together, we already feel like one big family. Linda and her husband, William, a very handsome and energetic man, and their young daughter, all make us feel so welcome. They are extremely well-read and worldly people, and there are so many questions we want to ask them – about Chinese culture, politics, education, the class system, and so on. But we satisfy ourselves with the knowledge that we will have many more conversations with them over the next few days, while trekking up the glorious Moon Hill, taking a cruise down the Li River, or walking through the rice paddies.

Linda and William are devoted to their daughter. It is a sad reality that many Chinese would rather have a boy: only the male line can carry the family name into the future, which is such an important part of China's traditional Confucian values; the expense of raising a girl is also lost when she marries away from the home. Furthermore, in rural areas, sons are perceived to be more help in the fields. The One Child policy, which was introduced in 1979 in an attempt to limit the escalating population in a country already struggling to

West Street, Yangshuo's main thoroughfare

find enough food, power and water for its citizens, has only led to further marginalisation of women, as families desperate for a male heir offer baby girls for adoption or worse, and abort female embryos. All of these factors have combined to create a nationwide imbalance in the sexes – even now there are places in China where the absence of little girls is striking. Ironically, this same imbalance might in the end restore some prestige to women, as finding a wife becomes ever more difficult for Chinese men.

As a Chinese chef, I've always felt it was only natural for me to be an avid supporter of Traditional Chinese Medicine in all its forms, including herbal medicine, acupuncture and acupressure. The principles of Chinese cuisine and traditional medicine overlap: not only do they share the same idea of balance – one in taste and texture, the other in bodily health – but there's also a whole tradition of medicinal cookery, creating restorative dishes based around the healing qualities of the ingredients. Various foods are considered to have attributes such as 'warming' (chicken, beef, ginger, chilli) and 'cooling' (fish, seafood, tea), and these in turn affect how energy flows around the body and so complement massage and acupuncture treatments, which also seek to even out and strengthen this flow. In my dream world, I would have a masseuse on hand 24 hours a day (I actually studied massage myself many years ago when I contemplated becoming a homoeopath).

Hearing of my belief in the wisdom of Chinese massage and medicine, the next day Linda affectionately drags me and my friend by the arm through the crowded backstreets of Yangshuo. We are both excited about the promise she has made to introduce us to the renowned Dr Lily Li. 'She is like a magician – the best Chinese doctor in town, and she has healed so many of my friends over the years. She will fix up your aching joints and sore lower backs.'

Dr Lily (pictured left) is beautiful proof of her own medical skills. She has glistening, clear skin, a warm, open face with exquisitely high cheekbones and boasts a trim, athletic physique. I can tell that Dr Lily has integrity, and is a true healer. As gentle and graceful as a gazelle, she presses, prods and palpates all areas of my back and then she skilfully reads my pulses. This is an integral part of traditional diagnosis, with several pulse points on each wrist not only revealing the health of specific organs and their associated energy systems, but also indicating – by their 'deep', 'ropy' or 'slippery' character – the nature of any illness that might be affecting the body. Dr Lily then listens to my breathing, studies my pupils, and carefully twists and turns my body, observing everything about me. Having consulted her colleagues, Dr Lily instructs them to give me a one-hour back and neck massage, and promises to return later to check on my progress. Lying face down on the massage table, I feel safe and warm, loved and looked after.

My friend receives the same concentrated attention. Dr Lily says she can feel some weakness in the lower back area. 'Have you ever had any trauma to this area?' she enquires. 'Yes,' my friend replies, 'you are right on the spot!' Dr Lily then exercises her greatest skill – acupuncture, which works directly on the meridian system, the foundation of Traditional Chinese Medicine.

Traditional Chinese Medicine

To be healthy, the Chinese believe that the whole body has to exist in harmony with a host of physical, mental and spiritual forces. Traditional Chinese Medicine (TCM) approaches illness as a loss of this balance – which can be caused by physical injury, stress, disease or even the weather and climatic conditions – leading to symptoms of illness. Restore the balance, and the patient becomes well again.

At its most basic, this balance is seen as the interaction of yin and yang, the two opposing forces that exist within everything. Good health is to be found at neither extreme, when the body would be either sluggish and cold or frantically overheated, but in the subtle blending of the two. However, diagnosing an illness is not easy, as someone could be sluggish either because they were too yin, which would need one treatment, or because they lacked enough yang energy, which would need another. A Chinese doctor might try to restore the balance using herbs, diet, acupuncture or acupressure and exercise remedies.

Herbal medicine is possibly the oldest form of TCM, dating back over 5000 years. It uses a model that studies the interaction of the five elements – fire, earth, metal, water and wood – which are in turn linked to specific tastes and organs. Herbs (which in TCM encompass plants, minerals and even animal products) are also classed by their 'warming' or 'cooling' effects. For instance, walnuts are warming and sweet, and affect the lung, kidney and large intestine, so they might be used to treat general weakness (the kidneys being seen as the body's major power reserve) or constipation.

Diet is an extension of herbal medicine, and the reason why the Chinese concept of balance in food is so vital: if you balance tastes, colours, textures and the 'warming' or 'cooling' properties of food, you are, quite simply, making sure that you stay well.

Eating healthy food is also one of the few ways you can top up the body's reserves of qi, or life force. We are all born with a supply of qi, which is stored in the organs and flows around the body along channels known as meridians; if the channels become blocked because of trauma, stress or disease, qi will either be unable to reach the affected area, causing a lack of energy, or will pool there, causing stagnation.

Acupuncture works by inserting needles into the meridians at specific, effective points to alter the qi flow in the meridian. This unblocks obstructions and restores an even flow of energy through the body, thus bringing the patient back to health. As some meridians are very long, the point being needled might seem to have no relevance to the problem: lower back pain – a sign of weak kidneys in TCM – might require treatment anywhere along the kidney meridian, which runs down the front of the body between the collarbone and sole of the foot.

The other way to increase qi is by a group of exercises collectively known as qigong, or 'breath skills'. These exercises use a combination of breathing techniques and various postures to encourage qi to flow in particular ways around the body, raising or lowering the qi level as required in each area.
It's perhaps the closest that TCM comes to the mystic, and is indeed closely associated with both Taoist and Buddhist meditation.

We float out of Dr Lily's treatment rooms relaxed and rejuvenated, if a little tender! Dr Lily is our new heroine, and we promise to return the following day for more of her healing light. But for now, sound in body and mind, we resolve to make the most of a glorious day by heading out of town and taking a cruise up the Li River. While it is possible to travel all the way between Yangshuo and Guilin, it's the middle part that holds the pick of the famous peaks (a scene from this stretch of the river even appears on the 20-yuan note), so we plan to make a shorter return trip from the old village and ferry port of Xingping, 20 kilometres upstream from Yangshuo. The cruise will take several hours, I'm told, and my ears prick up when I hear that there is a 'wok on board' – plenty of time, then, for us to cook lunch on the back of the boat. We set out early, and stop at a market on the way to Xingping. I find it so hard to resist such beautifully fresh fruit and vegetables and, as usual, I get teased for buying far too much. I swiftly pounce on freshly blanched mung bean noodle sheets and big clumps of fresh rice noodles sold by the kilo. I buy a soy sauce chicken, which the vendor promptly chops with a cleaver. We come across a woman who makes fresh peanut oil by crushing and grinding freshly roasted peanuts – what a find. What we buy is effectively extra virgin peanut oil, the absolute first pressing: rich in colour, intense in aroma, round and complex in flavour. I want to take her back to my restaurant . . .

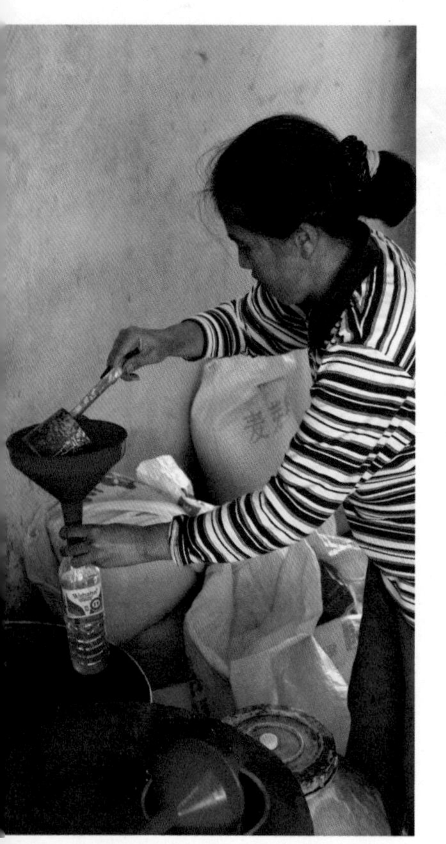

We set off upstream aboard the long, narrow craft towards the towering peaks flanking the river up ahead, the banks peppered with shingle beaches and clumps of graceful bamboo. About 10 minutes into the cruise, the riverboat stops and the boatman points out a particular set of mountains, a grey mass of cliffs with yellow-brown patches resembling galloping horses that have resulted in its name of Jiuma Hua Shan, or Nine Horse Fresco Mountain. The breathtaking scenery continues to unfold over the next hour, each peak with a romantic name and legend explaining it – Eight Immortals Crossing the River Hill, Fish-tail Peak, Penholder Peak, even a Hen-coop Mountain. It all appears to be lifted straight out of traditional Chinese landscape paintings, and is the classic scenery described so eloquently in the works of the great Chinese poets, such as Li Po.

A VIEW OF TIAN MEN SHAN *(Heaven Gate Mountain)*
Mountains split by the river
Two facing peaks
Pale pine trees along the shore
Reflections shattering on the wave-torn rocks
A vague horizon
Distant patches of rosy cloud
Sinking sun, a boat departing
I turn my head
Blued with shadow

Making fresh peanut oil

OPPOSITE: Boats of all kinds ply the Li River, passing dramatic limestone pinnacles

We lie on the bow of the boat, soaking up the intense heat and watching a passing parade of almost-submerged bamboo rafts being poled past.

These rudimentary vessels are little more than a half-dozen sturdy bamboo stems roped together, some with cormorants perched on them, looking like dishevelled figureheads as they stretch out their wings to dry. Trained by the locals to catch fish for them, the birds are allowed to swallow every seventh fish as 'payment'. We all look at one another, shaking our heads in disbelief. We are rendered utterly speechless by the overwhelming natural beauty that surrounds us.

My mind drifts back to the days when I studied Chinese landscape painting at the Julian Ashton Art School in The Rocks, Sydney. My teacher, Mr Lee, was a gentle, philosophical man who took great pride in his lessons. He painted landscapes so easily – the unmistakable karst pinnacles and shallow, flat rivers just seemed to flow from his brush. Observing the subject of his art in real life, I could finally see and appreciate where he and all the other great Chinese artists learned their sense of perspective, so clearly does the naked eye see foreground, middle ground and background in this layered landscape. And just as important are the gaps in between, for Chinese landscape painting embraces the power of suggestion by leaving blank spaces for the viewer's mind to fill in. As with so many aspects of Chinese culture, the philosophy of Taoism underlay much of Mr Lee's teachings – it was all about going with the flow and striving for an effortless, natural quality.

Lunchtime is upon us. The mung bean noodle sheets, all gorgeously slippery and velvety, are tossed with some soy sauce, grated ginger, sesame oil and sugar, just enough to give their reserved flavour a boost. To accompany the soy sauce chicken, I make a refreshing and piquant salad from pomegranate seeds, pomegranate juice, coriander and fresh oranges. I make a light dressing for the rice noodles from finely sliced coriander stems, finely chopped ginger, soy sauce, vinegar, a scant amount of chilli oil, that amazing peanut oil, and a teaspoon of sugar – all the ingredients are simply combined over low heat in a wok, to melt the sugar and allow the flavours to infuse. When drizzled over the freshly cooked rice noodles, this is a near-religious experience. They are too good to be true. Think white, think warm, think silky, think velvety, think fluffy, think . . . heaven. I can't believe I am cooking on a wok-equipped boat while journeying through such a dramatic landscape – I find it hard to wipe the smile from my face. *Oh well, that's China for you.*

Mung Bean Noodle Salad with Soy Sauce and Ginger

100 g (3 ½ oz) dried mung bean noodles

Dressing
1 large red chilli, finely chopped
2.5 cm (1 in) piece ginger, finely chopped
2 tablespoons light soy sauce
1 tablespoon brown sugar
1 tablespoon brown rice vinegar
1 teaspoon sesame oil
3 tablespoons peanut oil

First, make the dressing. Combine all ingredients except peanut oil in a large, heatproof bowl and mix well. Heat peanut oil in a small pan until surface seems to shimmer slightly. Carefully pour hot oil over dressing to 'scald' the chilli and ginger.

Place mung bean noodles in a heatproof bowl, then cover with boiling water and leave for 5 minutes. Drain noodles in a colander, then tip into bowl with dressing. Mix well with tongs and serve.

Serves 4–6 as part of a shared meal

For this fresh and simple noodle salad, you can use flat mung bean noodles (as shown in the photo) or the very fine ones that are also known as bean-thread noodles or vermicelli.

Pomegranate and Orange Salad

1 ripe pomegranate
3 oranges
⅓ cup coriander (cilantro) leaves
2 tablespoons good-quality extra virgin olive oil
1 teaspoon sea salt

Cut pomegranate in half and, holding each half cut-side down over a bowl, tap the skin all over with a wooden spoon. Gradually, the jewel-like seeds will loosen and fall into the bowl. To extract the juice, squeeze each half over the bowl.

Remove skin and pith from oranges and cut flesh into 5 mm (¼ in) slices. Add to bowl with pomegranate seeds and juice. Add remaining ingredients, mix well and serve.

Serves 4–6 as part of a shared meal

Stir-Fried Rice Noodles with Coriander, Ginger and Chilli

500 g (1 lb) fresh rice noodle sheets
¼ cup peanut oil
5 cm (2 in) piece ginger, cut into thin strips
1 bunch coriander (cilantro), stems only, finely sliced
1 large red chilli, finely sliced
2 teaspoons brown sugar
4 tablespoons light soy sauce
1 teaspoon brown rice vinegar

Cut noodle sheets into 5 mm (¼ in) strips and carefully separate them.

Heat oil in a wok until surface seems to shimmer slightly. Add ginger, coriander stems and chilli and stir-fry for 3 minutes. Add noodles and stir-fry for 4 minutes or until they begin to soften.

Add sugar and stir-fry for 30 seconds, then add soy sauce and vinegar and stir-fry for 1 minute. Serve immediately.

Serves 4–6 as part of a shared meal

We alight from the boat a few kilometres from Yangshuo, for an amazing one-hour walk along the banks of the Li River through sand, pebbles, boulders, grass and families of ducks. We all walk separately, tuning into the moment, like a moving meditation. I especially love being so close to the water buffaloes, such gentle giants. Writing this now, I long to experience this walk again, to relive the feeling of surrendering to nature.

Back in Yangshuo, we befriend another enchanting character. Pam Dimond is an Australian who packed up her corporate life several years ago and set herself up in this small highway town among hills, rivers and rice paddies. From her unusually beautiful property – rather like a Chinese–Tuscan villa, if you can imagine such a thing – Pam runs the Yangshuo Cooking School.

We share an unforgettable day together at the famous outdoor Baisha market, which takes place every three days, starting on the first of the month. My first impression of the market is a curious one: out of the corner of my eye, I see what appears to be an al fresco dentist's surgery. In a rickety old dentist's chair sits an old Chinese woman, mouth wide open, with a young dentist busily inspecting her teeth with fingers and sinister-looking metal instruments. *Only in China*, I think . . . *dentistry as a spectator sport*. Elsewhere on our trip, we see city dentists performing their operations right at the front of their modern clinics, with nothing between them and the crowded streets but a pane of glass. Perhaps it's good for business to let people see the dentist doing a painless job, though I imagine the patient's reluctance to lose face by showing any discomfort also plays a part!

The profoundly vibrant Baisha market is one of the area's great cultural experiences. Sacks and sacks of Chinese green and black tea leaves, plastic red tubs piled precariously high with eggs of all kinds – quail, duck, chicken, salted, preserved, fresh. There are rows and rows of the most exquisite fresh young ginger. I run my hands through the ginger in silent disbelief – the roots are light caramel-coloured and unblemished, with wonderful soft-pink highlights. Widely used in Chinese cookery, ginger root helps to moderate the flavour of meat and add a warming, zesty kick to underlying tastes; it's also an important medicinal herb, warming the body against chills and helping to clear toxins from the system.

An elderly woman sits cross-legged on the ground, patiently trimming the fibrous outer layers from her baby bamboo shoots. An ancient but very practical three-wheeled buggy sits behind her, perhaps her only mode of transport . . . I wonder if my goong goong (my mother's father) got around town in one of these? Another old woman, clad in a Mao-style blue jacket, carefully weighs the bunches of Chinese lettuce that are her livelihood. I love the old scales the vendors all seem to use here – no fancy digital machines, just plain, slightly rusty scales. And calculators are replaced with much more aesthetically appealing wooden abacuses, exactly like my goong goong used to use.

With Pam Dimond, of Yangshuo Cooking School

OPPOSITE & OVERLEAF: Lunchtime at Baisha market

阳大排档
正宗啤酒鱼
干锅牛排

The markets in China are such a direct reflection of the society and of the people that frequent them.

Each one is the heart of its community, the central meeting area, the place where everyone goes to buy food, and to eat in the tea houses. When I first visited China, in 1998, I was struck by the charming character of the traditional Chinese tea houses. Back in Sydney, I used this inspiration to shape my very own 'tea house' – my restaurant, Billy Kwong. Today, at Baisha, I encounter the quintessential Chinese tea house. We walk into a vast area about half the size of a football field, every inch of it covered by low round wooden tables and tiny wooden chairs. It's quite a sight to behold because the tables and chairs appear to be child-sized yet are occupied by adults, many of them elderly. Surrounded by scenes and faces that tell a lifetime of stories, I don't know where to turn next; there is so much to absorb in China – it feels like sensory overload at times.

The array of food stalls lining the perimeter of this central eating area is staggering. Each stall is set in its own little booth, with every surface finished in the fabulous big blocky white ceramic tiles that are so particular to China and lend everything a bright and often misleadingly hygienic air. Between them they offer everything: noodle soups and roasted meats; bean curd in all its glorious forms; pickled beans, carrots and pulses; boiled pork dumplings and fried spring onion pancakes. 'It doesn't get any better than this!' I exclaim to my friends.

A group of men huddle cosily around a table, woofing into what looks like a Mongolian hotpot-style meal. One legend traces the origins of this dish right back to the late Song dynasty, when Mongol soldiers were fighting with China north of the Great Wall. The Mongols' military strength lay in using their horses to launch lightning raids; they couldn't allow themselves to be slowed down by carrying any surplus gear and so used their shields as cooking vessels, heating water and braising their food over an open fire.

Overcome by the mouth-watering aroma and the sheer irresistibility of the whole ritual, I rudely and impulsively plonk myself right down beside them. As I lick my lips and rub my belly, the men all dissolve into laughter, and promptly offer me a bowl and some chopsticks as if I am a long-lost friend. A cooking pot of bubbling stock sits in the centre of the table, placed over a naked gas flame, and chopsticks are ferociously dipping in and out. Each of the men has a piping-hot bowl of rice seemingly stuck to their chin, eating their rice in that inimitable – and noisy – shovelling way that the Chinese do. Local styles of hotpot exist all over China, and the meal reminds me of the similar steamboat that my mother used to dish up every Sunday in winter. For me, these sorts of meals embody the pleasures of sharing food. I love the preparation of the stock and the ingredients, and handling all the different vegetables, meats and seafood.

Later, as we stroll around the food stalls, we are besotted by two darling little children who are merrily slurping away on their breakfast of hot noodle soup. Their mother is right beside them, busily filling and shaping dumplings to sell. We are also drawn to the endearing scene of a grandmother chopstick-feeding her grandchild, and behind this, an adoring mother nursing her little baby.

I tell you, all we Chinese do is *eat*! And if we are not eating, we are feeding everyone else around us. According to my mother, from the moment I came into the world, I have always had a 'very good appetite' – and, some thirty years on, I still possess that same insatiable appetite. Among my friends and family I am well known for my tendency to over-cater: if I have four guests for a meal, I cook enough for eight; if I have eight guests, there is enough for sixteen.

I love all the activity and industriousness in China.

Everyone is always doing something: bike-riding, fishing, plucking, massaging, drinking, gambling, cooking, teaching, practising martial arts, and so on. I really admire the way the Chinese use their hands and their fingers with such deftness, patience, precision and craftsmanship.

All the Chinese chefs I have worked with have had these qualities, and my Chinese masseuse of many years exercises the same instinctive sensitivity. In fact, this idea of refined skill acquired through long practice is such a recognised trait in China that there is even a word for it, *gongfu*. There's no exact translation of *gongfu* in English, but somebody who has it would be described as a master of their profession. This is where our word 'kung fu' comes from, but the Chinese meaning is not confined to the martial arts.

At dawn the next day we meet Mei, a beautiful Chinese woman who teaches tai chi and yoga. The setting is idyllic as the sun rises behind the rocky outcrops. Mei is taut, lean and composed; she is a walking advertisement for her art. There are five of us this morning, all attempting to do tai chi on the banks of the Li River, and Mei has her work cut out. Watching Mei doing tai chi in her red silk Mao-style outfit is like watching an elegant bird in full flight – she moves so gracefully and is completely present and focused in the moment.

I am so distracted by all the activity in and alongside the river, however, that I leave the tai chi class midway through and start snapping away with my camera: simple scenes of men and women doing their family laundry in the river, scrubbing blouses and trousers against the rocks, nattering and bantering the whole time. One woman perches herself on a rock in the river, with water lapping at her knees as she scrubs away contentedly. *Well*, I think to myself, *if you have to do a huge load of hand-washing, you may as well do it in such a beautiful setting.*

By 7 a.m., we're more than ready for breakfast. I've found a great café in the main street that does a decent cup of coffee – I swiftly down two espressos and a glass of fresh orange juice. Today Arnie, our warm and obliging local guide, is taking us to a local farming village, where we've been invited to cook lunch in a traditional house. We drive in an open bus and are ambushed by hawkers with postcards, water, soft drinks, wooden toys, you name it. We drive on through incredibly picturesque country, dominated by swathes of lush green paddy fields. *Just like the photos in the books,* I think to myself, *unbelievable*. Traditional mud-brick houses line the bumpy gravel roads, and we notice that none of the houses appear to have windows. They have the openings carved out for windows, but there are no panes of glass in them. Arnie tells us this is typical of the local architecture: 'Good ventilation in the warm months', he proclaims. We pass the famous Moon Hill, a towering mountain pierced by a huge hole shaped like a half-moon. We plan to climb the peak on our return in the late afternoon, when it will be cooler.

My mental image of the farming village we are about to drive into is one of wooden huts and sheds. I picture pigs drinking from troughs, chooks running around everywhere, farmers tending to their crops. But rather a different scene unravels before us. The bitumen road narrows until it becomes a concrete path,so we hop out of our minibus and start to walk into the village. Arnie acquires a motorbike from somewhere and I jump on the back and speed off with him, armed with bags of fresh produce. We pass not wooden huts but sturdy brick-built homes with white-tiled walls, concrete-floored large rooms, and green-painted front doors.

Inside, I am amazed at the simplicity of these homes, which consist of a main living area, a small kitchen with a gas wok rigged up in the middle of the floor, a bathroom and a bedroom upstairs. I begin cooking lunch straightaway, with the help of a sweet, shy man who washes and trims vegetables, peels garlic, and chops some pork that's destined for an omelette. I cook several small dishes, true to the Chinese peasant tradition. This is my preferred way of eating: I love savouring all the little morsels, and it is a healthy way to eat as you tend not to feel bloated and over-full. As usual, we foreigners are warmly welcomed and immediately given water and Chinese tea. Rolls of toilet paper in the living room are proffered as serviettes!

Lunch finished, we make our way back to Moon Hill. The afternoon heat of the sun has faded and we feel ready to take on the rather steep climb. In fact, the 45-minute ascent from the road is not too bad, as there are stone steps most of the way, the path weaving through thick groves of bamboo until we emerge just below the strangely shaped summit. We walk under the 20-metre-high arch, and the view back through it is like something from a fairy-tale, with all these unbelievable peaks soaring out of a patchwork of flat fields spread far below. Magical.

OPPOSITE: Moon Hill, near Yangshuo

PREVIOUS PAGE: Early morning on the Li River

Caramelised Lotus Root

2 tablespoons peanut oil
1 garlic bulb, unpeeled and cut in half crossways
2 garlic cloves, finely sliced
5 cm (2 in) piece ginger, finely sliced
550 g (1 lb 2 oz) fresh lotus root, peeled and cut into 5 mm (¼ in) slices
¼ cup brown sugar
2 tablespoons shao hsing wine
1 tablespoon brown rice vinegar
2 teaspoons light soy sauce
1 large red chilli, finely sliced on the diagonal – optional

Heat oil in a hot wok until surface seems to shimmer slightly. Add garlic, cut-side down, and sear over medium heat for 1 minute. Add sliced garlic and ginger and lotus root and stir-fry for 3 minutes. Add sugar and stir-fry for 2 minutes or until slightly caramelised.

Add shao hsing wine and stir-fry for 1 minute. Lastly, add vinegar and soy sauce and stir-fry for a further minute. Serve immediately, garnished with chilli, if desired.

Serves 4–6 as part of a shared meal

As this is such a simple dish, the crunch and delicate flavour of fresh lotus root is essential. The halved and seared garlic bulb infuses the oil with a subtle garlic flavour, but is not meant to be eaten.

Omelette with Pork and Mint

6 free-range eggs
125 g (4 oz) pork mince (ground pork)
½ cup finely sliced mint leaves
12 fine slices ginger, cut into thin strips
1 teaspoon light soy sauce
1 teaspoon oyster sauce
½ teaspoon brown sugar
½ teaspoon sesame oil
½ cup peanut oil
1 tablespoon oyster sauce, extra

Place all ingredients except peanut oil and extra oyster sauce in a bowl and mix with chopsticks.

Heat peanut oil in a hot wok until surface seems to shimmer slightly. Slowly pour egg mixture into hot oil and cook, without stirring, for 3–4 minutes over medium heat. Using a spatula, turn omelette over and leave to cook for another 2 minutes or until just set.

Carefully lift omelette from wok onto a serving platter and drizzle with extra oyster sauce.

Serves 4–6 as part of a shared meal

Stir-Fried Celery with Pickled Chillies

2 tablespoons peanut oil
5 cm (2 in) piece ginger, cut into thin strips
½ bunch celery, trimmed and finely sliced on the diagonal
4 pickled red chillies
2 tablespoons shao hsing wine
2 tablespoons light soy sauce
2 teaspoons brown sugar
1 teaspoon brown rice vinegar

Heat oil in a hot wok until surface seems to shimmer slightly. Add ginger and stir-fry for 30 seconds. Add celery and stir-fry for 2 minutes. Add chillies and stir-fry for 30 seconds. Add remaining ingredients and stir-fry for a further 30 seconds. Serve immediately.

Serves 4–6 as part of a shared meal

Stir-Fried Bean Sprouts, Snow Peas and Garlic Chives

2 tablespoons peanut oil
1 garlic bulb, unpeeled and cut in half crossways
150 g (5 oz) snow peas (mange tout), trimmed
1 teaspoon sea salt
2 tablespoons shao hsing wine
150 g (5 oz) fresh bean sprouts
1 small handful green or yellow garlic chives,
cut into 5 cm (2 in) lengths
1 teaspoon sesame oil

Heat peanut oil in a hot wok until surface seems to shimmer slightly. Add garlic, cut-side down, and sear over medium heat for 1 minute. Add snow peas and salt and stir-fry for 1 minute. Add shao hsing wine and stir-fry for 1 minute.

Add remaining ingredients and stir-fry for a further minute. Serve immediately.

Serves 4–6 as part of a shared meal

The halved and seared garlic bulb infuses the oil with a subtle garlic flavour, but is not meant to be eaten.

This evening we are heading to a 600-year-old village called Liu Gong, about 25 minutes' drive from Yangshuo.

We have a dinner date in Liu Gong with Malcolm, an Australian-born Chinese who resides in Yangshuo for six months of the year and returns to Australia for the rest of the year. Our paths first crossed when Pam pointed me in the direction of Malcolm's cafés on Yangshuo's main street as the source of that rare commodity in China, good coffee – and we never looked back.

Malcolm also runs an incredibly special restaurant in an extraordinary village setting: situated on the Li River, the Pavilion Restaurant is set inside an ancient two-storey house that's a work of art in itself. Crafted from beautifully fine, rustic bricks, it is furnished with traditional Chinese furniture and antiques, including stunning rosewood chairs, and illuminated by sultry swaying lanterns. Large wooden shutters open onto a crop of lotus leaves, and wafts of fragrant smoke rise from incense and candles, creating a haunting yet serene ambience. Climbing up the antique wooden stairs, we reach the most beautiful private dining area that looks out over the breathtaking Li River in all its stillness. As instructed by Malcolm, we arrive at 5.45 p.m., in time to have an aperitif on the outside terrace, to see the sunset, to watch the limestone pinnacles turn into black silhouettes in minutes, to witness the ducks and geese coming in from the river's edge to roost for the night, and to see bamboo rafts laden with watermelon and other market-fresh produce gliding across the glassy surface of the river. We stand and gaze in awe, smiling contentedly at one another, and shaking our heads in amazement and disbelief at the scene spread out before us.

Before dinner we go for a walk through the village. The fifty or so villagers seem to lead very simple lives: farming their crops, fishing from the river and tending to their animals. The front doors of all the houses are wide open – and behind the doors, families sit glued to blaring television sets. I am struck by this image of two worlds colliding. Outside, in the cobblestoned alleys, men perched atop rickety old wagons wave to herders with wooden crooks – they appear to belong to a very different time and space.

My attention is also caught by the brightly coloured and proudly displayed posters of Chairman Mao that are pasted onto the concrete walls in most of the houses. Although the facts of this historic leader's life are now largely irrelevant to most Chinese – and to a country racing ever further away from his political beliefs – he's remembered and still revered in an abstract way for the immense power and respect he gained during his lifetime. He was also, like these people, born a peasant, and his image serves as a constant reminder that even the poorest Chinese might one day aspire to fame and fortune.

The riverside village of Liu Gong

This makes him especially popular in the rural districts of China's interior, among a population increasingly left behind by the modernisation sweeping through the favoured eastern half of the country.

Back at the restaurant, we sit down to an eagerly anticipated ten-course meal that the chef has created especially for us. Pam has let slip to Malcolm that we are desperate to get our hands on some good-quality wine. And that was all it took for him to raid the secret stash of Margaret River wines in his cellar, and to give instructions for some white wine to be chilled ready for the Aussie visitors! In fact, the Chinese don't usually drink wine at all, so we rarely have the chance on our travels to enjoy a glass of crisp, dry riesling or semillon sauvignon blanc, which seem to go so well with Chinese food. In China, the favoured drink to accompany a meal is beer – usually served warm, since cold drinks are held to be bad for the digestion. First introduced by the Germans in the nineteenth century, beer is now so popular it seems that almost every town has its own brand. In the countryside, we also occasionally come across home-made sticky rice wine, which arrives in plastic jerrycans but tastes quite pleasant, a bit like sake or a sweet sherry. But the drink of choice for partying men is *baijiu*, clear and potent grain spirits – strong enough to make your eyes water.

We sit down to an elegant meal that includes steamed chicken wrapped in bamboo leaves and permeated by the earthy, straw-like scent of bamboo; claypots full of sticky rice flavoured with Chinese duck sausage, ginger and shao hsing wine; and refreshingly simple stir-fried Chinese greens with garlic and soy sauce. Malcolm's unique restaurant is not known to many people. It is not advertised, but has gained quite a following through word-of-mouth, and it does not keep regular hours, opening only for special bookings. Like Malcolm, it is one of a kind. I suspect it is his passion, his hobby, his indulgence. The two cafés are his livelihood and run like a normal business with regular opening hours, but this place is truly special and remains an indelible memory for me.

It is hard saying goodbye to Yangshuo.

With heavy hearts, we farewell our new friends Malcolm, Pam, Linda and William, who have shown us such warmth and fed us so generously with the best of Chinese home cooking. We feel privileged to have glimpsed the slower, more traditional way of life that still exists in the countryside – not to mention Yangshuo's awesome landscape. Now it is time to leave all this and head deeper into China's southwest, to the remote and mountainous province of Yunnan.

Lijiang and Tiger Leaping Gorge

LIJIANG AND TIGER LEAPING GORGE

有

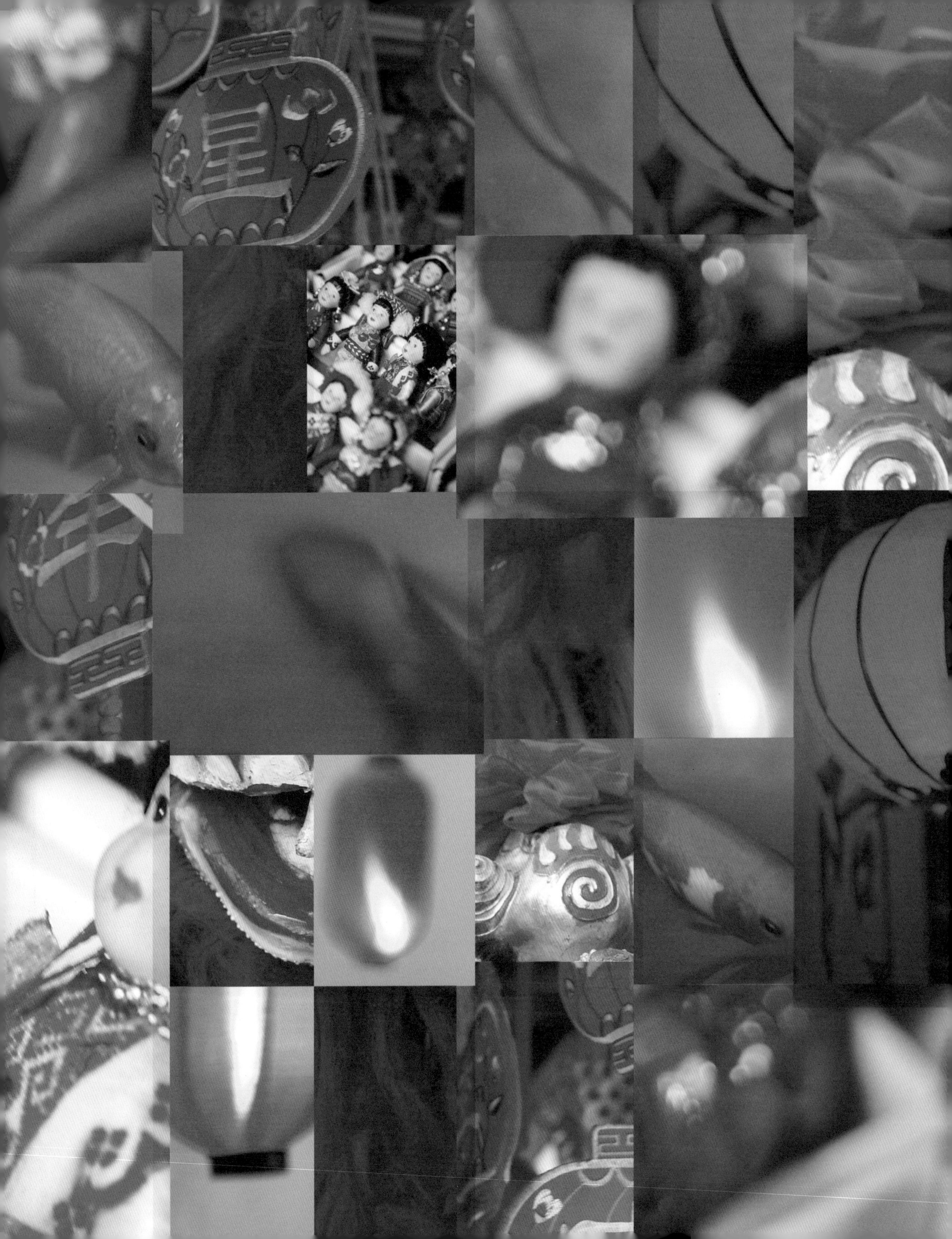
星

地和顺财
如意万事兴

The province of Yunnan occupies a strange place in the Chinese psyche.

Stuck way down in the far southwest of the country and bordering Vietnam, Laos and Myanmar, Yunnan used to be considered a wild backwater, far from eastern China's familiar comforts. But it's also intriguing, with its myriad ethnic 'minority' cultures and famously sunny weather – Yunnan actually means 'south of the clouds'.

There's no one cooking style as such, but there are several famous foods produced here, including the deliciously smoky Yunnan ham, and I grew up hearing about steampot chicken, cooked in a broth gently scented with fragrant medicinal herbs. There's a lovely story attached to Yunnan's best-known dish, 'crossing the bridge' noodles, which is really a local version of the hotpot or steamboat, consisting of a bowl of oily, piping-hot chicken stock to which diners add their own selection of paper-thin meat slices, noodles, vegetables and spices. The tale goes that during the Ming dynasty, a scholar used to study on the far side of a lake in his garden, and because of the great distance from his house, his lunch of noodle soup was always cold by the time it arrived. His wife eventually hit on a solution: she cut the food thinly, poured boiling stock over it, topped it off with a layer of oil to keep the heat in, and carried it over the bridge to her husband, who was delighted to find his lunch perfectly cooked – and hot.

A province of wild parts, Yunnan's most spectacular corner is its mountainous northwest, which adjoins the Tibetan plateau. Here, in a band no more than 150 kilometres across, three of Asia's greatest rivers – the Yangtze, Salween and Mekong – run in deep, parallel valleys separated by serried ranks of towering peaks. And it is here that we are headed, to the town of Lijiang, nestled at the foot of the mighty Yulong Xue Shan, the Jade Dragon Snow Mountain.

Flying into Lijiang airport, we are welcomed very warmly by Joanne, our local guide, who speaks excellent English. It's a 45-minute bus trip into town, and on the way, Joanne tells us all about the local Naxi people, a minority group numbering about 295,000 who took Lijiang as their capital back in the thirteenth century.

Joanne also explains that Lijiang is separated into an old town and a new town. Going by what we can see from the bus window, the new town looks rather dull, resembling the usual urban Chinese landscape of concrete and tiled buildings. But behind the little bump of Lion Hill lies the charming old town of Dayan, a maze of cobbled lanes, carved stone bridges and wooden homes that form the Naxi quarter, which has been a World Heritage site since 1999.

Founded in AD 600, Dayan comprises the largest collection of traditional houses anywhere in China, now carefully restored following a devastating earthquake that struck in February 1996, killing more than 300 people and destroying much of the south of the town. In the aftermath, the government spent a huge amount on rebuilding, and has since encouraged tourism as a way of recouping its costs.

A traditional Naxi house

PREVIOUS PAGE: Black Dragon Pool, Lijiang, looking across to the Jade Dragon Snow Mountain

近
水
楼
餐
厅
福
四
高
有
平
安
餐
厅

You still see many Naxi among Dayan's markets, streets and public squares, but it's clear that they're gradually being pushed away by the town's massive tourist industry, which is almost entirely run by outsiders.

There's no doubt, though, that Dayan is almost poetically beautiful. The streets are threaded with neatly paved canals, and the constant sound of running water creates a calming and fresh atmosphere; the water is extremely clean, which is another pleasant surprise. I buy some goldfish from a man by the side of the canal, then gently release them back into the water to earn merit and luck.

When a group of Naxi women walk past, we are intrigued by their long cotton navy skirts trimmed with white worn with a burgundy-coloured pinafore over a wide-sleeved cotton shirt. They wear blue caps on their heads and Chinese slipper-type shoes on their feet, but it is their blue-and-white shawls that are particularly fascinating, the patterns representing the sun, moon, stars and the eyes of frogs, once an important Naxi deity.

Because the alleys in the old town are so narrow, Dayan is closed to traffic, apart from bicycles, making its labyrinth of cobbled streets very pleasant to explore on foot. Its rickety old stone houses with wooden frames and balconies, and the backstreets lined with eating places, arts and crafts stalls and artisans' workshops, are all criss-crossed by bridges and gushing canals. There are so many different people on the streets, and there is so much life everywhere we look.

All these distractions mean that our 15-minute walk from the bus to our hotel turns into 45 minutes. The Jian Nan Chun Hotel is a traditional building with pagoda-style rooftops, wooden beams and ornately carved and red-painted columns everywhere. A serene Chinese garden occupies the central courtyard, and calligraphic scrolls and porcelain vases adorn the walls. The women behind the front desk are delightfully dressed in traditional Naxi costume. When travelling on a budget in China, you consider yourself lucky if your pillow and bed are not hard as rock, and if the plumbing works. Fortunately, these rooms are great, if rather small.

The colourful sights of Dayan, Lijiang's old town

The Naxi

The Naxi are Tibetan in origin and probably settled the Lijiang area about 2000 years ago. Though coming into conflict with outsiders from time to time – especially the Mongols, when they invaded China in the thirteenth century – they have maintained a good deal of their culture to the present day. The Naxi religion, dongba, is animist but has absorbed a dusting of Chinese beliefs, especially Taoism. Of the host of deities they used to worship, the main survivor is the war god Sanduo, whose statues adorn many temples around Lijiang. The Naxi also have their own writing system, which uses thousands of pictograms to record their scriptures; sadly, its use is dying out and few modern Naxi can read the ancient texts. The Naxi are also renowned for their orchestral music, which, uniquely in China, includes in its repertoire some compositions dating back 1300 years to the court music of the Tang dynasty.

But what really raises eyebrows among other Chinese is that the Naxi are the last ethnic group in China with a matriarchal society. Politically, almost all their chieftains have been men, but in other aspects of life it's the women who rule the roost. Paternity traditionally counted for very little, as all inheritance was traced through the female branch of the family, and women did most of the domestic and agricultural work. Today, these traditions remain strongest in the countryside, though women retain a good deal of community authority and respect even in larger towns and cities.

雲南普洱
中國

Eager to explore Lijiang some more, I soon find myself back in the maze of alleyways.

I come across the sweetest eating house, filled with tiny tables and chairs that are surprisingly comfortable once you bend right down and sit on them. Further along the street, I stand for ages watching a local woman deftly tossing spring onion pancakes, the delicious smells of sizzling onion and cooking dough arousing my appetite. Next door to her, another woman is adding the finishing touches to a hearty noodle soup full of thin white noodles. The eating houses and stalls are so simple, with naked gas flames, Chinese claypots filled with stock and well-used bowls of sugar, salt, MSG and soy sauce.

Lijiang's many Western-style bars and restaurants are a reflection of its status as a major tourist attraction – although, thankfully, this time the town is not as jam-packed as it was on my previous visit several months ago. While Westerners have been coming to Lijiang for years, after the reconstruction the government was also keen to encourage domestic tourism, which they did by promoting the differences between the Naxi and the country's Han Chinese majority. At the time, this was something new; now, the notion of cultural tourism has really taken off in China, with many younger Chinese even beginning to idealise and envy the minority groups, whose lives – from the outside, at least – seem far simpler than their own struggles for financial success and happiness in China's overcrowded and sometimes turbulent eastern cities. All of which means that the streets of Lijiang are often thronged with busloads of Chinese tourists.

An abundance of excellent-quality antique shops call for much personal restraint on my part. They are chock-full of stunning amber jewellery from Tibet, wooden prayer beads, rustic and irregular-shaped wooden bowls, Chinese wooden scales with mother of pearl inlay, ancient cooking implements, traditional bamboo baskets, jade snuff bottles lined with the most exquisite miniature paintings, ancient hand-woven fabrics, gadgets, trinkets, bits of fur and copies of ancient texts. Many are clearly 'new antiques' made for the tourist trade, but they are all so enticing. A pile of worn and character-filled granite mortar and pestles momentarily send me into a buying frenzy until I realise there is simply *no way* I can carry them around in my luggage.

I love the vibrant colours of Chinese textiles and jewellery, and spend about half an hour in a wooden-bead shop, entranced by the spectrum of strands, from striking azure blue, deep burgundy, bright orange and purple to deep sea-green, magenta and pink – a seeming mish-mash of tones, yet somehow they all work together. I also buy three beautiful shawls for their interesting patterning and colour combinations. Later, I come across a little hole-in-the-wall shop that belongs to an old man who sits at his desk all day, hand-stitching cute toys for children. I buy the quirkiest frog-like creature and, although it is only tiny, the level of detail and craftsmanship is astounding.

I come across some amazing scenes: lining one alley is a row of aluminium steamers and boiling pots holding barbecued pork buns, dumplings, Chinese bread and deep-fried gluten sticks – all warming and hearty, and all extremely hard to resist. Lijiang feels like the kind of relaxing place you could retire in. It is so colourful and culturally diverse that you'd never be bored. It is also one of the cleanest places I have been to in China; today, in keeping with the meaning of Yunnan's name, there are glimpses of blue sky to be had – a rarity elsewhere, even on the hottest of days, because of the stifling pollution that hangs over much of the country.

Each morning we begin our day at a quaint eating place called the Well Bistro, a rustic, artsy wooden café with fresh chrysanthemums on the tables, really good coffee and delicious fresh fruit and yoghurt. The Yunnanese are extremely unusual in China for eating dairy products – shunned in most of the rest of the country – and growing coffee, which was successfully introduced during the nineteenth century despite stiff competition from the national beverage, tea. Having sat through one too many bad breakfasts of MSG-laden soups, gloopy dim sum and cold cuts of meat in Chinese hotels, it is especially refreshing to be able to start the day with something really appetising. The young woman who runs the café is very cool. She has a knitted beanie pulled down over her ears, and black hair that perfectly frames her face.

In the evening we enjoy a great dinner in an unusual place called the Monkey Bar. It is situated near our hotel, down one of the many winding alleyways, and only opens for bookings, so you must make a reservation several days beforehand. When they know guests are coming, they make a special trip to the market that day. Entering the restaurant is like walking into an Aladdin's cave: on one side of the tiny dining area is a huge, knobbly rock wall with cascading waterfalls and fish ponds. There are vines and exotic plants hanging everywhere, and the room is furnished with rustic wooden stools, benches and tables, antique lanterns, artwork and colourful cushions. Off to one side of the room is an expanse of solid timber planks: push open the door and you find yourself in a den-like area with a central fire surrounded by piles of cushions and pillows, where many a good time has clearly been had! Pictures of reggae musician Bob Marley adorn the walls.

The food is divine – pure and home-cooked, with none of that tell-tale MSG taint. The dish that stands out for me is the braised pork belly: chunks of shimmering, clean-tasting pork long-braised in dark and light soy sauces, rock sugar and star anise.

During our meal, the restaurant owner's two little girls sit on the sofa beside us, giggling and eating their own delicious dinner, while their father attends to our every need, making us fresh watermelon juice and giving us some of his beautiful green tea to sample. After dinner, he takes us across the alleyway to his other business, an antique store. I really like this man, who is unusual, quirky and arty, with a sharp sense of humour, and an appealing cheekiness. When we leave, he gives me a silver bell engraved with the face of a Buddhist deity.

Lijiang has plenty of relaxing places to eat, drink and watch the world go by

WELL
井卓
餐馆
1996
BISTRO

MONKEY BAR

Braised Pork Belly with Rock Sugar and Soy Sauce

800 g (1lb 10 oz) pork belly, cut into 8 cm (3 in) chunks
4 tablespoons peanut oil
7 cm (2¾ in) piece ginger, finely sliced
½ cup shao hsing wine
3 tablespoons light soy sauce
2 tablespoons dark soy sauce
1 cup yellow rock sugar
4 star anise
5 cups water

To remove any impurities from meat, place pork belly in a large pan or stockpot, cover with cold water and bring to the boil. Simmer for 5 minutes, then drain, discarding water. Rinse pork thoroughly under cold running water and drain well.

Heat oil in a hot wok until surface seems to shimmer slightly. Reduce heat to low, then add pork and fry for about 10 minutes, or until skin is golden and crisp. Carefully remove pork and drain on kitchen paper.

Place pork in a heavy-based saucepan with remaining ingredients. Bring to the boil, then immediately reduce heat to a gentle simmer. Cook, covered, for 50 minutes or until pork is tender. Transfer pork to a serving platter and ladle over sauce.

Serves 4–6 as part of a shared meal

We set out early the next morning, as we are going to walk a stretch of the famous Tiger Leaping Gorge, a two-hour drive north of Lijiang and the scenic highlight of any trip to Yunnan.

Tiger Leaping Gorge is where the mighty Yangtze River – China's longest, at 6400 kilometres – cuts deeply into the foot of a mountain range, through a gorge so narrow at one point that it's said a tiger could leap across the raging water.

Our bus pulls up at Qiaotou, a small township on the main road. We walk into the gorge along a path lined with beautiful pale-grey paving stones, and are overtaken by rickshaws carrying tourists who like to see things without their feet touching the ground! There are men on every corner who guard the gorge and ensure that tourists do not smoke or drop litter – a refreshing sight, actually, as I've found that cleanliness and environmentally sound rubbish disposal are not high priorities in many parts of China I've travelled through.

It's a beautiful day and we welcome the blue sky and devour the clean, fresh air, marvelling at the sight of the stark mountains rising all around us. Again I am filled with wonderment at this incredible country – the diversity of *everything* is rather hard to get your head around at times. You can be in the tiniest, cobblestoned, crowded, hustling and bustling alleyway one minute and then, in just a few hours, you can be alone amid majestic natural landscapes.

Musing on this, we walk around a bend and get our first glimpse of the gorge – wow! The terraced hillside we are on drops steeply down into the rapids, on the other side of which a 3000-metre-high wall of rock rears up sheer and grey, its peaks faintly sprinkled with snow. The river is tucked in shadow as we follow it downstream, the force of its gushing torrent of brown water awe-inspiring as it tears down the narrow chasm. In such a wild setting, with nothing nearby save for a smattering of small villages, it's a testament to nature's raw power.

Sadly all this may soon be tamed, as there are plans to dam the gorge in order to produce hydroelectricity. China desperately needs power for its 1.3 billion citizens and is seeking alternatives to coal, before the whole country vanishes beneath a cloud of smog. Huge wind farms have been set up in the northwest of the country, with hydroelectric dams elsewhere – most famously at the Three Gorges, several thousand kilometres downstream along the Yangtze, near the city of Chongqing. While improving people's

Paths hewn from sheer rock walls wend their way through Tiger Leaping Gorge

lives and reducing pollution are admirable aims, it's still awful to think that where we are walking might one day vanish under water, displacing the local people and sacrificing such dramatic scenery.

Though the full hike through the gorge takes two days, we only have time for a leisurely two-hour walk before returning to Qiaotou. Here we have lunch at a local restaurant, which has many interesting dishes that are new to me. We opt for some slinky rice noodles, a delicious dish of lotus root with shiitake mushrooms, and beautifully crunchy black cloud ear fungus with cucumber, but also can't resist indulging in some more pork, this time stir-fried with gai choy. Next comes a dish of stir-fried Naxi-style chicken with chillies, green peppers and peanuts, and our feast is rounded off by some stunning water chestnuts braised with carrots and dried pork.

I love the kitchen at this local restaurant, and keep sneaking up to the door to peer in at the leaping flames and the fresh produce piled everywhere. The walls are lined with the ubiquitous giant square white tiles, there is a central cooking bench with a wooden frame and a stainless-steel top, and stacks of the distinctively Chinese, brightly painted enamel bowls that border on the kitsch and with which I am slightly obsessed. Standing in the doorway, I watch as a woman swings a cleaver and hacks into a piece of pork bone with all her might. But what really catches my eye is her chopping board – a round of wood about 15 centimetres thick, with a 5-centimetre-deep hollow worn into it from many years of use. I don't know how she manages to chop effectively on such an uneven surface, but she succeeds somehow. To me, this scene speaks volumes about the Chinese capacity to make do with whatever they have.

Stir-Fried Rice Noodles with Black Beans, Chillies and Coriander

500 g (1 lb) fresh rice noodle sheets
¼ cup peanut oil
2 tablespoons salted black beans
⅓ cup finely chopped coriander (cilantro) roots and stems
2 large red chillies, finely chopped
2 tablespoons light soy sauce
1 tablespoon dark soy sauce
1 teaspoon sesame oil

Cut noodle sheets into 1 cm (½ in) strips and carefully separate them.

Heat peanut oil in a hot wok until surface seems to shimmer slightly. Add black beans, coriander and chilli and stir-fry for 1½ minutes, stirring constantly to ensure the black beans do not burn. Toss in rice noodles and stir-fry for 1 minute.

Add remaining ingredients and stir-fry for a further 3 minutes or until noodles are heated through. Serve immediately.

Serves 4–6 as part of a shared meal

Stir-Fried Lotus Root with Fresh Shiitake Mushrooms, Ginger and Carrot

1 medium carrot, peeled
2 tablespoons peanut oil
5 cm (2 in) piece ginger, finely sliced
150 g (5 oz) fresh lotus root, peeled and cut into 1 cm (½ in) slices
100 g (3½ oz) fresh shiitake mushrooms, stems discarded
2 tablespoons shao hsing wine
1 teaspoon brown sugar
1 tablespoon light soy sauce
1 teaspoon brown rice vinegar
½ teaspoon sesame oil

Cut carrot in half lengthways and then into 5 mm (¼ in) slices on the diagonal.

Heat peanut oil in a hot wok until surface seems to shimmer slightly, then add ginger and lotus root and stir-fry for 2 minutes. Add carrots and mushrooms and stir-fry for 1 minute. Add shao hsing wine and sugar and stir-fry for 1 minute. Add remaining ingredients and stir-fry for a further minute. Serve immediately.

Serves 4–6 as part of a shared meal

Fresh lotus root is essential for this simple stir-fry.

Stir-Fried Black Cloud Ear Fungus with Garlic, Chilli and Cucumber

1 small cucumber
2 tablespoons peanut oil
1 garlic bulb, unpeeled and cut in half crossways
5 cm (2 in) piece ginger, cut into thin strips
4 spring onions (scallions), trimmed and cut into 5 cm (2 in) lengths
100 g (3½ oz) fresh black cloud ear fungus
2 tablespoons shao hsing wine
3–4 large red chillies
1 teaspoon brown sugar
3 teaspoons light soy sauce
1 teaspoon brown rice vinegar
½ teaspoon sesame oil

Peel cucumber, cut in half lengthways and then slice on the diagonal.

Heat peanut oil in a hot wok until surface seems to shimmer slightly. Add garlic, cut-side down, and sear over medium heat for 1 minute. Add cucumber, ginger and spring onions and stir-fry for 2 minutes. Add cloud ear fungus, shao hsing wine, chillies and sugar and stir-fry for 1 minute.

Add soy sauce and vinegar and stir-fry for a further 2 minutes. Stir through sesame oil and serve immediately.

Serves 4–6 as part of a shared meal

The halved and seared garlic bulb infuses the oil with a subtle garlic flavour, but is not meant to be eaten.

Stir-fried Pork with Gai Choy

½ bunch gai choy (mustard greens) – about 150 g (5 oz)
2 tablespoons peanut oil
600 g (1 lb 4 oz) pork neck fillet, cut into 5 mm (¼ in) slices
1 tablespoon peanut oil, extra
5 cm (2 in) piece ginger, cut into thin strips
2 garlic cloves, roughly chopped
2 tablespoons shao hsing wine
½ teaspoon brown sugar
2 tablespoons oyster sauce
1 teaspoon sesame oil
1 teaspoon brown rice vinegar
pinch ground white pepper

Trim 5 cm (2 in) from stem ends of gai choy. Wash leaves thoroughly, drain well and slice finely.

Heat peanut oil in a hot wok until surface seems to shimmer slightly. Add half the pork and stir-fry for 30 seconds. Remove pork from wok with a slotted spoon and drain on kitchen paper. Add extra oil to wok with remaining pork and stir-fry for 30 seconds. Return all pork to wok, along with ginger and garlic, and stir-fry for 30 seconds.

Toss in gai choy and stir-fry for a further 30 seconds. Add remaining ingredients except pepper and stir-fry for about 2 minutes or until pork is just tender. Serve immediately, sprinkled with pepper.

Serves 4–6 as part of a shared meal

Naxi-Style Chicken with Chillies, Green Pepper and Peanuts

600 g (1 lb 4 oz) chicken thigh fillets, cut into 1 cm (½ in) cubes
2 tablespoons cornflour (cornstarch)
2 tablespoons shao hsing wine
2 tablespoons peanut oil
10 small dried red chillies
2 tablespoons peanut oil, extra
5 cm (2 in) piece ginger, cut into thin strips
1 green pepper, cut into 1 cm (½ in) squares
1 small cucumber, cut into 1 cm (½ in) squares
1 tablespoon brown sugar
½ cup roasted unsalted peanuts
2 tablespoons light soy sauce
1 tablespoon brown rice vinegar

Combine chicken with cornflour and shao hsing wine in a bowl. Cover, place in refrigerator and leave to marinate for 1 hour.

Place oil and chillies in a cold wok and *then* turn heat to low. Cook for about 1½ minutes or until chillies begin to darken slightly. Using a slotted spoon, immediately remove chillies and drain on kitchen paper.

Leaving chilli-infused oil in wok, turn heat up to high and stir-fry half the chicken for 3 minutes. Remove chicken with a slotted spoon. Add extra oil to wok with remaining chicken and stir-fry for 3 minutes. Return all chicken to wok, along with reserved chillies, ginger, pepper and cucumber, and stir-fry for 1 minute.

Add sugar and stir-fry for 30 seconds. Add remaining ingredients and stir-fry for 30 seconds. Serve immediately.

Serves 4–6 as part of a shared meal

Braised Water Chestnuts with Carrots, Lup Yook and Ginger

1 medium carrot, peeled
1 tablespoon peanut oil
5 cm (2 in) piece ginger, finely sliced
3 garlic cloves, crushed
75 g (2½ oz) lup yook (Chinese dried pork) or rindless bacon rashers, finely sliced
300 g (10 oz) fresh water chestnuts, peeled
1 teaspoon brown sugar
2 tablespoons shao hsing wine
1 tablespoon light soy sauce
1 tablespoon brown rice vinegar

Cut carrot in half lengthways and then into 5 mm (¼ in) slices on the diagonal.

Heat oil in a hot wok until surface seems to shimmer slightly. Add ginger, garlic and lup yook and stir-fry for 1 minute. Add carrot and water chestnuts and stir-fry for 3 minutes.

Add sugar and shao hsing wine and stir-fry for 1 minute. Add soy sauce and vinegar and stir-fry for a further 30 seconds, then serve immediately.

Serves 4–6 as part of a shared meal

You'll need to visit an Asian supermarket to find fresh water chestnuts and lup yook. This recipe relies on the sweet crispness of fresh water chestnuts for its taste and texture, so only attempt this dish when they're available.

On our way back to the old town, we pass golden fields of corn and sunflowers.

I am absolutely amazed when the bus overtakes a huge truck jam-packed with Chinese cabbage – there must be at least 600 cabbages crammed onto that truck. We also pass lines of people by the side of the road selling beautifully fresh, crunchy apples, and we make the bus pull over, so we can buy a basketful. But what should be a simple exchange turns into a major event. All the apple-sellers spot our tourist bus stopping and about a dozen of them descend on us as the bus door opens, mobbing us as we try to clamber out, and exclaiming loudly in Chinese why we should buy their apples above the others. I want to buy a basket from *all* of them, as it is so obvious that they could do with the income. I feel humbled by these roadside apple-sellers, who spend all day struggling to sell their produce, when maybe only a handful of people will stop and buy during the course of a day . . . It is indeed a hard life, and it makes me feel so fortunate for all that I have back home in Australia.

A few kilometres down the road we zoom past a bunch of people selling large baskets of bright-red long chillies. We all ooh and aaahhh, and once again urge the bus driver to slam on the brakes and do a swift reverse – we just *have to buy* a basket of chillies. You just never know what you might come across on the side of the road in rural China!

By now it is about 3 p.m., and we're all snoozing in the bus, in order to muster up energy for some food shopping on the way back home. In homage to the famous Yunnanese dish of 'crossing the bridge' noodles, this evening I plan to cook my Chinese steamboat, half the joy of which lies in buying up big at the markets and then making up the menu as you go along. So on our way home, we take a detour to the produce markets, a 15-minute walk from the old town. These enormous markets are among the best we have experienced so far on our trip in terms of freshness and variety, and are packed with local buyers and sellers. There are men walking around with a recent purchase of slaughtered chickens; noodle makers carrying bamboo baskets laden with all types and sizes of rice noodles; wooden boxes of the earthiest-looking mushrooms, shiitake, oyster, enoki; there are fabulous melons of all descriptions, bitter melon, silk squash, cucumbers, gherkins, prickly melons, hairy melons; there are plump white long radish, and round red radish; tables piled high with iceberg lettuce and Chinese celery. I just let the ingredients guide me,

Lijiang produce markets

and soon we are like packhorses, carrying old rice sacks filled with delicious, fine-smelling food. Next I spot an enamelware stall, where I buy all manner of dishes (small, medium and large), plates, shallow bowls, lidded pots – they'll be perfect for all the marinated raw ingredients.

I also spot a beautiful display of hand-beaten copper pots, woks, buckets and ladles, and can't resist purchasing several items, imagining how wonderful they will look in my restaurant back in Sydney. (In the centre of a large table at Billy Kwong, I now have a copper wok filled with fresh organic ginger, and it looks stunning.)

We are surrounded by artisans: bread and bun makers, a woman shelling and selling fresh soy beans and *only* soy beans, old-fashioned butchers, elderly women sorting through dried chillies, fabric weavers, blacksmiths, mushroom pickers, wool knitters, bead threaders, chestnut roasters, chilli grinders, tofu makers, tea masters. I am like a kid in a lolly shop.

Although there is an abundance of fresh pork and chicken, I give it a wide berth – I just can't deal with raw meat laid out on old wooden slabs in the 30-degree heat . . . Besides, I ordered all the beef, pork and chicken I need for tonight's meal yesterday from The Mill restaurant, just minutes from our hotel. When I am in China, I have a terrible, cheeky habit of overtaking people's kitchens and restaurants. The people at The Mill have obligingly allowed us to use their private room upstairs, so, after our splurge in the markets, we take all our bounty to the restaurant's kitchens, where the chefs assist me with the cleaning and trimming of the vegetables.

I couldn't be happier. We have had the most wonderfully stimulating and mind-opening day, and here I am with a bottle of chilled Chinese beer to hand, preparing and cooking food – washing, peeling, trimming, scoring, marinating, slicing, dicing, chopping, pickling, salting and arranging.

We set the table with tie-dyed tablecloths we bought in Yangshuo – a lime green one with white embroidery and a vibrant orange one.

When I have a steamboat at home I usually place electric woks in the centre of the table, and the homemade stock bubbles away all night, as my guests dip all sorts of ingredients into it. Tonight we don't have electric woks, so we set up charcoal braziers at each end of the table instead. The restaurant manager lights the charcoal for me, then rests ancient claypots over the flame, and I promptly fill the pots with my fragrant and aromatic stock. My stock consists of water, shao hsing wine, salt, ginger, garlic, lemongrass, red onion and spring onions. I always make my stocks light to begin with, knowing that they will thicken and gain character and intensity as the meal progresses. It all makes quite a spectacle, and is the most perfect setting for a steamboat.

There are about twenty dishes on the table. There are separate plates of beef, pork, chicken and squid, the last of which is finely sliced and lightly marinated in salt, sugar, wine, ginger, garlic and spring onions. Side dishes include pickled white radish, pickled cucumber, halved cherry tomatoes, fresh red chillies with soy sauce, pickled mustard greens, gai choy, Chinese cabbage, garlic chives, wads of handmade noodles and fresh silken tofu and, of course, the irresistibly refreshing plates of mint, coriander and bean sprouts.

The Mill's private dining room is a beautiful space lined with traditional Chinese windows framed with ornate woodwork. You can sit comfortably in the deep window seats and stare out at timeless scenes of cobblestones, glowing red lanterns, Naxi people dressed in their distinctive traditional costumes, silhouettes of towering mountain ranges – and feel surrounded by so much culture, history and potential.

Da daaaaarrrrrrr! The table is set and we are ready to begin the epic steamboat. With flames licking the sides of the bubbling claypots and warming the stock, the drama begins. Everyone drops ingredients into all the pots and suddenly the clear, serene stock becomes animated and alive. What I look forward to most when hosting a Chinese steamboat party is the sense of conviviality, the intense social interaction that occurs around the table. Something about this kind of meal pushes people out of their comfort zone: everyone has so much fun and there is always lots of laughter.

The stock becomes richer as time goes by. Toward the end of the meal, in keeping with tradition, noodles and tofu are cooked in the stock to produce an extraordinary broth: to me, this is like a secret, magical potion, a healing elixir of life. Not only is it full of flavour, but it also contains people's energy and joy.

Just as well our hotel is close to The Mill restaurant – we all roll out of there with extremely full, happy bellies. That is another thing I must warn you about in China: be prepared to put on a few extra kilos around the waistline. The food is irresistible and because you are in such exotic places most of the time, you find yourself wanting to try *everything* on offer . . .

A steamboat feast at The Mill restaurant in Lijiang

Chengdu and the Le Shan Buddha

CHENGDU AND THE LESHAN BUDDHA

Between Yunnan and Tibet, Sichuan province feels very different from anywhere else in China.

For a start, its western half is stuck up on the rugged Tibetan plateau and inhabited almost totally by Khampa Tibetans, noted for their colourful dress and independent spirit. Its eastern half comprises a wonderfully fertile, very 'Chinese-looking' bowl of farmland that surrounds the capital of Chengdu, but is cut off from the rest of the country by even more mountains. This isolation has led to many aspects of life in Sichuan evolving in unique ways, including the cuisine: Sichuanese is among the most incredibly spicy, complex, fresh and delicious food you could ever experience, and I simply couldn't come to China without tasting it in its homeland. I also wanted to visit Chengdu's spice market, having seen some sensational photos of it. Last, but not least, Sichuan is also where pandas come from, and we've heard it's possible to visit them just outside Chengdu.

To be honest, our first impression of Chengdu is that it feels like the most overpopulated, oppressive city in China. The pavements are insanely crowded with market stalls, hawkers and pedestrians, and the roads so clogged with traffic that driving anywhere is incredibly frustrating and soul-destroying – so much of our time is spent sitting in traffic jams that are going *nowhere*! But when we insist on abandoning our vehicle and walking, we find ourselves struggling with overwhelming levels of pollution, although we do get there in half the time. Many locals wear surgical masks outdoors and I must say, self-consciousness aside, I am tempted to followed their lead.

Realising it is going to take a while to acclimatise, we settle into our hotel and then make a beeline for the nearest produce markets. Travelling in China, I find myself fixated with the local markets and food streets; aside from being hugely enjoyable in their own right and great places to watch the hustle and bustle of daily life, they also seem to offer a clue as to the essential character of a place. However, we find the Chengdu fresh food markets rather lame and disappointing, full of dubious-looking meats and limp vegetables – perhaps not so surprising, given the city's choking pollution.

But as we explore over the next few days we discover another side to the city. We find that the Sichuanese are a pretty laid-back crowd and that Chengdu, while an entirely modern-looking city, has plenty of spacious parks planted with gingko trees and trellises of wisteria, under which people laze around in bamboo chairs, chewing melon seeds and drinking tea. We begin to notice that there are open-air tea houses everywhere – along canal banks, in temple courtyards, or just filling a vacant patch of pavement. All you have to do is sit down and an attendant appears to take your money and give you a cup of Chinese tea (which gets refilled for free), before leaving you to sit in peace.

On our first evening, we are taken to a local Sichuanese restaurant and, from this point on, our opinion of Chengdu is totally transformed. When I am in a foreign country and cannot speak the language, I make it my duty to case the joint before I order – and I find

Dodging the traffic in Chengdu

PREVIOUS PAGE: The Giant Buddha at Le Shan

Chinese Feeling

that this restaurant is enormous, able to seat hundreds of guests. Weaving in and out of other diners' tables, I grab a waitress and point to dishes I like the look of. This is an accepted way to order in China, and not just for foreign tourists: because of the fanciful names given to many regional dishes, even out-of-town Chinese can be completely baffled by reading a menu and finding names like 'tiger-skin peppers' (scorched green peppers with vinegar and salt) or 'strange-flavour chicken' (chicken with a sour, hot and sweet sesame sauce). Many Chinese restaurants have menus with photos of all the dishes on offer – I now understand why. The menu this evening runs to about fifteen pages, divided into starters, soups, dim sum, wontons and noodles, meat, poultry, beef and game, rice and congee, vegetables, eggs and tofu, house specialities, chef's recommendations . . .

Soon I am in raptures over a starter of fresh soy beans, stir-fried with garlic, chilli and black beans. There is another great dish of braised eggplant drowned in oil, chillies and Sichuan pepper. Next to arrive are sublimely soft rice noodles, served at room temperature in a coil and swimming in a heavenly sauce that must have a hundred ingredients in it. A secret recipe of this particular restaurant, the sauce is a vibrant, deep-orange colour, with a texture that is sort of oily without being indigestible. I suspect it is chilli oil with stock added to it, which 'thins out' the oil content. There is also soy sauce, plenty of ground Sichuan pepper, freshly sliced cucumber and fresh Chinese herbs, plus a dollop of a mouth-watering dark blackish-brown paste on top, made from caramelising garlic and chillies with sugar and salt. Having only eaten rice noodles hot before, whether in a soup, stir-fried or steamed, to have them served like this is a completely new experience. A feeding frenzy erupts at our table as the waitresses bring plate after plate of weird and wonderful delicacies, all with flavours that are *so different* from any of the Chinese food we are familiar with in the West. Add to this the now-familiar spicy heat, and we quickly realise that Sichuanese cuisine is one for the brave-hearted, thick-skinned, iron-stomached and gastronomically courageous – and we can't wait to try more of it!

Stir-Fried Fresh Soy Beans with Garlic, Ginger and Black Beans

2 tablespoons peanut oil
5 cm (2 in) piece ginger, finely chopped
4 garlic cloves, finely chopped
1 tablespoon salted black beans
400 g (13 oz) fresh or frozen soy beans
2 tablespoons shao hsing wine
1 teaspoon brown sugar
2 teaspoons oyster sauce
2 teaspoons light soy sauce
1 cup water
1 large red chilli, finely sliced lengthways
1 teaspoon sesame oil

Heat peanut oil in a hot wok until surface seems to shimmer slightly. Add ginger, garlic and black beans and stir-fry for 30 seconds. Add soy beans and stir-fry for 2 minutes, stirring constantly to ensure nothing catches and burns.

Add shao hsing wine and stir-fry for 30 seconds. Add sugar, 1 teaspoon of the oyster sauce and 1 teaspoon of the soy sauce and stir-fry a further 30 seconds.

Pour in water and simmer, uncovered, for about 7 minutes or until soy beans are just cooked but still have some 'bite'. Lastly, add remaining oyster sauce and soy sauce with the chilli and sesame oil. Serve immediately.

Serves 4–6 as a snack or as part of a shared meal

Braised Eggplant with Sichuan Pepper and Chilli

3 medium eggplants (aubergines), peeled
2 tablespoons sea salt
4 tablespoons peanut oil
5 cm (2 in) piece ginger, finely sliced
3 garlic cloves, crushed
2 tablespoons brown sugar
½ cup shao hsing wine
½ cup water
2 tablespoons light soy sauce
1 tablespoon brown rice vinegar
1 large red chilli, finely chopped
pinch Sichuan pepper and salt
1 large red chilli, finely sliced on the diagonal – optional

Cut eggplants into 2 cm (¾ in) slices, then cut each slice into 2.5 (1 in) cm strips. Sprinkle eggplant strips with salt and place on a tray in a single layer. Set aside for 1 hour.

Rinse eggplant in a colander under cold running water, then drain and pat dry with kitchen paper.

Heat peanut oil in a hot wok until surface seems to shimmer slightly. Add ginger, garlic and eggplant and stir-fry for 3 minutes. Add sugar and allow to caramelise for 30 seconds, stirring constantly to prevent eggplant from burning. Add shao hsing wine and stir-fry for 1 minute, then add water and cook for 2 minutes.

Add soy sauce, vinegar and chopped chilli and stir-fry for 2 minutes. Serve immediately, sprinkled with Sichuan pepper and salt, and garnished with sliced chilli, if desired.

Serves 4–6 as part of a shared meal

Fresh Rice Noodles with Sichuan Chilli Oil and Cucumber

500 g (1 lb) fresh rice noodle sheets
1 small cucumber, cut into thin strips
pinch Sichuan pepper and salt

Sichuan chilli oil
2 teaspoons dried chilli flakes
½ cup vegetable oil
2 tablespoons light soy sauce
2 tablespoons hot water
1 tablespoon brown rice vinegar
2 teaspoons brown sugar

First, make the chilli oil. Place chilli flakes in a heatproof bowl. Heat oil in a small heavy-based pan until surface seems to shimmer slightly. Carefully pour hot oil over chilli in bowl to release heat and flavour. Stir to combine and set aside, uncovered, for 30 minutes. Strain cooled oil mixture through a fine sieve set over a bowl and discard chilli flakes remaining in sieve. Stir remaining ingredients into oil.

Cut noodle sheets into 2.5 cm (1 in) strips and carefully separate them. Place noodles in a shallow heatproof bowl that will fit inside a steamer basket. Place bowl inside steamer and position over a deep saucepan or wok of boiling water and steam, covered, for 5–6 minutes or until noodles are hot.

Carefully transfer noodles to a serving platter and pour over Sichuan chilli oil, garnish with cucumber and sprinkle with Sichuan pepper and salt.

Serves 4–6 as part of a shared meal

This is my simplified version of the dish we had in Chengdu that changed my view of rice noodles forever. There we enjoyed super-fresh rice noodles – literally cooked that morning and served to us at room temperature, deliciously wobbly and slinky. For the most part, the rice noodles found on the shelves of Chinese supermarkets in the West are at least a day old and require some form of initial cooking (whether it be steaming or stir-frying or plunging into soup), as a hard rice noodle is rather unpleasant.

Next day, we visit the Sichuan Advanced Cooking School, and are thrilled to find a campus with a wonderful spirit and dynamism.

We arrive during the students' lunch break, and instead of the usual harsh sounds of Chinese propaganda, the loudspeakers are pumping out the boppy, energising tunes of Mando-pop, modern Chinese rock music. This creates a sense of fun and freedom that we are more acutely aware of since in much of China, there is a looming sense that 'big Communist brother is watching you'.

We are taken on a brief tour of the cooking school, where students are taught restaurant- and hotel-standard Chinese cuisine and kitchen skills. Long white corridors lead into rooms filled with wok-stalls, gas stoves, stainless-steel benches, pots, pans and all sorts of cooking equipment. A very well-spoken Sichuanese woman with a lovely, encouraging manner takes us through several famous Sichuanese dishes, including ma po tofu. She tells us how this deliciously spicy dish – whose name means 'pock-marked mother's tofu' – was invented here in Chengdu in the 1860s by a widow who ran a stall selling tofu in chilli and black bean sauce to local tradesmen. Her cooking was so good that her customers helped her to open a proper restaurant, which is still going – in fact, there's a chain of them spread across the city. I just love these stories, and the way they illustrate the level of engagement of ordinary people with their country's rich history and culture. The smells of spices and cooking and the sense of pride and tradition here are a world away from an awful cooking college I once visited in Guangzhou, which taught its students to cook lemon chicken using custard powder and lemon essence!

Five minutes' walk from the college is a typical Sichuanese supermarket. I've been here before and I urge my friends to come along for the experience. The sheer scale of the place is staggering, with everything sold in bulk: there are whole sections of different brands of packaged cooking staples like tea, soy sauce and MSG; piles of fruit and vegetables; and massive walk-in cold rooms for meats – quite a change from the average Chinese outdoor market, with meat gently decaying in the sun. Other sections are devoted to white goods, clothes, furniture, and electronics. You name it, it has it.

Sichuanese Cuisine

Sichuan cooking is unique in China in that, unlike other regional traditions, it is less concerned with bringing out the natural qualities of ingredients, such as taste, colour and texture, than with striving to create a dish of compound flavours and textures in accordance with local preferences. And, although this involves a lot more than just lacing everything with chillies, the Sichuanese are certainly addicted to them. Some dishes, such as the nationally famous Sichuan hotpot, are so spicy that even locals turn bright red and start sweating at the first mouthful, at the same time insisting it is beneficial for warding off chills in winter and cooling the body in summer.

Other Chinese cooking styles use almost as many chillies, but what distinguishes Sichuanese food is the widespread use of Sichuan pepper. This extraordinary, reddish-brown 'peppercorn' is actually the dried berry of the prickly ash, a spiky shrub that grows in the mountains of northwestern Sichuan. It is intensely aromatic with a haunting woody fragrance, and leaves a weird, tingling sensation on your tongue that many find enticing, even mildly addictive. When combined with the heat of chillies, the effect is simultaneously numbing and spicy. It also has other uses: one romantic story goes that little bags of Sichuan pepper used to be exchanged between lovers as tokens of their affection.

As for texture, the Sichuanese love the chewiness that results from dry-frying, a technique which basically involves deep-frying meat or vegetables until they are completely dehydrated but not yet crisp, then adding a thin, herb-infused sauce, along with sugar and sometimes black vinegar, that is promptly soaked up. A similar result is achieved by simmering meat in an aromatic stock, before it is thinly sliced and served cold with a pungent sauce. By way of contrast, soft and slippery textures are also popular, with delicate 'rippled-silk' dumplings and particularly fine wontons served in many places.

The Sichuanese have a huge range of small dishes similar to Cantonese dim sum, though with fewer dumplings, called *xiao chi* ('little eats'). Many of these dishes were originally snacks hawked by vendors who used to roam the streets with their wares hung from poles slung across their shoulders, selling bowlfuls for a few coins a serving – one classic noodle dish is even called *dandan mian*, or 'carrypole noodles', after the way it used to be sold.

Ma Po Tofu

1 × 300 g (10 oz) packet silken tofu
2 tablespoons peanut oil
200 g (6½ oz) fatty pork mince (ground pork)
2.5 cm (1 in) piece ginger, cut into thin strips
2 garlic cloves, finely chopped
1 teaspoon salted black beans
¼ cup shao hsing wine
1 teaspoon dark soy sauce
1 teaspoon brown sugar
1 cup water
½ teaspoon Sichuan pepper and salt
1 large red chilli, finely sliced on the diagonal – optional

Chilli paste

1 large red chilli
1 teaspoon sea salt
1 teaspoon dried chilli flakes
½ teaspoon Sichuan peppercorns
1 tablespoon vegetable oil

First, make the chilli paste. Cut chilli in half lengthways and scrape out seeds using a spoon. Finely dice chilli and pound to a fine paste with salt, chilli flakes and peppercorns using a mortar and pestle, blender or small food processor. Stir in vegetable oil and set aside.

Gently remove tofu from packet and invert onto a plate. Carefully cut into 20 cubes by cutting lengthways into four equal slices, then widthways into five slices, draining off any excess liquid.

Meanwhile, heat oil in a hot wok until surface seems to shimmer slightly. Add pork and stir-fry for 3 minutes. Remove pork with a slotted spoon and set aside.

Add chilli paste to wok with ginger, garlic and black beans, then reduce heat and stir-fry on low heat for 2 minutes, stirring constantly.

Return pork to wok with wine and stir-fry for 1 minute. Add soy sauce and sugar and stir-fry for 30 seconds. Pour in water and bring to the boil. Reduce heat to a gentle simmer and carefully slide tofu into wok, gently separating the cubes as they fall into the pork mixture. Simmer, covered, for 3 minutes.

Spoon into a shallow bowl, sprinkle with Sichuan pepper and salt. Garnish with sliced chilli, if desired, and serve immediately.

Serves 4–6 as part of a shared meal

Kung Po Chicken

600 g (1 lb 4 oz) chicken thigh fillets, cut into 1 cm (½ in) cubes
2 tablespoons cornflour (cornstarch)
2 tablespoons shao hsing wine
2 tablespoons peanut oil
10 small dried red chillies
2 tablespoons peanut oil, extra
5 cm (2 in) piece ginger, cut into thin strips
1 tablespoon brown sugar
½ cup roasted unsalted peanuts
2 tablespoons light soy sauce
1 tablespoon Chinese black vinegar
pinch Sichuan pepper and salt

Combine chicken with cornflour and shao hsing wine in a bowl. Cover, place in refrigerator and leave to marinate for 1 hour.

Place oil and chillies in a cold wok and *then* turn heat to low. Cook for about 1½ minutes or until chillies begin to darken slightly. Using a slotted spoon, immediately remove chillies and drain on kitchen paper.

Leaving chilli-infused oil in wok, turn heat up to high and stir-fry half the chicken cubes for 3 minutes. Remove with a slotted spoon. Add extra oil to wok with remaining chicken and stir-fry for 3 minutes. Return all chicken to wok, along with ginger and reserved chillies and stir-fry for 30 seconds.

Add sugar and stir-fry for 30 seconds. Add peanuts, soy sauce and vinegar and stir-fry for 30 seconds. Serve immediately, sprinkled with Sichuan pepper and salt.

Serves 4–6 as part of a shared meal

Although I have eaten several versions of Kung Po chicken in Chinese restaurants around the world, none of them prepared me for this lip-smacking authentic version. A mouth-watering combination of fried chicken cubes, chillies and peanuts dressed with soy sauce and black vinegar, Kung Po chicken (or *gongbao jiding* in Chinese, meaning 'Governor's Diced Chicken') is named after a nineteenth-century Sichuanese governor.

Our next task is to try and find Chengdu's spice market.

Despite being a native of the city, our guide Lily has never been to the spice market, but makes phone calls and studies maps in order to locate it for us. Lily is amazing; just shy of 23 years of age, she is engaging, informative, obliging and very, very kind. She has what it takes to be a great guide – she is purely interested in what you want to do and see, and puts herself out to make sure your wishes are fulfilled.

Having got her directions, Lily tells our driver how to reach the market and, when we get there, she is just as dumbstruck as the rest of us. Imagine a vast expanse, divided up into about a hundred spaces like small rooms, each selling a different spice. The floor is concrete and dirt, and there are some low walls in between, but mostly each space is separated by wooden tables displaying spices. Now try to imagine that some of these spaces are essentially homes for the world's largest bags of dried chillies: there are plastic bags the size of a king bed, absolutely jam-packed with large dried chillies and just stacked on top of one another, right up to the ceiling and with some of them in rows ten deep. We suppose these are ready for export – I suspect that much of China's dried chilli products come from Sichuan.

Then there are huge sacks about 2 metres high and 1 metre wide, brimming with the most exotic spices and dried goods: whole white peppercorns, star anise, mung beans, green tea leaves, black tea leaves, liquorice root, dried bamboo shoots, dried sheets of bean curd, red beans, black beans, dried tiger lily buds, dried red dates, dried wolfberries, salted and preserved calamari and cuttlefish, stinky dried fish, peanuts, nutmeg, dried Chinese mushrooms and every type of black fungus – every pulse, grain and spice imaginable. I run my fingers through sack after sack, absorbing all the heady aromas and scents, and feeling the textures of each spice, pulse and grain in my hand. And sure enough, there's a whole section for Sichuan peppercorns – I ask if they're fresh and the vendors hold up their scratched hands to prove that they picked the berries from the spiky bushes themselves.

Discovering an unimaginable array of spices in Chengdu

PREVIOUS PAGE: The spice market's cavernous central hall

The next sight to behold are piles of cassia bark, which in China takes the place of cinnamon and is more subtly scented. I have never seen such beauty: it is sold in parchment-like sheets and wonderful scrolls of brown bark and, as for that dizzying, earthy, musty smell . . . I just want to buy a whole tableful of this cassia bark and take it home to Sydney, where I would display it like a work of art in my restaurant, to show its character, texture and composition to full advantage.

The spice market is a sensual delight. We walk past every stall, into every corner, along every lane of these markets – I touch and smell everything I see. In the outside area, we marvel at Chinese women sitting happily on plastic tarpaulins, virtually engulfed by the mass of large dried red chillies they are sorting through, as they prepare them for sale and export. All day, every day, this is their job, their livelihood.

A glance to the left and we see huge black plastic barrels filled with all types of chilli products: red chilli paste, green chilli paste, pickled large red chillies, pickled small red chillies, ground dried chillies and so on, and so on. There are big spoons in each barrel so you can help yourself. And, of course, I can't help myself and have to play with every spoon and every barrel! Rows and rows of hessian sacks are filled with chillies and tied neatly, ready for transportation. We find ourselves sneezing uncontrollably due to the spice-filled air, but I just adore the whole experience: it is so unfamiliar, striking, bizarre, fascinating and colourful.

大熊猫产房
Giant Panda Nursery Facility
亚成年大熊猫
Sub-Adult Pandas
成年大熊猫
Adult Giant Pandas

Entranced as we are by Sichuanese food, we feel we cannot leave without seeing the pandas that are native to western Sichuan's wild, high-altitude bamboo forests.

Fortunately for us, these adorable creatures are much easier to see at the famous Panda Breeding Center, about 10 kilometres northeast of Chengdu, so we set off there the next morning, the time of day when the pandas are at their most playful. We arrive in the misty dawn with many other tourists to find the pandas putting on an almighty performance, as if playing to the crowd. They are just *so* cute, as they roll around in the grass, chew on sticks of bamboo and slide down grass hills. The younger pandas wrestle with one another, their fluffy bottoms up in the air, then sit on their hind legs just like a human does, then it's back to more hugging and rolling around with one another. Their mother is scolding them and adoring them at the same time, in exactly the way any mother does with her child – those big black-ringed 'bedroom' eyes staring right back at you. We are all reduced to two-year-olds within seconds, giggling and chuckling in response to their playfulness, their cheekiness. We can't take our eyes of them as they cavort around, rubbing their bellies, climbing up tree trunks and just flopping in the branches – big, wobbly, slovenly yet beautiful.

The highlight is seeing a newborn just a few weeks old. We are only able to view this baby panda through a glass window, as it stays by its mother's side in an enclosed area until it is three months old and strong enough to brave the outside environment. With only about 1200 pandas left in the wild, the breeding program here is playing an important part in their survival; the idea is to build up the numbers in captivity and then return them to the wild. I stay glued to the window for about half an hour, watching the mother panda reclining on her back with her baby, a 20-centimetre-long ball of white fluff with those distinctive black rings around its eyes, and black booties on its tiny paws – so vulnerable and dependent. The panda cub is lying there so contentedly on its mother's warm belly, drifting off to asleep and slowly sliding down before she gently drags her baby back up to nestle between her big furry chin and warm, cosy neck. It is a sight I will never forget.

Eventually, we all fall back into the car, clutching fluffy-toy panda souvenirs – a bit daggy, I know, but the pandas have transformed us into hopeless, sooky messes and we are unable to resist.

Irresistible pandas at the Panda Breeding Center, just outside Chengdu

Having long been interested in the esoteric and metaphysical side of life, I can't wait to see one of the world's largest sculptures of Buddha, at Le Shan.

The next morning we rise early, looking forward to the fresh country air that lies ahead, and enjoy a fascinating two-and-a-half-hour drive southwest from Chengdu.

Le Shan is a large town situated at the confluence of the Min, Dadu and Qingyi rivers, which tear around the red sandstone cliffs in a swirl of rapids. In AD 713, a monk named Haitong decided that the only way to protect ships along this rough stretch of water was to carve a Buddha image into the 71-metre-high cliffs. He was extremely devout, to the extent of blinding himself to shame a corrupt official who delayed funding for the project, which meant that the Buddha eventually took ninety years to complete. As this incredible carving is recessed into the cliff face, you can't quite see it from town, but have to either catch a bus to the parkland around the Buddha's head, or, as we did, take a boat. The best vantage point is from the water, and there are public ferries, but we opt for a private speed boat, which turns out to be a shifty little business. We are ushered down a rickety old wooden path onto a gangplank where a Chinese woman sits. Looking suspiciously gangster-like, she appears to be the 'collector of the money' and swiftly demands 50 yuan from each of us before pointing us in the direction of a waiting speed boat. At the helm is an old Chinese bloke with a half-smoked cigarette hanging from the corner of his mouth. He prompts us to put on life jackets before we climb into the boat onto old, mouldy seats, and *vroom, vroom*, off we speed in the direction of the Buddha. We all look at each other nervously, not knowing whether to laugh or cry – this bloke is speeding at what feels like 200 kilometres an hour, with cigarette smoke and ash flying everywhere. We just hold onto our hats and anything else we can reach . . . very, very tightly!

Five minutes later, the boat throttle is thrown into 'hover' mode. Arriving at the sacred site, all our fear and despair fall away, replaced by an overwhelming sense of peace as we encounter the all-embracing Buddha, looking immensely powerful as he gazes down serenely at us through half-lidded eyes. From our viewpoint at the Buddha's feet, we can see hundreds of people climbing the adjacent cliffs, like ants climbing a hill, in a zig-zag fashion along stairs and pathways, beginning from his big toe, right up to the level of his curly hair. Our boat weaves slowly to the left, then to the right, so we can take in this magnificent sight from all angles. Then *vroom, vroom*, off we go again, at 200 kilometres an hour, with another cigarette now hanging from our boatman's mouth. We are just laughing helplessly by this point. Off the boat we hop, with a renewed zest for life and gratitude for the safety of dry land, ready for a quick look around the nearby streets and a hasty lunch of steamed chicken, tomatoes and stir-fried corn. As we walk back to our bus, ready for the drive back to Chengdu, we come across many beautiful and unusually dressed men and women – we are told they are Khampa, Tibetans who live high in the mountainous areas of western Sichuan. I am thrilled by the ethnic richness and diversity of this province, and seeing these people only fuels our excitement and anticipation about our journey to Lhasa, Tibet, the following day.

Steamed Chicken with Hot and Sour Dressing

400 g (13 oz) chicken thigh fillets

Dressing
2 tablespoons finely chopped coriander (cilantro) stems
5 cm (2 in) piece ginger, cut into thin strips
2 tablespoons trimmed and finely sliced spring onions (scallions)
2 garlic cloves, finely chopped
1 large red chilli, finely sliced
2½ tablespoons light soy sauce
1 tablespoon brown rice vinegar
1 teaspoon brown sugar
1 teaspoon sesame oil
2 tablespoons peanut oil

First, make the dressing. Combine all ingredients except peanut oil in a heatproof bowl. Heat peanut oil in a small heavy-based pan until surface shimmers slightly, then carefully pour over ingredients in bowl. Stir to combine and set aside, uncovered.

Arrange chicken in a single layer on a heatproof plate that will fit inside a steamer basket. Place plate inside steamer, position over a deep saucepan or wok of boiling water and steam, covered, for about 14 minutes or until chicken is just tender. Remove plate from steamer basket and allow chicken to rest for 5 minutes.

Drain off excess liquid and transfer chicken to a chopping board. Cut chicken on the diagonal into 1 cm (½ in) slices and arrange on a platter. Spoon over dressing and serve at room temperature.

Serves 4–6 as part of a shared meal

Caramelised Tomatoes with Ginger and Vinegar

2 tablespoons peanut oil
375 g (12 oz) grape or cherry tomatoes
5 cm (2 in) piece ginger, finely sliced
1 large red chilli, finely chopped
3 tablespoons shao hsing wine
1 tablespoon brown sugar
1 tablespoon brown rice vinegar
1 tablespoon light soy sauce

Heat oil in a hot wok until surface seems to shimmer slightly. Add tomatoes and stir-fry for 2 minutes to 'blister'. Add ginger and chilli and stir-fry for 30 seconds.

Add shao hsing wine and stir-fry for 30 seconds. Add sugar and stir-fry for 1 minute until slightly caramelised.

Lastly, add vinegar and soy sauce and stir-fry for a further 30 seconds. Serve immediately.

Serves 4–6 as part of a shared meal

Stir-Fried Corn with Red Onions and Lup Cheong

4 sweet corn cobs
2 lup cheong (Chinese dried sausage) or rindless bacon rashers
2 tablespoons peanut oil
1 small red onion, finely sliced
2 garlic cloves, finely chopped
5 cm (2 in) piece ginger, finely chopped
1 large red chilli, finely chopped
1 teaspoon sea salt
2 tablespoons shao hsing wine
2 teaspoons brown sugar
2 tablespoons light soy sauce
1 tablespoon brown rice vinegar
1 teaspoon sesame oil
pinch ground white pepper

Remove kernels from corn cobs by running a sharp knife down the sides of each cob – you should have about 3 cups corn kernels. Finely slice sausage or bacon on the diagonal.

Heat peanut oil in a hot wok until surface seems to shimmer slightly. Add onion, garlic, ginger, chilli and salt and stir-fry for 1 minute. Toss in corn and sausage and stir-fry for 2 minutes.

Add shao hsing wine, sugar and soy sauce and stir-fry a further 2 minutes. Stir through vinegar and sesame oil and serve immediately, sprinkled with pepper.

Serves 4–6 as part of a shared meal

Lhasa: Momos and Monasteries

LHASA: MOMOS AND MONASTERIES

The hour-long flight west from Chengdu to Lhasa, Tibet's ancient capital, is a real eye-opener.

We soar over the 'roof of the world' and onto the green-brown Tibetan Plateau, which is completely surrounded by majestic snow-capped mountains. The sky suddenly turns a bright, deep blue – a much longed-for sight after China's choking pollution. It's such a magnificent setting that Tibet's history seems doubly sad. A loose confederation of states unified by their deep attachment to Buddhism, Tibet had the misfortune to lie between China, Russia and British India, and so became a pawn in the protracted struggle for supremacy between these powers during the nineteenth century. It was the Chinese who finally invaded and annexed the country in 1950, usurping the power of the monasteries, which had been centres of learning and culture. In 1959, Tibet's supreme spiritual leader, the Dalai Lama, fled across the Himalayas into India. In response to an uprising in Tibet, the Chinese authorities instigated an appalling thirty-year crackdown, which saw the monasteries ransacked and monks hounded or worse.

Today, while the temples have been rebuilt and many restrictions on religious freedoms lifted, the 2 million Tibetans are possibly outnumbered in their own country by Chinese immigrants, while the brand-new rail line from eastern China – despite being a marvel of engineering – only emphasises the Chinese government's intent to hold onto the region for good. It's a situation that can't help but stir the emotions.

We are met at the airport by our Tibetan guide, who drapes a white silk scarf around each of our necks: 'A Tibetan sacred scarf to welcome you all to my country,' he announces proudly. We all pile into a minibus for the hour-long ride to Lhasa, a journey that gives us a fascinating first impression of the country. We are mesmerised by the grandeur of the mountains – graceful, haunting and wild all at once – but not so delighted by a huge, ugly neon billboard advertising one of China's largest telecommunications companies.

Then we pass a crowd of people thronging around a huge boulder painted with a vivid yellow image of Sakyamuni (probably the most common representation of Buddha in Tibet), blue-haired and sitting cross-legged on a lotus flower. There are fragments of white silk fabric strewn all over the rock, which turn out to be weathered versions of the white scarves we are all sporting, offered in homage by passing pilgrims. It's our first experience of the Tibetan people's deep spirituality, and this awe-inspiring sight suddenly makes me realise that I am really, truly in Tibet, somewhere I have wanted to come all my life.

A little further on we come across a serene and peaceful lake fringed in light-green grass, on which a couple of stocky yaks are grazing. For Tibetans, these shaggy, short but sturdy creatures serve as both a source of food and as beasts of burden, but these two seem to be intended more as tourist attractions, and have been lovingly decked out in coloured woollen blankets and ribbons. They are accompanied by two Tibetan women selling knick-knacks, and together they make a splendid picture: the lake in the background, yellowy-green-leaved trees along the banks, and the natural beauty and aura of the tall

Buddha images draped with white silk scarves

PREVIOUS PAGE: View from the Potala Palace, Lhasa

women, their bright clothes and chunky jewellery contrasting with their dark hair, wind-burned skin and hard-working hands.

Tibetans are a most staggeringly beautiful race of people, with strikingly high cheekbones, the blackest of hair, muscular physiques, and faces animated by almond-shaped dark-brown eyes and flashes of sparkling white teeth. This despite the fact that they live incredibly tough lives in one of the harshest inhabited environments on earth, where there is barely any agricultural land and the winters are so cold that rocks shatter. Some Tibetans, known as *drokpa*, still lead a nomadic life, herding yaks between summer and winter pastures and living in felt tents, though most are farmers (*rongpa*), living a more settled existence in small hamlets. In addition, there is the monastic community, or *sangha*, of monks and nuns.

As we near Lhasa, we pass several clusters of squarish, flat-roofed white mud-brick houses with ornate front doors. Interestingly, every home is also flying a big, flashy red Chinese flag. Our guide tells us that the Chinese authorities make the locals put these up, reasoning that it creates the 'right' impression for visitors driving in from the airport. We also notice the huge number of military personnel here, and pass a large army barracks – clearly, the Chinese government is determined to keep a very tight hold on this region.

Finally, we enter Lhasa. The name 'Tibet' conjures up such incredible expectations that it's perhaps impossible for the reality to live up to them, but I am still taken aback by my initial view of modern-looking main roads, large department stores, mobile-phone shops, fast-food outlets and neon signs. Then I am suddenly brought into the present by a staggering sight: the enormous and magnificent Potala Palace rising up ahead. We all just stare in wonderment and disbelief, and again it hits me that I've actually made it to Tibet at last. I have goose bumps all over and my heart is thumping with emotion.

We arrive at our hotel, which is situated right in the centre of the city; one of the better places to stay in Lhasa, it's still a bit basic and ordinary. Jumping on my bed I am disappointed to find a dead-hard mattress and even harder pillow. *Oh no, stiff neck*, I think – next time I must bring my own pillow.

We had planned to do a little sightseeing, but our guide advises against this, suggesting that we rest and acclimatise for the remainder of the day. Lhasa sits at a whopping 3595 metres above sea level, and because the air is thinner up here there is less oxygen in each lungful you breathe in, so you get tired far more easily. Even simple things like climbing stairs can really take it out of you until your body adapts; at first I am constantly lethargic and slightly dizzy, with no appetite – most unusual! Although we all shake off our symptoms within a couple of days, it's important not to ignore the early signs of acute mountain sickness, such as headaches and nausea, since it can be fatal in extreme cases (see 'Resources').

Pooh
西藏

Witnessing the *kora* around the Jokhang Temple in Lhasa is a humbling and uplifting experience

The next morning, feeling far more rested, we head out to explore Lhasa's ancient sights. The old town sits east of the Potala Palace, focused on the Barkhor district, a maze of streets surrounding the Jokhang Temple, the holiest and busiest in all of Tibet. Though you never seem to be far from some loud, tacky Chinese advertising billboard, the old town remains a fascinating area, with the 'real' Tibet easy to find in the rustic, characterful side streets and alleyways, with their tea houses, fabric shops and markets. Most of all, though, Tibet exists in its amazing people: living below the poverty line by Western standards, and with their national identity severely threatened, the Tibetan people are inspiringly charismatic and spirited. What holds them together is their shared spirituality, their devotion to Buddhism.

We find evidence of this as soon as we enter the old town, where hundreds of pilgrims are making their daily religious circuit (*kora*) clockwise around the Jokhang Temple. The dynamic force and spiritual energy created by this ritual is truly transforming; when we break into the flow and join the circuit, it is like being caught up in an almighty whirlpool.

The participants are equally extraordinary: tall, strikingly built men from the mountains, dressed in theatrical, woolly, long-sleeved jackets lined with leopard fur; monks in ruby-red and saffron robes; young men draped in layers and layers of different fabrics, sashes and necklaces, their hair in ponytails, or matted into dreadlocks. One old woman, who looks about 95 years old with her lined, character-etched face, smiles at me and reveals a mouth filled with no teeth and a lot of gum. Girls parade past wearing low-slung bronze belts studded with turquoise stones over cobalt-blue skirts with playfully embroidered multicoloured trims.

Many Tibetan women adorn themselves in heavy chunks of coral, silver, amber and turquoise jewellery, along with *zee*, elongated beads made from a type of agate with unusual black markings. Both men and women wear earrings, which are often tied on with a piece of cord. I'm surrounded by a magical sea of colour, tone, texture and beauty. The charming thing, of course, is that the Tibetans are unaware of how utterly fashionable, funky and brilliant they look, and certainly have no attachment to such concepts.

There is no doubt as to these pilgrims' religious devotion – some are locals, but others have walked to Lhasa from the remotest regions of Tibet just to pray here. As they circumambulate the Jokhang, many spin hand-held prayer wheels, a small metal cylinder mounted on a stick that 'speaks' a prayer for every time it is rotated. Hundreds of others are prostrating themselves at every step, kneeling, then stretching out to touch their heads to the ground. They have squares of cardboard or wood tied to their elbows and knees to protect their joints from the continual battering, and the sound of wood and cardboard scraping against the ground sets up a hypnotic rhythm. One old man has a big lump worn into his

forehead from years and years of prostrating himself to Buddha in this way, up and down all day. Tibetans may have little materially, yet it is clear that spiritually they are so, so rich – the communal spirit of it all was profound.

I am struck by the beauty of a group of handsome Tibetan men in dark-brown suits and cowboy hats who are hanging out with one another in the morning sun, projecting an incredible intensity of mood. Several older Tibetan women chat among themselves, all wearing traditional long dresses with colourful striped aprons, and leather boots with turned-up toes.

A young mother with her daughter catches my attention. She smiles at me and one hand comes out seeking money, as the other points to her child. I hand over a few dollars – enough for several days' food – and pull out my camera to take some photos. The mother obligingly straightens up the little girl's matted hair and dirt-stained shirt before I take the shot . . . such a beautiful, priceless moment. I am deeply touched by the level of human contact here: it brings you out of yourself, and somehow compels you to be a better person. Witnessing the *kora* around the Jokhang is so utterly moving and so other-worldly that I am having trouble holding in the tears – I am so stirred by this rich and ancient culture.

The Potala Palace, Tibet's most famous landmark, looks down over the city from the top of Marpo Hill.

Built during the seventeenth century as the centre of Tibetan government and the winter residence of the Dalai Lama, the Potala's sheer white walls enclose a vast complex of halls, shrines, tombs, apartments and terraces. The main section comprises the easterly White Palace, where the Dalai Lama had his living quarters, and the central Red Palace, which offers a spectacular view of the city from its rooftop.

At the main entrance to the Potala, we are confused to see two traditional Chinese lion statues guarding the gates, which our guide says were installed by the Chinese authorities. Placed here, at the entrance to Tibet's old spiritual and administrative heart, they feel like a heavy-handed reminder of China's control, and I am saddened that the Tibetans' fragile yet divine culture is being eroded in this way.

A row of brass prayer wheels lines the wall to the right of the entrance gate. The custom is to touch and spin these metre-high cylinders as you pass: each is mounted on a vertical spindle and filled with printed prayers, which are 'spoken' as they tumble about inside the moving wheel. Then we are engulfed by a sea of hawkers as we try to enter the gates, and we get waylaid haggling and buying wonderful sets of beads and bracelets.

As we climb one of the steep access ramps that snake up the southern side of the hill, we witness some extremely moving sights. Boldly coloured prayer flags flutter in the breeze, their colours symbolising the five elements of earth (yellow), green (wood), red (fire), white (metal) and blue (water), and their movement conveying prayers to the deities.

The colourful temples of Lhasa are redolent of yak butter and incense

PREVIOUS PAGE: The Potala Palace

A long wall of mani stones – flat, grey tablets inscribed with Buddhist sutras and placed here by pilgrims as an act of merit – flanks the path, while nearby two women with braided hair and exquisite coral jewellery sit cross-legged on the ground, nursing their babies. It's this extraordinary mix of extreme devotion and everyday life, aspects that are so separate in our culture but so intertwined here, that makes Tibet such a unique place.

As our guide leads us through the Potala, he demonstrates a profound depth of knowledge not just about the palace but about Buddhism as well. He stops to recount the meaning and virtue, the story and history, the tradition and belief behind every single deity, statue, room, shrine, jewel and vessel we pass. Listening to him is like listening to poetry. His story-telling is layered, complex and rich; he speaks with so much compassion, wisdom and warmth for his beloved Tibet.

We move from one room to the next, sliding in and out of dark wooden corridors and hallways, sometimes finding ourselves scaling very steep and rickety narrow wooden staircases. Compared with the bustle surrounding the Jokhang, the Potala is more like a museum – not surprising, as nobody has lived here since the Dalai Lama fled in 1959 – but the experience of being here is still deeply moving. The walls are covered in intricate, boldly coloured murals illuminated by flickering yak butter lamps, or *chomay*. The lamps emit a strong, lingering aroma that permeates your entire being, and wafts of smoke that irritate your eyes. They are topped up by passing devotees as another act of merit; I watch a passing group with matted hair and rosy-brown complexions carefully scoop some yak butter from a plastic bag and add it to one of the lamps as their offering.

There is a lifetime's worth of visual beauty to take in here but after two hours we all feel rather over-stimulated on *every* level, and

adjourn to a tea house. I slump on the wooden settle, feeling completely blissed-out and speechless, struggling to take in all that I have just experienced. The tea we have is most refreshing – a green brew infused with dried red dates, which add a subtle, complementary sweetness. Our break also makes us realise that we have mustered up quite an appetite, and we head back to town, where we end up at a fairly traditional Tibetan restaurant, kneeling on cushions around a square, low wooden table. We tuck into delicious bowls of *thugpa* – thin white rice noodles, drenched in a thick, spicy, brisket-based stock, scattered with finely sliced spring onions. We also order a few plates of stuffed dumplings called *momos*, which turn out to be rather tasteless: good stomach-fillers but with no particular quality, texture or flavour. I become fascinated by the table next to us, where a man – perhaps the head of a family – skilfully rolls *tsampa* with one hand into perfect football shapes and passes them around to each of his companions. *Tsampa* is a Tibetan staple, made by kneading together roasted barley flour, yak butter and tea, and it has a pleasantly nutty sort of flavour.

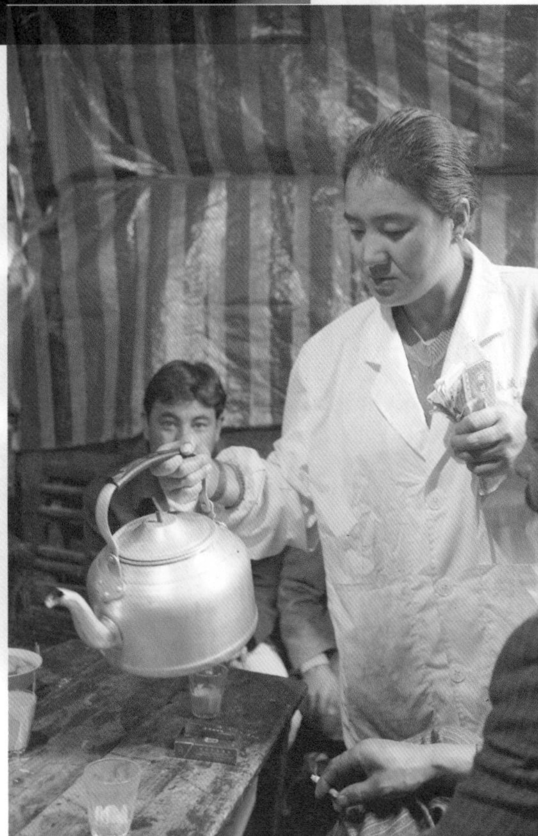

Now, I must admit that you wouldn't really go to Tibet for gastronomic inspiration.

The climate here is so harsh that the Tibetan diet is largely limited to what you can make from barley and yak meat: *tsampa*, soups, *momos*, and a few other variations on the same theme. In this context, it's also perhaps not so strange that Tibetans, unlike other Buddhists, eat meat – if they didn't, they'd starve.

As a result, one thing that seems to be everywhere in Tibet is the distinctive smell of yak butter, which is not just used in temple lamps (and, incredibly, temple sculptures) but also in just about every Tibetan dish, even the tea. It seems to seep out of the pores of every Tibetan, and is so overpowering that at times I'm ashamed to say I have to cover my nose with a scarf to lessen the acrid, slightly rancid smell.

I find Tibetan butter tea – *bo cha* – a difficult subject in itself. It is made from yak butter mixed with salt, milk, soda, tea leaves and hot water all churned up in a wooden tube (or, in more modern homes, huge electric blenders). It looks exactly like regular milky tea, but it tastes *very* different – salty, thicker and with the taste of melted butter through it. Tibetans consume vast quantities and always offer tea to guests, but though I tried so hard to like it, my taste buds got in the way every time.

Speaking of Tibetan tea, on a morning stroll we stumble across the most incredible tea house in Lhasa, a really magical place. Inside it is dark but with shafts of morning sunshine streaming through wooden-framed windows. When our eyes grow accustomed to the dim light, we can make out a rectangular room with mustard-yellow walls. Running down the centre of the ceiling is a line of wooden beams, worn dark burgundy by age and painted with blue and yellow motifs. The place is packed with wooden tables, where mostly men – nomads, locals and monks – are just hanging out with one another, chatting and sipping tea.

Despite being the only obvious 'outsiders', we feel immediately at home here, and are welcomed with wide, warm smiles. A young woman tirelessly orbits the room with an aluminium teapot in one hand and a wad of money in the other, filling up people's cups and taking their money. By chance, our guide happens to be there too, and he invites us over to join him and his friends. With typical Tibetan hospitality, he buys us each a glass of butter tea.

We stay for about half an hour, just people-watching and soaking up the beautiful, easy, neighbourhood atmosphere. The kitchen area is simply a small open space occupied by two women tending huge stockpots filled with a delicious-looking *thugpa* broth bubbling away over a naked flame. A whole shelf is lined with Chinese porcelain bowls filled with fine, slippery rice noodles, condiments, some fresh herbs and braised meat, each awaiting a splash of the piping hot broth before being taken out to a hungry customer. You could even have this same broth in a bowl overflowing with freshly steamed *momos*.

Sampling Tibetan butter tea

OPPOSITE: Bowls of noodles ready to go in the kitchen area of a tea house in Lhasa

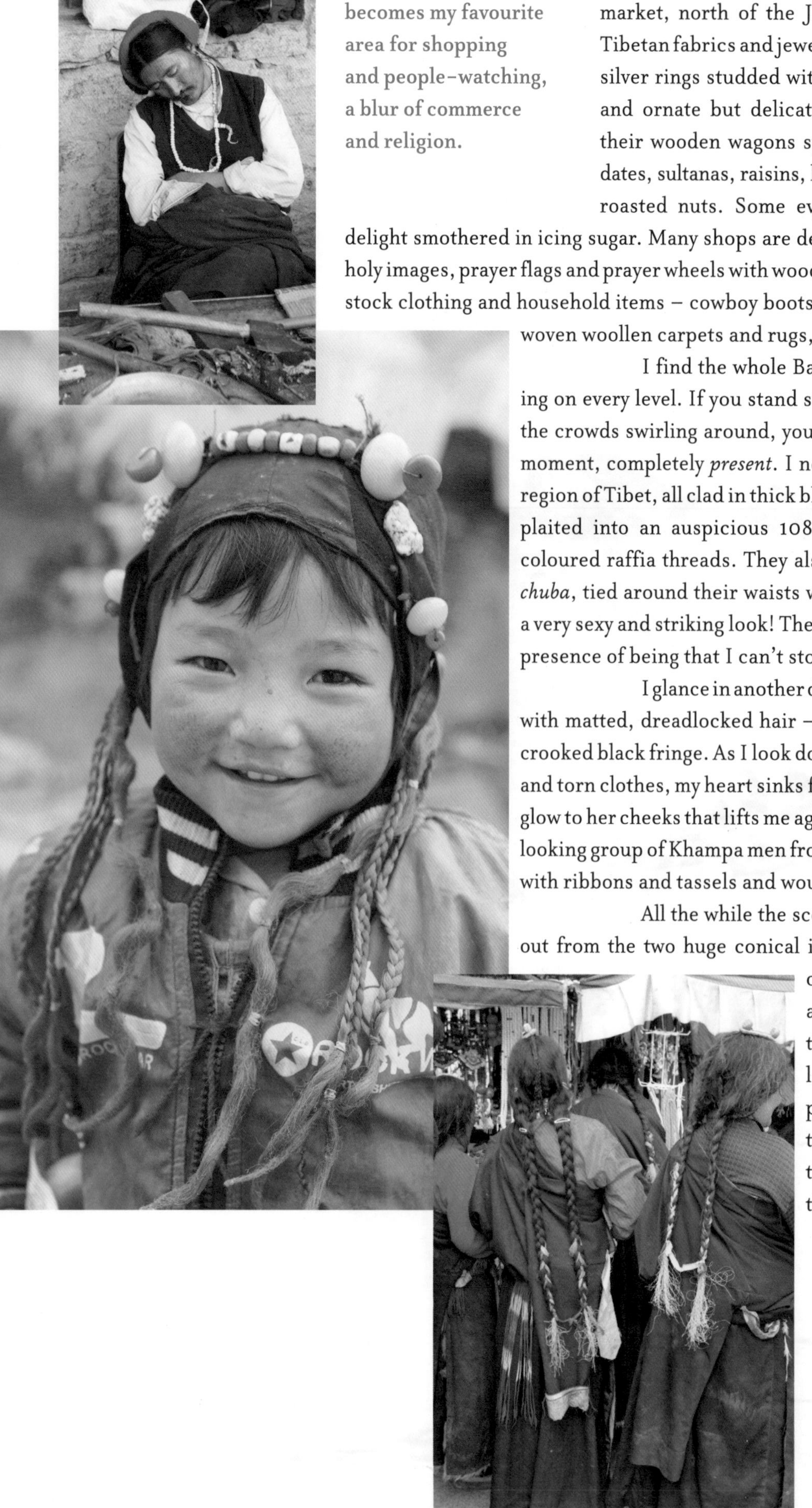

The Barkhor soon becomes my favourite area for shopping and people-watching, a blur of commerce and religion.

The shopping in Lhasa is such fun – especially the Tromzikhang market, north of the Jokhang. There is such a rich array of Tibetan fabrics and jewellery, from scarves and throws to chunky silver rings studded with turquoise, dazzling amber necklaces, and ornate but delicate earrings. Street hawkers stand near their wooden wagons spruiking delectable dried apricots, red dates, sultanas, raisins, bananas, mangoes and mounds of freshly roasted nuts. Some even sell pale-pink squares of Turkish delight smothered in icing sugar. Many shops are devoted to the spiritual accoutrements of holy images, prayer flags and prayer wheels with wooden handles and brass inlay, while others stock clothing and household items – cowboy boots, fabulous jackets lined with fur, hand-woven woollen carpets and rugs, and drapes for covering doorways.

I find the whole Barkhor area so stimulating and awakening on every level. If you stand still in the middle of all the activity, with the crowds swirling around, you just become completely tuned into the moment, completely *present*. I notice a group of women from the Amdo region of Tibet, all clad in thick black skirts, their backside-length braids plaited into an auspicious 108 strands and intertwined with multi-coloured raffia threads. They also have long-sleeved sheepskin cloaks, *chuba*, tied around their waists with a sash and worn off the shoulder – a very sexy and striking look! They all exude such a profound, remarkable presence of being that I can't stop staring at them.

I glance in another direction and spot a beautiful young child with matted, dreadlocked hair – a little black scarf reveals an adorable crooked black fringe. As I look down at her grubby little fingers, her worn and torn clothes, my heart sinks for a moment, but there is a healthy, rosy glow to her cheeks that lifts me again. In another direction is an amazing-looking group of Khampa men from eastern Tibet, their raven hair plaited with ribbons and tassels and wound up over their heads.

All the while the scent of juniper and clouds of smoke seep out from the two huge conical incense burners, or *sangkangs*, in front of the Jokhang, sweetening that inescapable buttery smell. Then, underneath all the other noises, I become aware of a low, vocal hum, the sound of uncounted people soulfully mouthing sacred mantras under their breath as they go about their daily tasks, adding another layer to the spirituality of ordinary Tibetans.

Southeast of the Barkhor is a small Muslim quarter, distinguishable by a couple of small mosques. Muslims have probably lived in Lhasa since the Mongols extended their influence here in the thirteenth century, and today many are metalworkers and butchers – we pass stalls selling deep-red, smelly cuts of yak hung from wire racks in all their gory glory.

We also find an area specialising in traditional Tibetan handicrafts, with proceeds going to villagers and local artisans. The hand-woven fabrics here are exquisite, with some superb carpets and mats, and there's a whole section devoted to wooden furniture and wood-carving, all lovingly finished with intricate, hand-painted designs. We enquire here about *thangkas*, portable religious images of Buddha or Tibetan deities, painted on cloth and mounted on scrolls. We are led upstairs to a studio, an inspiring, light-filled space of brightly coloured wooden beams and pale-green walls. A low table in the middle of the studio is covered with vessels of all kinds – plastic cups, claypots and beer cans cut in half – filled with every shade of colour. Four artists work quietly and intensely, sitting cross-legged with their backs to the window, a frame holding an unfinished *thangka* before each of them. The *thangkas* are immensely detailed works, every inch redolent with meaning, and we are all left speechless by the painstaking effort being put into them, the focus, adroitness and sheer mastery shown by the artists.

My second-favourite place to be, after my kitchen, is in an art studio. I peer over the shoulder of one of the artists and he does not stir, so comfortable is he with this inquisitive onlooker. Another boy sits on the floor sketching the hands of the Buddha in each of their symbolic gestures, or *mudras*. I am taken aback by his exactness and talent; not only does he draw well, but he also has the most exquisite artistic hands with very long fingers. I am desperate to see the rest of his beautiful work and ask to see his sketch pad. He shows me reluctantly, obviously shy at having to deal with this crazy foreign woman! His sketches show immense talent: perfect geometric grids are drawn up on each page, overlain with various images of the Buddha and other deities. Impulsively, I ask if I can buy the sketch pad from him. He looks at me in confusion, giggles, and consults his colleagues; worried he will refuse, I offer him a silly amount of money. He cannot believe it – the whole studio erupts with laughter.

Colourful pigments used for painting *thangkas*

OPPOSITE: A Muslim boy perches in a Lhasa doorway

The studio owner leads us into the next room to show us how all the dyes and paints used in the *thangkas* are made from scratch, ground from stone. A woman sits in the corner, highlighted by an ethereal shaft of light pouring in through the window, clutching her babe with one arm and operating the grinding machine with the other. An enormous *thangka* rests in the corner, unfinished, and again I admire the astounding craftsmanship. I am particularly taken with the shade of pale eucalyptus green that illuminates a deity's halo. The Tibetan sense of colour and design is among the most inspired I have ever seen: burnt oranges mix with flashes of cobalt-blue and chocolate-brown – it is all so daring and *alive*.

The owner is so thrilled with our obvious interest in his studio that he shows us through to another workshop downstairs, where several men sit cross-legged on cushions performing the most staggeringly intricate wood carving – their eyes must take an absolute beating after years and years of such immense concentration. Another man sits on a stool totally engrossed in his copper work, moulding and beating the metal into a forearm that will be attached to a beautiful Buddha statue. Body parts of horses and other sacred animals are strewn over the workshop floor awaiting repair or completion.

By now we are absolutely exhausted with everything: the altitude, the emotion, and the sheer intensity of all we have experienced. It is time for an early supper and a long night's rest. We find ourselves at a hotel run by Westerners and catering to foreign travellers. All I want is a simple bowl of fresh lettuce leaves dressed with olive oil and lemon, and I find it here, along with a huge bowl of spaghetti bolognaise, something I almost never eat at home but unexpectedly crave. We return another night, partly because they serve a very good *cold* Australian white wine, but also because when you have been immersed in Tibetan culture all day long, it helps to have a familiar environment where you can relax in the evening and reflect on your experiences.

A *thangka* studio in the Barkhor

The next day we set off for a picnic to Yamdrok-Tso, a sacred lake some 50 kilometres southwest of Lhasa.

Yamdrok-Tso is the third-largest lake in Tibet and one of the most holy, with disaster predicted should it ever dry up, so it's particularly depressing that the Chinese have made it the centre of a hydroelectric scheme.

On the way to the lake, we stop in the centre of Lhasa at the main food market, which – despite the basic diet that most Tibetans live on – turns out to have excellent vegetables, fruit, noodles and tofu. I go wild over the wads of yellow garlic chives, bright-red tomatoes, huge mounds of fresh green soy beans, shiny purple eggplants, clusters of wild mushrooms and piles of cabbages. One side of the market has the biggest range of tofu I've ever seen – silken tofu, firm tofu, deep-fried tofu, soy-braised tofu, large blocks of it, small squares of it . . .

Then I stumble across a real treasure, a young Tibetan woman selling a mouth-watering variety of pickled vegetables. Yum! I buy several bags to have with our picnic lunch, together with a roast duck. Back home, inspired by the pickles from the market, I decide to create my own versions.

Pickled Carrot and Celery with Tofu and Sweet Paprika

1 small carrot, peeled
1 teaspoon sea salt
2 sticks celery, cut into 5 mm (¼ in) cubes
150 g (5 oz) five-spice firm tofu
1 cup brown rice vinegar
¼ cup brown sugar
3 spring onions (scallions), trimmed and cut into thin strips
½ cup finely shredded Chinese cabbage

Dressing
1 tablespoon light soy sauce
½ teaspoon sesame oil
1 tablespoon brown rice vinegar
1 teaspoon sweet paprika powder

Using a vegetable peeler, finely slice carrot lengthways into ribbons. Cut carrot ribbons into thin strips then place in a bowl with half the salt and mix well. Place celery in a separate bowl with the rest of the salt and mix well. Set carrot and celery aside for 1 hour.

Combine vinegar and sugar in a small heavy-based saucepan and stir over medium heat until sugar dissolves. Simmer, uncovered and without stirring, for about 10 minutes or until reduced and slightly syrupy. Set aside to cool.

Drain carrot and celery and, using your hands, gently squeeze out any excess liquid. Place vegetables in the cooled syrup to pickle them lightly.

In a large bowl, combine pickled vegetables with remaining ingredients. Mix thoroughly using your hands.

To make the dressing, combine ingredients in a small bowl. Spoon dressing over vegetables and toss gently.

Serves 4–6 as part of a shared meal

Braised Green Beans with Chilli

400 g (13 oz) green beans, trimmed and cut into 5 cm (2 in) lengths
2 tablespoons peanut oil
2.5 cm (1 in) piece ginger, finely chopped
2 garlic cloves, finely chopped
2 large red chillies, finely sliced
2 tablespoons shao hsing wine
1 teaspoon brown sugar
2 tablespoons light soy sauce
1 teaspoon brown rice vinegar
½ teaspoon sesame oil

Add beans to a wok or saucepan of boiling water and simmer for 8 minutes. Drain and set aside.

Heat peanut oil in a hot wok until surface seems to shimmer slightly. Add ginger, garlic and chillies and stir-fry for 2 minutes. Add beans and cook for 1 minute, then add shao hsing wine and cook for 30 seconds.

Add sugar and allow to caramelise for 30 seconds. Add remaining ingredients and cook for 30 seconds. Serve immediately.

Serves 4–6 as part of a shared meal

Pickled White Radish with Chilli

500 g (1 lb) white radish (daikon), peeled and cut into 1 cm (½ in) cubes
1 tablespoon sea salt
2 tablespoons brown sugar
2 tablespoons brown rice vinegar
1 large red chilli, finely sliced

Place radish in a bowl and sprinkle with salt and sugar, mix well to combine, then cover and refrigerate overnight.

Tip radish into a colander to drain and, using your hands, squeeze out any excess liquid. Add vinegar and chilli, then mix well and serve.

Refrigerated and sealed in airtight container, this pickle will keep for up to 2 weeks.

Serves 4–6 as part of a shared meal

Cannellini Bean Salad with Carrot and Celery

1 cup dried cannellini beans
1 small carrot, peeled and cut into
  5 mm (¼ in) cubes
2 sticks celery, cut into 5 mm (¼ in) cubes
½ cup mint leaves
½ cup coriander (cilantro) leaves

Dressing
1 egg yolk
2 tablespoons brown sugar
¼ cup light soy sauce
¼ cup brown rice vinegar
¼ cup extra virgin olive oil

Soak beans overnight in water. Drain and place in a heavy-based saucepan with enough cold water to cover. Bring to the boil, then reduce heat and simmer for 1–1½ hours or until tender, adding more water during cooking if necessary. Drain and leave to cool.

To make dressing, whisk egg yolk and sugar until light and fluffy. Add soy sauce and vinegar and whisk to combine, then add oil and whisk again.

Place beans, carrot, celery, mint and coriander in a large bowl. Add dressing and toss gently.

Serves 4–6 as part of a shared meal

If you don't have time to soak and cook dried beans, you can use canned – you'll need two 400 g (13 oz) cans of cannellini beans, rinsed and drained. You could also use chickpeas in this salad.

When we set out for Yamdrok-Tso, it is cold, overcast and drizzling with rain, but our guide assures us that by the time we get to the lake the sky will be bright blue and clear – and, as always, he is right.

As the bus climbs up to the 4488-metre-high plateau on which the lake sits, winding its way around treacherous bends and passing over-enthusiastic cyclists and triathletes in training, we are all rendered speechless by the overwhelming beauty of the country: untouched, wild, sacred and profound.

After almost two hours we suddenly round a bend and there is the lake below us. We are all desperate to stretch our legs but are prevented from leaving the bus by a rough horde of Tibetan men, who actually start pushing their way inside the door in their eagerness to sell us souvenirs. An elderly man, complete with grey hat and burgundy-coloured gloves, points to his magnificent white yak and exclaims 'Five yuan, picture, picture!' We all fall for it and line up to get the once-in-a-lifetime snapshot, complete with him, his yak and the magnificent, milky-blue Yamdrok-Tso Lake in the background.

As soon as the other Tibetans see us giving money to him, we are again besieged. Being pushed around by these guys makes me rather frustrated – I want to be free to simply view the lake. Then, out of the corner of my eye, I spot two huge, sinister-looking black dogs straining at their leashes: they're Tibetan mastiffs – very, very scary! We decide it's time to get back in the bus and head downhill to the lake shore for our picnic.

Our simple lunch turns out be quite a feast: along with the pickles and roast duck from the market, our guide has packed us a hearty lunch of bread, soy-braised chicken drumsticks, hard-boiled eggs, nashi pears and bananas. The time spent at the lake is an unforgettable experience – sitting on the banks of this magical place in the middle of the Tibetan Plateau, far away from the distraction and noise of tourists, not a soul in sight . . . just us and the mountains. I am reminded of the words of a poem written by my friend Subhana Barzaghi:

SACRED MOUNTAIN HOME
Zen master Dogen said,
'Mountains and rivers of the immediate present
are the ancient way of all Buddhas.'
At dawn you recognise your true home –
Sandstone cliffs, steep valleys,
golden wax flowers
all abide in you.
Sacred mountain,
home of my original dwelling place,
shelter for the many beings.

Time is getting on, so we set off on the two-hour drive back down to Lhasa. However, as we are negotiating the steepest part of the road an hour later, the bus suddenly comes to a clunking stop. Our guide gets out of the bus with the driver and both men lift the bonnet to assess the situation. There is a rather unpleasant smell of burning rubber in the air, wafting in through the cabin and, feeling slightly anxious, we all stick our heads out of the window.

'Don't worry, just the brakes,' says our guide. 'Don't worry, we have brake fluid!' *OK, fine, the brakes have gone on us while we're descending one of the steepest mountains in Tibet,* I think to myself. We grab the opportunity to take a few shots of the surrounding landscape, and realise that even though we're in the middle of nowhere, we have actually pulled up at a small roadside village. Several women are digging dirt ditches with big shovels. Our guide – always thinking ahead – casually goes up to one of the women and asks her if there is anywhere nearby where a group of foreigners could cook some food and take some photos?

Roadside scenery on the way to Yamdrok-Tso

OPPOSITE: The sacred lake of Yamdrok-Tso, southwest of Lhasa

The experience that follows is one of the highlights of my life.

Next thing we know, the woman is motioning all of us to come into her home, while her three beautiful children come racing out to fetch all our stuff. From the outside, her house is an unassuming rectangular mud-brick structure, with small, square wooden-framed windows and Tibetan prayer flags poking out from the chimneys. So we are completely unprepared for the beautiful, artistic, vibrant and rich interior, which feels just like a family home should – welcoming, abundant and cosy.

We enter through a rather intriguing doorway, hung with a white piece of fabric decorated with a navy blue, yellow and red trim. This leads to a sun-drenched outdoor patio given colour and life by bushes of chrysanthemums, a scattering of tins and rusty copper pots, tables made from old timber, and a tall, wooden cylinder wrapped in stripy fabric, which we later discover is a butter churn. There's also an old wooden settle covered with fabulous bits of mismatched hand-woven fabric and embroidery, all strewn with faded, well-used cushions – a great place for reading, I think to myself.

Surrounding the courtyard are the bedrooms, the kitchen area and the living room, their walls and wooden shutters picked out with white, blue and yellow highlights. We are led into the living room, which is a sight to behold. In fact, it is the most exquisite living room I have ever been in, with an amazing ceiling crafted from warped wooden beams, walls lined with chests of drawers and cabinetry, and every last bit of free space draped with fabrics, scarves and *thangkas* depicting sacred deities. We are asked to sit on a long couch which is covered with beautiful tapestry work and embroidery.

The woman's three children – a boy of about ten and two girls who look eight or so run around, giggling and chuckling. They are beside themselves with glee and excitement; they have really beautiful, rosy complexions and they are just so full of life and love.

The compound of a Tibetan village house

OPPOSITE & OVERLEAF: Richly decorated rooms surround the house's internal courtyard

Their mother and grandmother offer us butter tea and barley beer, while the children stand in the doorway staring at us with big, soft brown eyes, still giggling and chuckling. Next minute, their grandmother disappears and returns with a crying babe in her arms, the youngest addition to this close-knit family. I can't help myself and promptly borrow the baby for a cuddle. There is no male presence at this point except for the young boy – they are all out working the land.

After our refreshments we roll up our sleeves and get down to some serious work. We are directed into the kitchen, and I am bowled over by the sheer beauty of this modest, square-ish room. Painted a rich chocolate-aubergine colour, the walls are decorated with white outlines of the eight auspicious symbols – parasol, conch shell, golden fish, lotus flower, knot of eternity, vase of great treasure, wheel of law and banner of victory – all representing the gifts bestowed on Sakyamuni after his enlightenment and widely used as protective motifs in Tibetan houses, monasteries and temples. The room is lined with more wooden shelves and cabinets, one of which boasts an electric blender and large television – just to remind us that we are in Tibet, land of the devout and the everyday. In one corner sits a wooden tub full of fresh, cold water with a beautiful bronze ladle hanging from the rim. Next to this is a double-burner gas stove, which proves to be super hot and efficient. For my preparation bench, a wooden chest in the middle of the rammed-earth floor is covered with a cloth and I begin my washing, trimming, pickling and slicing. As I prepare the food, the kids are outside helpfully washing and scrubbing all the dishes and utensils we've brought with us. I become aware of the remarkably friendly atmosphere, of how everyone seems comfortable with everyone else, even though we cannot speak one another's language. Our guide has gone way beyond the call of duty to make all this possible, and it's entirely due to him that we're able to experience such a memorable and life-enhancing afternoon.

The cooking frenzy begins. I purchased some soy-braised pork at the market, which I slice into chunks and then caramelise with brown sugar, soy sauce and Chinese black vinegar. The woman hands me a beautiful, black cast-iron pot – perfect for such a dish. I stare at a bag of small, yellow potatoes I bought on a whim, enchanted by their tiny size, wondering what to do with them. In the end I boil them, then stir-fry them with a splash of peanut oil, some freshly sliced ginger, brown sugar, shao hsing wine and soy sauce, serving them with a sprinkle of Sichuan pepper and salt. They turn out to be a bit of a hit! A couple of tomatoes are stir-fried with a luscious clump of fresh, earthy shiitake mushrooms, some smashed cloves of garlic, more ginger, soy sauce, sesame oil and sugar. As the cooking smells waft out of the kitchen, the family gathers around the kitchen door. By this time, the men have returned from the fields and, when our guide explains the situation to them, they too smile at us warmly and make us feel welcome. Compared to the women, the men are shy and retiring – it seems that the women definitely rule the roost in this family . . .

At last we are finished, the food photographed and eaten. In recognition of the family's extraordinary hospitality, we offer some money, as our guide suggests, but we also clean up the huge mess we've made and give them all our cooking utensils and equipment to keep – it feels like the least we can do in return for the privilege of being welcomed into their home.

By the time we climb back into the bus, waving goodbye to our new friends, we've forgotten all about the dud brakes (which are all fixed and ready to go by this time). When we get back to Lhasa, it's already 7 p.m., and we soon collapse into bed, utterly exhausted once again. We are all feeling the altitude and the sheer energy-drain that accompanies the moving experiences and sensory overload that Tibet constantly provides.

Caramelised Pork with Ginger and Vinegar

600 g (1 lb 4 oz) pork belly
2 tablespoons peanut oil
¼ cup shao hsing wine
1 tablespoon brown sugar
3 star anise
5 cups water
2 tablespoons Chinese black vinegar
1 tablespoon light soy sauce
1 teaspoon dark soy sauce

Marinade
1 teaspoon cornflour (cornstarch)
1 teaspoon sea salt
¼ cup shao hsing wine
10 cm (4 in) piece ginger, cut into thin strips

To remove any impurities from meat, place pork belly in a large pan or stockpot, cover with cold water and bring to the boil. Simmer for 5 minutes, then drain, discarding water. Rinse pork thoroughly under cold running water and drain well.

Cut pork belly into 5 cm × 2.5 cm (2 in × 1 in) pieces. Combine marinade ingredients in a large bowl. Add pork and leave to marinate in the refrigerator for 30 minutes.

Heat oil in a hot wok until surface seems to shimmer slightly. Add marinated pork and stir-fry for 4 minutes.

Add remaining ingredients and simmer gently, covered, for 50 minutes or until pork is tender. Serve immediately.

Serves 4–6 as part of a shared meal

Cooking in Tibet, I garnished this rich dish with some pickles from the market in Lhasa, but at home you could just use some very finely shredded fresh ginger.

正宗牛肉面

Caramelised Potatoes

(1 lb) baby new potatoes
spoons peanut oil
in) piece ginger, finely sliced
spoons brown sugar
spoons shao hsing wine
spoon light soy sauce
Sichuan pepper and salt

whole unpeeled potatoes to a large pan of cold salted water. Bring to the boil, reduce and simmer for about 35 minutes or until potatoes are tender. Drain well and pat dry chen paper. Cut potatoes in half if they are not tiny, and leave to cool slightly.
eat oil in a hot wok until surface seems to shimmer slightly. Add potatoes and stir-fry bout 3 minutes or until lightly browned all over.
dd ginger and stir-fry for 30 seconds. Add sugar, wine and soy sauce and stir-fry for t 1 minute or until slightly caramelised. Serve immediately, sprinkled with Sichuan per and salt.

Serves 4–6 as part of a shared meal

Stir-fried Fresh Shiitake Mushrooms, Tomatoes and Ginger

2 small tomatoes
2 tablespoons peanut oil
100 g (3½ oz) fresh shiitake mushrooms, stems discarded and caps halved
3 garlic cloves, roughly crushed
7 cm (2¾ in) piece ginger, finely sliced
½ teaspoon sea salt
3 spring onions (scallions), trimmed and cut into 5 cm (2 in) lengths
2 tablespoons shao hsing wine
1 teaspoon brown sugar
1 large red chilli, finely sliced
1 teaspoon light soy sauce
½ teaspoon sesame oil

Cut tomatoes in half lengthways, then cut each half into quarters and set aside.

Heat peanut oil in a hot wok until surface seems to shimmer slightly. Add mushrooms, garlic, ginger and salt and stir-fry for 2 minutes. Add tomatoes and spring onions and stir-fry for 1 minute.

Add shao hsing wine and sugar and stir-fry for 30 seconds. Add chilli and soy sauce and stir-fry a further 30 seconds. Stir through sesame oil and serve immediately.

Serves 4–6 as part of a shared meal

Carrot, Radish, Celery, Bean Sprout and Black Sesame Seed Salad

1 small carrot, peeled
1 small cucumber, cut in half lengthways
1 teaspoon sea salt
1 cup brown rice vinegar
¼ cup brown sugar
2 sticks celery, sliced on the diagonal
1 cup fresh bean sprouts
3 red radishes, trimmed and cut into 5 mm (¼ in) slices, then into thin strips
3 spring onions (scallions), trimmed and cut into thin strips
½ cup finely shredded Chinese cabbage
2 teaspoons black sesame seeds
pinch Sichuan pepper and salt

Dressing

1 tablespoon light soy sauce
½ teaspoon sesame oil
1 tablespoon brown rice vinegar

Using a vegetable peeler, finely slice carrot and cucumber lengthways into ribbons. Cut carrot ribbons into thin strips then place in a bowl with half the salt and mix well. Place cucumber in a separate bowl with remaining salt and mix well. Set cucumber and carrot aside for 1 hour.

Combine vinegar and sugar in a small heavy-based saucepan and stir over medium heat until sugar dissolves. Simmer, uncovered and without stirring, for about 10 minutes or until reduced and slightly syrupy. Set aside to cool.

Drain cucumber and carrot and, using your hands, gently squeeze out any excess liquid. Place vegetables in the cooled syrup to pickle them lightly.

In a large bowl, combine pickled vegetables with celery, bean sprouts, radishes, spring onions and cabbage. Mix thoroughly using your hands.

To make the dressing, combine ingredients in a small bowl. Spoon dressing over salad. Serve salad on a platter, sprinkled with sesame seeds and Sichuan pepper and salt.

Serves 4–6 as part of a shared meal

Black sesame seeds have a more pungent flavour than white sesame seeds, and are available from Asian supermarkets. If you can't find them, white sesame seeds or even black poppy seeds will add a similar textural contrast.

Ganden Monastery occupies an important place in Tibetan religion.

About 45 kilometres east of Lhasa, the monastery was established in 1410 by Tsongkhapa, the founder of the Gelugpa or Yellow Hat sect, which became the dominant strand of Tibetan Buddhism and is now led by the Dalai Lama. Along with Sera and Drepung monasteries, Ganden was also one of the main seats of learning in Tibet (traditionally, education was the sole province of the monasteries).

Although it is a glorious and clear morning, we all feel slightly edgy and excited, since our main reason for visiting Ganden is not to see the monastery but to visit a nearby sky-burial site. Sky burials are the most common Tibetan funeral ceremony, however many Tibetans are understandably reluctant for these sacred rites to be turned into a tourist attraction. In deference to their wishes, we plan to arrive at Ganden around 9.30 a.m., since sky burials generally take place early in the morning.

The scenery along the way is amazing, despite it being the dry season, with the sparse mountains coloured a raw brown without a shred of greenery. Our bus climbs the long, zig-zagging dirt road to the monastery, revealing stupendous views of the surrounding Kyi-chu Valley and the snow-capped peaks of the Himalayas. As we approach Ganden, our guide is quick to point out several big black vultures circling in the sky above us. 'That is the sky-burial site,' he says. 'Come on, we go there – I want to show you.'

We get out of our bus at the start of the low *kora*, the easier of the two pilgrim trails that encircle the monastery – and one of the most profound 45-minute walks I have ever taken. We follow the dirt track in single file, passing offerings left by the faithful: piles of *mani* stones, bushes draped in Tibetan scarves, wads of printed prayers and prayer flags; there are shreds of fabric and string everywhere.

When the trail finally comes to the sky-burial site, I find my heart thumping loudly, and I have butterflies in my belly. The air is thick with the scent of burning juniper, and it is clear that a burial has recently taken place. Apparently, the wood smoke attracts the attention of the vultures, which then descend from the sky and eat the human remains, returning the body to nature, in accordance with the Tibetan saying: 'We enter this earth naturally, and so when we die, we must return to the earth naturally.' Needless to say, the vulture is one of the most highly esteemed creatures in Tibetan tradition.

Ganden Monastery

PREVIOUS PAGE: Mountain scenery on the way to Ganden

OPPOSITE: The trail to the sky-burial site

We quietly walk up to the site, which occupies a large, open slope on the side of the mountain. A paved square marks where the deceased's body was lain to be ritually dismembered before being burned; several primitive-looking cutting implements are strewn around, and nearby bushes are covered with remnants of clothing, scarves and human hair – all from previous burials.

The site is an incredibly moving place to be and to think about the Tibetan view of death: unlike the taboos and fears surrounding death in most Western traditions, Tibetan Buddhism meets it head on, and this is one of the aspects of the Tibetan way of life I love most. Buddhism constantly reminds us that from the moment we are born, we begin to die – but that this is not something to fear. Rather it is motivation for us to live each moment as if it were our last, with the greatest love and the deepest compassion for others. This also allows us to grasp the idea of impermanence – the notion that all that arises, ceases and that everything is transient – and allows us to *let go* of so much unnecessary pain and suffering, and so create more room for true happiness in life.

One of the books that has had the most profound influence on my life is *The Tibetan Book of Living and Dying*, by Sogyal Rinpoche, and particularly these words: 'Do I remember at every moment that I am dying, and everyone and everything else is, and so treat all beings at all times with compassion? Has my understanding of death and impermanence become so keen and so urgent that I am devoting every second to the pursuit of enlightenment? If you can answer "yes" to both of these, then you have really understood impermanence.'

The trail to the sky-burial site is strewn with offerings and prayer flags

OPPOSITE: The zig-zagging road to Ganden Monastery

BELOW RIGHT: Monks creating a sand mandala at Ganden Monastery

Sera Monastery, just 5 kilometres north of Lhasa, is famous for its three colleges dedicated to various aspects of religious study.

Dating from the fifteenth century, Sera also boasts a beautiful *kora*, which takes less than one hour to complete. However, the most impressive sight here takes place every afternoon between 3.30 and 5.30 p.m., when all the young monks congregate in the central courtyard and 'debate'. It is quite a spectacle: about a hundred beautiful, healthy young men, dressed in burgundy robes and clutching wooden prayer beads, taking part in highly passionate philosophical discussions.

One monk stands up and delivers a question, moving his whole body in an extraordinary, emphatic way: he leans back on his right foot with his right arm extended behind him, and then comes forward and slaps his left palm with his right in a terrific clap. At the same moment, he yells out his question to the receiving monk – who sits on the ground, cross-legged. It is a wonderful sight, full of vigour and vibrant energy.

I try to imagine what 15-year-old boys do each afternoon back home – and to then see boys of the same age, debating the meaning of life in this intensely dynamic fashion, for two hours, is truly amazing.

Feeling a bit 'templed out', we spend more and more time in Lhasa, just watching the ebb and flow of Tibetan daily life.

I am still curious, though, to find out what monks cook and eat. When I tell our guide how I long to see a monastery kitchen, he suggests a visit to Drepung, which was founded in 1416 and was once the largest monastery in the world, home to over 8000 monks.

The next day dawns overcast and cloudy and, as we drive the 8 kilometres to Drepung, the sight of the mist rolling in and around the white-washed monastic structures is eerie and mystical. Huge piles of wood are neatly stacked in every corner of the monastery, striking chocolate-brown fabrics and materials are draped from the window frames and doorways of the halls, and stunning gold sculptures depicting the eight auspicious symbols, such as the wheel of law (which represents the Buddhist eightfold path to enlightenment) detail the rooftops. The steps are crowded with pilgrims in all their glorious colours and rags, spinning prayer wheels with one hand, begging with the other. As always, I give them some money – I just cannot walk past and not acknowledge them.

I look over to our guide, who has even more of a twinkle in his eye than he usually does. He motions me over to where he is standing, at the doorway to the monastery's kitchen. I bolt over, eager to see what I am convinced will be one of the world's most interesting and unusual kitchens. I am not disappointed.

Huge timber doors with a thick wooden latch open to reveal the most gorgeous space: a dimly lit, almost cavernous room with a hard, well-worn dirt floor, white-washed walls and beautiful sturdy, thick wooden columns and ceiling beams. Wide shafts of natural light seep in through windows, creating an ethereal aura. A middle-aged man stands on top of a mighty mud-brick oven, stoking the fire while carefully lifting the lid off a huge bubbling stockpot with a wooden paddle. Stretched across the top of the oven is a taut wire that holds copper and bronze ladles; to the left is a rustic, black wooden shelf holding tidy rows of copper and bronze water jugs, kettles and wooden pails. Nearby stands a grand antique cupboard, made from caramel-coloured wood, complete with intricate inlay and carving. In another corner several monks sit chatting peacefully on wooden settles draped with Tibetan rugs and embroidered fabric; beautifully ornate *thangkas* are pinned to the mustard-coloured walls.

One monk is dextrously making meat dumplings. I stand and watch him for a while, and he just carries on as if I'm not there. Beside him is the biggest block of yak butter

I've ever seen. Outside, several young monks sit cross-legged, dutifully peeling a huge bronze vessel full of potatoes.

After having a good look around, we all stand back and watch, completely mesmerised, as the monks get their dinner. One by one, they go into the kitchen, clutching a big silver jug with gold trim, which they hand to the cook. The cook then fills the jug with hot broth, and the monk bows and leaves. The whole scene is made all the more enchanting by the fantastic rays of light shining into the gloom, illuminating the deep hue of the monks' robes and the steam rising off the piping-hot broth. The silence that accompanies it all is exquisite and adds an air of divinity to the entire ritual.

Although our time in Tibet is over, nowhere else in the world has made such a deep, personal impact on me.

I feel that every Westerner would benefit greatly by visiting Tibet at least once in their lifetime to learn about 'true' life values. For so many of us Westerners, who get so caught up in materialism and superficial worries, Tibetans, with their total devotion to a spiritual life, remind us of what is *real*, and of what *really matters*.

Xi'an and the Terracotta Army

XI'AN AND THE TERRACOTTA ARMY

Now the capital of Shaanxi province, Xi'an was once the capital of all China.

The nation's first emperor, Qin Shi Huang, reigned from Xi'an and was buried just outside the modern city in 210 BC, his tomb guarded by the famous Terracotta Army. Xi'an remained China's capital, off and on, for the next thousand years, most notably during the Tang dynasty (AD 618–907), when it sat at the eastern end of the fabled Silk Road and was for a time the largest, wealthiest city in the world.

Things went downhill for Xi'an after the Mongols conquered China and made Beijing their base in 1264, and our first impression of the place is that Xi'an looks just like any other hustling and bustling Chinese city, with the same polluted skies, bumper-to-bumper traffic and high-rises everywhere. We do, however, notice the grid-like street plan that is a legacy of the carefully designed city of the Tang era, and the impressive 12-metre-high, grey-brick city walls that date back to the Ming dynasty (1368–1644) and encircle the heart of the city.

The Bell Tower Hotel, where we are staying, turns out to be in the centre of town where the four main streets converge, just opposite the wood and brick Bell Tower, which was built in 1582 and is one the city's main landmarks. Starving, and itching to explore this new place, we head straight to lunch at Dafachang Fast Food, a famous restaurant near the Bell Tower, just off the main square. The restaurant is one of many across northern China specialising in boiled, steamed or shallow-fried dumplings known as *jiaozi*, stuffed with a range of fillings. Though many people tend to think of the Chinese as avid rice-eaters, this is really only true for the south of the country – here in the north it's too cold to grow rice, so hearty wheat noodles and dumplings wrapped in wheat-flour skins are the staple instead.

We decide to try an exciting-sounding 'special banquet', which allows you to sample '16 types of Chinese dumplings', but are disappointed and a bit baffled when a selection of curiously shaped bright orange and brown dumplings arrives at the table. 'This is the "pumpkin" wonton, and this is the "chestnut" dumpling,' says the waitress. We stare at these strange things and then look at one another with sinking hearts, before turning to our long-suffering guide and interpreter, Chris, and telling him that we want the simply shaped dumplings – the unpretentious, authentic white-flour ones.

'OK, OK, now I understand!' Chris quickly pacifies us before steam comes out of our ears. Within 10 minutes, all the tourist-oriented nonsense is taken from our table and replaced with joyful, overflowing plates of fluffy, plump Chinese dumplings as we know and love them – in rustic half-moon shapes with thick frilly edges. Lamb is the most traditional filling for these dumplings, but we also get some stuffed with crab, some rich pork ones, some with garlic chives and mushrooms, and some delicate ones with prawns, all served with a soy and garlic dipping sauce.

Xi'an's Bell Tower, which marks the centre of the city

OPPOSITE: The finely sculpted features of a restored warrior

PREVIOUS PAGE: The massed ranks of the Terracotta Army

The restaurant also has a wonderful range of cold appetisers: when a trolley comes to a halt at our table, I think I order *all* of the dishes on offer – fresh soy bean sprouts with a hint of soy and garlic, a slithery glass noodle salad with chilli and coriander, an unusual dish of baby squid with red chilli and green pepper, a refreshing cucumber salad, and some beautifully crunchy jellyfish.

The Chinese traditionally eat these dishes before the main course. While travelling in China, I generally order six or seven at each meal, whether there are three of us at the table or ten of us. My guide always asks: 'Are you sure you want to order that many appetisers? Usually we only order two or three. The waitress thinks you have ordered far too many.'

'Yes, Chris, I am positive!' I like to eat lots of different bits and pieces during a meal, I like grazing and picking, so having an array of dishes on the table at once is perfect for me. Eating in this way also makes for an interesting and pleasant experience, not to mention encouraging the healthy consumption of small amounts of each dish. I have never really enjoyed eating rice with a meal, because it fills me up too much, like potatoes or bread. Interestingly, a similar preference is common in China, where the more expensive or formal the meal, the less likely it is that plain boiled rice (or noodles, for that matter) will be served. My mum still comments on the fact that I only ever liked to eat all the *soong*, the 'bits and pieces'.

An array of cold appetisers and dumplings at Xi'an's renowned Dafachang Fast Food restaurant

Poached Baby Squid with Red Chilli and Green Pepper

600 g (1 lb 4 oz) cleaned baby squid, including tentacles
½ green pepper
1 large red chilli, finely sliced

Dressing
5 cm (2 in) piece ginger, finely chopped
4 garlic cloves, finely chopped
2 tablespoons brown sugar
4 tablespoons light soy sauce
2 tablespoons brown rice vinegar
2 teaspoons sesame oil

Cut squid bodies and tentacles into 1 cm (½ in) pieces. Remove seeds and membrane from pepper, then cut into 1 cm (½ in) squares.

Combine all dressing ingredients in a large bowl and mix well, then add chilli and pepper squares.

Add squid to a large saucepan of boiling water and blanch for 4 minutes or until just tender. Quickly drain, then add to bowl with dressing and toss gently. Serve immediately.

Serves 4–6 as part of a shared meal

At night Xi'an really comes alive.

Neon from thousands of signs gives a luminous tinge to the black sky – parts of the city are so bright that they resemble a mini Times Square! There are masses of people everywhere shuttling between night clubs, bars and glitzy restaurants, and it has the buzz of a young, happening, modern city. Fashion-conscious teenagers fill the streets and public areas, über-chic department stores showcase all the international haute couture houses, and every restaurant is packed to the rafters.

We head to dinner at a Cantonese-style place called the Old Hong Kong Restaurant. When we arrive, as usual I grab the waitress and my guide and off we go, peering at dishes on each of the tables: I point, Chris translates, the waitress writes the order; I point, Chris translates, the waitress takes the order . . . The waitresses thinks I am mad – given my looks, why on earth can't I speak the language?

The crispy-skin pigeon is heavenly – cooked in my favourite way, it has been poached in soy sauce, before being deep-fried golden brown then sliced up and served with Sichuan pepper and salt and fresh lemon. The whole steamed flounder with ginger, spring onion and chilli is as good as my mother's, and the braised Chinese lettuce is crunchy and refreshing. I am curious to see a dish of deep-fried chicken with chilli and peanuts, but it turns out to be quite disappointing. The deep-fried cubes of chicken are skewered on toothpicks, and it is over-salty, laced with MSG and peppered with fiery-hot fried dried chillies – not really to my liking. The most stunning dish besides the pigeon is the braised fish head with whole garlic and chilli, served piping hot in a claypot. When the waiter presents the dish to us, he dramatically lifts the lid and *swoosh*, a billowing cloud of steam and a tantalising scent fill the air. The sound of the aromatics still charring and sizzling is so inviting, and we fight over the caramelised garlic cloves, the seared, crispy bits of sweet spring onion stem, and the subtle yet powerful slices of ginger. The fish head has absorbed all these flavours, plus a wonderful balance of shao hsing wine, sugar, chilli, soy sauce, sesame oil and stock, and it also has the most delectable, gelatinous cheeks, lips and eyes.

To end the meal, we drink a refreshing green tea, the perfect way to cleanse the palate. It comes in a charming, small glass teapot, which the waiter constantly refills. I notice that the lid of the teapot is neatly attached to the handle with a twist of red cord.

阳光丽都
娱乐广场
服务社会
健康·专业
欢乐·温馨
娱乐大众
lido
自助中西餐 烧烤 火锅
中国光大银行

The Big Goose Pagoda, Xi'an

We start the next day early, as we have a lot of sightseeing to pack in.

We head first to the Big Goose Pagoda, about 4 kilometres south of the city walls. Standing in the grounds of the Temple of Grace, this is Xi'an's largest Buddhist temple. The 60-metre-high, reddish-hued pagoda dates from the Tang dynasty and is of an unusual, square-sided design. It was built to store the Buddhist scriptures monk Xuan Zang (also known as Tripitaka) brought back to China while he translated them for posterity – but where the name comes from, nobody knows for sure. Xuan Zang had set off on a pilgrimage to India to study Buddhism in AD 629, returning sixteen years later, laden down with holy texts. His incredible journey passed into legend and was finally committed to paper during the Ming dynasty as the novel *Journey to the West*. Several centuries later, the same story gained a new generation of fans as the basis of the popular television series *Monkey*.

As I walk through the grounds of the pagoda I notice a beautiful old monk sitting wistfully under a willow tree. He is simply dressed in mustard-yellow Buddhist robes, a square-cut tunic with big buttons and a pair of wide-legged trousers. He has the softest, kindest face. Something about his energy draws me toward him and I walk over – he smiles at me and I sit down next to him, reaching my right arm out to him, with my hand open wide, palm facing upwards. I want to hold his hand and he lets me, and there we sit for about 10 minutes, just holding hands and smiling. He points to the beads around my neck, and I say, 'Lhasa'. He nods and smiles, 'Oh, Lhasa . . . ' Beyond that, we cannot speak English and I cannot speak Chinese, so we communicate just by 'being' together.

All too soon, it's time to return to the city – to explore its ancient heart, the Muslim Quarter.

The Muslim Quarter is the oldest and most vibrant part of Xi'an.

According to one story, the area was originally populated by descendants of the Arab traders who lived in the city during the Tang dynasty, when roads through central Asia to the Mediterranean were open.

Even though it is just a 10-minute stroll from the hotel, our first foray into the Muslim Quarter proves to be a little harrowing. Despite having been in town for only 24 hours, I am already deeply distressed by the number of homeless people and children begging on the streets – in fact, right outside our hotel. As many times as I have experienced this in my travels, I always find it devastating. Today, I can't take my eyes off a young woman of 20 or so, who sits blank-faced and dismal outside the local KFC with her two small children. Although her children are about the same age as my little niece and nephews, there the similarity ends, for these children are covered from head to toe in

dirt and grime from street living. The small girl is stuck to her mother's breast in hope of receiving some sustenance; however, the mother looks so skinny herself that I doubt she would have any milk to give. The little boy screams and screams and screams – he is tired, hungry, dirty, hot, bothered, frustrated.

This is the downside of the economic powerhouse that is shaping modern China: many rural people feel left out and so leave their home villages to try their luck in the cities, only to end up on the streets. The society is changing so fast that there are plenty of opportunities for those able to take them, but for any who fall behind there is no safety net, no government support or health care. I feel so blessed with what I have in my life; China constantly challenges everything that we so often take for granted, and this is one reason I will always come back here.

Somewhat unsettled, we cautiously enter the Muslim Quarter, a maze of narrow, cobbled alleyways, half-timbered houses and old shops. It's all a bit grotty but is jam-packed, with a sociable bustle in the streets, music in the background and children everywhere. It feels like pick-pocket central to me, and I find it faintly sinister and intimidating, but also compelling. With the smell of cumin, garlic, fennel and chilli filling the air, it's like walking into another country. Row upon row of restaurants are filled to the rafters with lively diners all chowing down on Central Asian food: lamb stew with bread, lamb kebabs, beef kebabs, chicken kebabs, whole grilled and spice-marinated baby fish, and mammoth portions of chicken stewed in what looks like a chilli and tomato sauce. In one corner, an ordinary-looking man turns out to be an expert noodle maker, pulling, twisting and banging a thick lump of dough until it magically separates between his hands into a mass of delicate, thin noodles over a metre long. Within a minute they're cooked, covered in a spicy sauce, and swirled onto a customer's plate. Elsewhere chefs are sweating over dancing flames, grilling and turning huge bundles of marinated-meat skewers over primitive, yet powerful-looking grills, while in the background a strange-looking machine roasts whole chestnuts, and a young boy keeps watch over a table of delicious-looking spring onion pancakes and sweet treats.

At the heart of the Muslim Quarter is Xi'an's Great Mosque, said to be one of the largest and oldest in all of China, and a haven of tranquillity after the surrounding streets. The main prayer hall has a beautiful turquoise-coloured roof and rows of shoes outside the door, removed by the white-turbanned worshippers as they enter, but I most like the four peaceful courtyards, scented by pink-flowered camellias and cooled by fountains. Entered through stone gateways carved with swirls and abstract designs, the courtyards are flanked by small halls, and their flagstones have been worn smooth over time.

Back on the streets again, we soon encounter more child beggars; some are deformed, and most are barely 10 years old. They are tugging at our coats, our legs and our arms, fixing us with hollow and despairing eyes. I am so upset and churned up inside that I have to head back to the hotel. On the way, we again pass the woman and her two

Street food in Xi'an's Muslim Quarter

Worshippers' shoes flank the entrance to the Great Mosque's main prayer hall

children outside KFC – the kids are still screaming and have become even more hysterical. I cannot bear it: I dash inside and buy three hamburgers, three cold drinks and two ice-creams, and hand them out. In an instant, the crying stops, and beautiful childish smiles and giggles return.

Entering the serene precincts of Xi'an's Great Mosque

Lamb Skewers

1 kg (2 lb) lamb fillets, cut into 1 cm (½ in) cubes
1 tablespoon sea salt
2 lemons, cut into wedges

Spice paste
1 teaspoon ground cumin
1 teaspoon sweet paprika powder
1 teaspoon ground fennel
1 teaspoon ground nutmeg
1 teaspoon ground cinnamon
1 teaspoon ground turmeric
1 teaspoon roasted and ground Sichuan pepper
1 teaspoon ground ginger
2 teaspoon dried chilli flakes
⅓ cup vegetable oil

First make the spice paste. Combine all the spices in a large bowl, then stir in the oil to form a paste. Add meat and mix well, cover, place in refrigerator and leave to marinate for 4 hours.

Soak sixteen 25 cm (10 in) bamboo skewers in cold water for 30 minutes. Thread lamb onto skewers and cook on a hot barbecue or chargrill.

Serve immediately, seasoned with sea salt and with lemon wedges alongside.

Serves 4 (makes about 16 skewers)

You can also use beef fillet or chicken thigh fillet for these succulent kebabs. Accompanied by a large salad, a plate of fresh herbs and some flatbread, they make a lovely simple meal.

The Terracotta Army was intended to guard the tomb of China's first emperor, Qin Shi Huang.

The site occupied by the Terracotta Army is an hour's drive east of town, and we are bursting with excitement at the thought of visiting this extraordinary place. Renowned for having unified China in 221 BC and building the first Great Wall, Qin Shi Huang was also a despotic ruler who endeavoured – like Mao – to destroy all evidence of history before his reign, ironically dying during a quest for magical herbs that would supposedly make him immortal. Court historians recorded the lavish design of his tomb, writing of rivers of mercury, ceilings studded with gems to represent stars and chambers dripping with gold, but nobody knew anything about the life-sized Terracotta Army until peasants digging a well in a field found the first soldiers in 1974. So far, more than 8000 figures have been located, although only a fraction have been excavated and restored to their original purpose: an implacable army guarding the emperor for eternity.

Before seeing the real-life warriors, we watch a fascinating 15-minute film on the history of Xi'an, setting the tone for our visit. The screen surrounds us on all sides and, with the dramatic acting and visuals, we feel like we are caught up in the action. By the time it is finished, I am desperate to see the warriors up close. We enter 'Pit 1', a huge area protected by a hangar, where the main army is assembled in battle formation – I am speechless. There before our very eyes stand thousands of life-size statues of warriors, all with distinct, expressive faces, their various hairstyles and clothing indicating each soldier's rank in the army. A warrior sporting a knot of hair on the side of his head is a common soldier, one with a big topknot in the middle of his head is a general, warriors wearing more armour are higher officials, and those of a more stocky build, with chunky legs and wearing tunics, are mid-ranking officials.

The intricacy of the craftsmanship is astonishing – not only the warriors' hand-sculpted heads but also their belts, their armour, their footwear, everything. And they look just as impressive from behind as from the front. What is extraordinary is the way each warrior is totally individual – in terms of physical stature, facial expression, outfit, hair-do, posture and body language. They sport so much personality and inner vibrancy: there are some warriors with small heads, some with round heads; some are rather middle-aged characters with sagging stomachs and slightly rounded shoulders, while others are skinny, tall and lanky. You almost feel that if you could touch them and talk to them, then they would talk right back to you.

All facing the same direction, the warriors lean slightly forward as if at the ready, propelled by a collective energy that is powerful and overwhelming, a visual rhythm born of unflinching clarity of intention and camaraderie. I am literally moved to tears by their faces, which radiate absolute devotion to their emperor, their god. They worship him, they protect him, and they will defend him no matter what; they are completely loyal and faithful to him. Qin Shi Huang needed them, too: he knew he was unpopular, and that after

his death, trouble would come from the descendants of those he'd slain or defeated during the course of his unification campaign. And, in time, it did – from the Han dynasty that duly overthrew his grandson.

In some areas, the pits have been plundered and the warriors have no heads, but even head-less, their posture is still proud and tall, and their aura noble and devoted. Nearby some tail-less terracotta horses patiently await restoration and repair. Like the warriors, the horses are noble, majestic and completely breath-taking. The body of each horse is perfectly formed – the attention to detail is reminiscent of the precision of a Leonardo Da Vinci anatomical sketch. You can sense the tendons, ligaments and musculature beneath the barrel of each horse's body, in its slender, long neck and elegantly sculpted legs and hooves. They are so lifelike, I want to reach out and touch them.

There are four or five pits altogether and we spend a good 30 minutes in each. I notice that not all the soldiers are lined up as for a battle – in one pit, identified as the 'army headquarters', a group are facing each other, having a meeting. There is a lifetime's worth of visual and aesthetic beauty to digest here, and we all marvel at some exquisitely crafted carriages that have been excavated from the emperor's tomb, along with a pair of bronze chariots. There are also several lifetimes of restorations work still to be done, and archaeologists are busily working around us.

Mr Yang, the farmer who first discovered the warriors by unearthing a terracotta head in his field, sits inside the souvenir shop, ready to sign books if asked. He is a white-haired old man, with fantastic, big black-framed round glasses, and sits quietly behind the desk, observing everyone. I get the impression that he is completely sick of being on show, of signing books for tourists – he is grumpy, tired and does not smile once.

After spending several hours being captivated by the warriors, we have all worked up quite an appetite.

Five minutes' drive away is a local village that caters for tourists, and we pull up outside some swanky-looking townhouses. Our guide explains that this area used to belong to farmers, but when the Terracotta Army was discovered here, the government purchased the land so they could restore the site and turn it into a major tourist destination. Some of the villagers chose to stay in the area, spending their compensation money on smart townhouses and capitalising on the influx of tourists.

We are warmly greeted by two sweet-faced young girls, who quickly usher us inside, out of the blistering 32-degree heat. The sitting area is modern, with new white tiles everywhere, fancy rosewood furniture, air-conditioning that works, and a big TV screen.

My guide speaks to the women of the household and tells them that we are keen 'foodies' from Australia, and asks whether we might be allowed to watch the resident noodle-maker perform her art? Of course! A lovely woman greets us with a big smile as she deftly rolls away at a piece of smooth, silky-looking dough. Most of the Chinese kitchens I have seen are as basic as this one, with big square tiles installed from floor to ceiling, a simple two-burner stovetop, a rice cooker, a bamboo steamer and a few cooking utensils. What is produced from this simple kitchen, however, is astounding. We watch in amazement as the cook transforms an ordinary-looking piece of dough into the finest noodles, and our mouths fall open as she fashions delicate diamond shapes out of another piece of dough. We spontaneously applaud as she turns a strand of dough into rustic 'ear-shaped' pasta. A young girl joins in the noodle making halfway through, and our guide explains that this girl is an apprentice noodle maker.

Tummies rumbling and mouths drooling, we return to the eating area, which is equipped with lovely square wooden tables and stools, and are offered refreshing green tea. Expecting a simple lunch, we are pleasantly surprised by the most amazing spread.

Out come the first dishes: a wonderful starter of choko pickles – beautiful slivers of silky green vegetable, cool and refreshing with a slightly sour and salty flavour – and two small plates of chopped spinach-like greens. On tasting them, I am sent into total raptures: they have the most exquisite, delicate flavour and the most pleasing texture. None of us have ever eaten these vegetables before and, when we ask, our guide explains that they are a type of 'wild Chinese weed'. I ask if the waitress can bring me out the raw ingredients, in case I recognise them. One of the weeds, pronounced *ren rah*, looks very similar to a bunch of mint but smells nothing like it, and the other does indeed look just like a green weed. The texture of both is similar to brewed and strained jasmine tea leaves – slightly chewy, slightly wet, but rather appealing. The flavour is harder to describe but is a combination of earthy, straw-like, aromatic and herbaceous tastes, with a lingering, almost intoxicating quality.

Next up are some delicious deep-fried fritters with meltingly sweet pumpkin inside, and a pickled, crunchy lotus-root salad flavoured with Sichuan peppercorns, dried red chillies and vinegar – all accompanied by three fabulous dishes of the noodles we'd seen being made. We are in heaven as we busily chomp and slurp away. The ear-shaped pasta is served in a beautifully comforting, home-style soup reminiscent of a Chinese-style minestrone. The diamond-shaped shreds are served stir-fried and laced with chilli, soy sauce and garlic; thin strips of cucumber dotted throughout soften the effect of the fiery chilli. A refreshing egg and tomato salad arrives, along with a totally wild dish of stir-fried green chillies. Enter at your own risk!

Then my favourite dish of the day appears: stir-fried matchsticks of potato with dried red chilli, spring onions and carrot. The sour and salty flavour is delicious, making for a wonderful dish, but whoever would have thought to *stir-fry* potatoes? Only the Chinese . . . actually, now I come to think of it, my family served me a similar dish when I visited them in Guangdong (see recipe on page 14). I remember being pleasantly surprised by the combination of ingredients, and I now proudly have a vegetarian version on my restaurant menu back in Sydney: 'Billy Kwong's Stir-Fry of Organic Potatoes with Carrot, Ginger, Brown Rice Vinegar and Soy'.

The dishes keep coming, we keep accepting them, and we keep eating them. There appears to be no room left on the table, but somehow we manage to fit everything on. That is the funniest thing about Chinese meals – in my restaurant, the tables are also tiny, but you wouldn't believe the amount of food we can fit onto them. Where there is a will there is a way, I guess. Every dish is so inviting that we just can't bear to send any back, or to waste anything. Just when we think we are going to burst, *more* food arrives – amazing Chinese dough buns to mop up all the sauces, and some luscious braised tofu. Unforgettable food, amazing textures and combinations of ingredients and flavours: we agree that this is the best meal we have had on our journey so far – it is all so fresh, clean-tasting and vibrant.

A feast is laid on for us at a local village
OPPOSITE: Making fresh pasta and noodles

Pumpkin Fritters

1 kg (2 lb) pumpkin, peeled and cut into 5 mm (¼ in) slices
5 cm (2 in) piece ginger, cut into thin strips
¼ cup plain (all-purpose) flour, plus extra for dusting
2 cups vegetable oil for deep-frying

Batter
¾ cup beer
¾ cup plain (all-purpose) flour
¾ cup ice

Place pumpkin on a heatproof plate that will fit inside a steamer basket. Place plate inside steamer and position over a deep saucepan or wok of boiling water and steam, covered, for 15 minutes or until pumpkin is tender. Remove plate from steamer and drain off any excess liquid. Transfer pumpkin to a cold plate and place in refrigerator to cool.

Using a fork, roughly mash cooled pumpkin, ginger and flour in a bowl, mixing well. Dust a tray or large plate with the extra flour. Take tablespoonfuls of the pumpkin mixture and, using your hands, shape into flattish cakes. Carefully place finished cakes onto the floured tray or plate ready for deep-frying.

Combine batter ingredients in a bowl with a slotted spoon (using a spoon rather than a whisk keeps the batter thick and lumpy, and the lumps become crunchy when deep-fried). You may need to add a little more flour to the batter if it is too runny – it all depends on the humidity. Leave batter at room temperature until ice has half-melted; start using *immediately* at this stage.

Heat oil in a hot wok until surface seems to shimmer slightly. Using a spatula, carefully lower fritters into oil, one at a time – you should be able to cook about five or six fritters in each batch. Deep-fry on each side for about 2 minutes or until golden brown. Remove fritters with a slotted spoon and drain well on kitchen paper. Repeat with remaining batches of fritters.

Arrange fritters on a platter and serve immediately.

Serves 4–6 as part of a shared meal (makes about 20 fritters)

These fritters are delicious served with a small bowl of soy sauce and sliced red chillies for dipping.

Country-Style Egg and Tomato Salad

1 medium red onion, finely sliced
1 teaspoon brown sugar
1 teaspoon sea salt
4 free-range eggs
2 medium tomatoes
2 tablespoons brown rice vinegar
1 tablespoon extra virgin olive oil
1 teaspoon light soy sauce
3 iceberg lettuce leaves, finely shredded
pinch Sichuan pepper and salt

Place onion in a bowl, sprinkle with sugar and salt and mix well. Cover and set aside to pickle for 30 minutes.

Meanwhile, place eggs in a small saucepan of simmering water and cook gently for 10–12 minutes. Remove eggs from saucepan using a slotted spoon and refresh under cold running water. Carefully peel eggs and cut in half.

Cut tomatoes in half lengthways, and then cut each half into quarters.

Drain pickled onion and, using your hands, gently squeeze out any excess liquid. Return onion to bowl, then add vinegar, oil and soy sauce and mix well.

Arrange lettuce on a platter and top with eggs and tomatoes. Garnish with pickled onion and sprinkle with Sichuan pepper and salt. Serve immediately.

Serves 4–6 as part of a shared meal

Stir-Fried Green Chillies with Garlic

2 tablespoons peanut oil
4 garlic cloves, crushed
300 g (10 oz) large green chillies,
cut into 5 mm (¼ in) slices
3 tablespoons light soy sauce
1 tablespoon brown rice vinegar

Heat oil in a hot wok until surface seems to shimmer slightly. Add garlic and chillies and stir-fry for 3 minutes. Add soy sauce and vinegar and stir-fry for a further 2 minutes. Serve immediately.

Serves 4–6 as part of a shared meal

Stir-Fried Duck Breasts with Pickled Ginger and Pickled Chillies

4 × 200 g (6½ oz) duck breasts, with skin
2 tablespoons peanut oil
100 g (3½ oz) sliced pickled ginger
100 g (3½ oz) pickled red chillies
4 spring onions (scallions), trimmed and
sliced on the diagonal
2 tablespoons light soy sauce
2 tablespoons brown sugar

Trim any excess fat from duck breasts – you should have about 600 g (1 lb 4 oz) duck after trimming – and cut meat and skin on the diagonal into 1 cm (½ in) slices.

Heat oil in a hot wok until surface seems to shimmer slightly. Add duck and stir-fry for 1 minute. Remove duck from wok with a slotted spoon and set aside.

Drain off half the oil from wok, then add pickled ginger and chillies and stir-fry for 30 seconds. Return duck to wok, along with remaining ingredients, and stir-fry for 2 minutes. Serve immediately.

Serves 4–6 as part of a shared meal

Pickled ginger and pickled red chillies are available from Asian supermarkets.

Braised Firm Tofu with Tomatoes

1 × 300 g (10 oz) packet firm tofu
3 small tomatoes
2 tablespoons peanut oil
5 cm (2 in) piece ginger, finely sliced
1 tablespoon brown sugar
2 tablespoons shao hsing wine
2 tablespoons brown rice vinegar
2 tablespoons light soy sauce
½ teaspoon sesame oil
2 spring onions (scallions), trimmed and cut into 5 cm (2 in) lengths
pinch ground white pepper

Cut tofu into 5 cm × 2.5 cm (2 in × 1 in) pieces and drain well on kitchen paper. Cut tomatoes in half lengthways, then cut each half into four wedges.

Heat peanut oil in a hot wok until surface seems to shimmer slightly. Carefully add tofu and sear for 1 minute or until lightly browned, then turn over and sear other side. Add tomatoes and ginger and stir-fry for 2 minutes, being careful not to break up tofu.

Add sugar and stir-fry for 1 minute until caramelised. Add shao hsing wine and stir-fry for a further minute.

Stir through vinegar, soy sauce, sesame oil and spring onions. Serve immediately, sprinkled with pepper.

Serves 4–6 as part of a shared meal

We fall into the bus and head back to Xi'an.

I am so full I really need to flop into bed for several hours to allow everything to digest, but as we sail down a busy city street I catch a glimpse of what looks very much like a Chinese herb and medicine market – I yell to the driver to stop. Taking a deep breath, we jump off the bus and into the market, and immediately the air is thick with yelps and screams, as we spot all manner of weird and wonderful things: dried starfish, coils of dried snake, dried cocoon-like pods, dried turtle shells and crab shells, dried over-sized fungus and mushrooms, dried black scorpions, cicadas, worms, seahorses, shells, dried squid . . .

For me, one of the most confronting sights is a sack of dead black ants. Imagine the physical sensation of picking up a 2 kilo bag of rice grains. Well, with this in mind, just think how many ants would have to be in the sack to make it weigh 2 kilos! I later learn that these ants are used to treat a variety of ailments, including rheumatism, hepatitis and ageing. Another surprising sight is a stall that sells the hairy, shrivelled-up genitals of male animals, including deer and dog – apparently, these help to reverse impotence in men.

After half an hour of this we are *definitely* ready for our hotel rooms. I collapse in a heap and stay there all evening, mentally preparing for our next exciting journey – to the capital city of Beijing.

Traditional remedies, ranging from ants to starfish and lizards, on display at a herbal medicine market near Xi'an

Beijing and the Great Wall

BEIJING AND THE GREAT WALL

装修
防水
福門財門幸福門
門財門幸
做防水

福門財門幸福門
門財門幸福門
宅王宅吉祥宅

大翔凤胡同
DAXIANGFENG HUTONG
危难时刻 迅速报警
110
中国移动通信

Without a doubt, Beijing is a striking and wonderful city: the heart of the nation, beating with life.

Yet Beijing's many contradictions can make it a difficult place to deal with, and for all its grandeur it often feels as though there are dark undercurrents lurking just beneath the surface. As the city is considered a showcase for everything that the government would like the country to be, there's a huge military and police presence, and daily life seems constrained by a plethora of rules and regulations. And the extreme pollution and soaring summer temperatures don't make it any easier to cope with simply getting around the place.

Beijing hasn't always been China's capital. In fact, it was the Mongols, under Kublai Khan, who set it up in the thirteenth century as the country's administrative centre. They built the city on a large scale, to humble those who came to pay homage – including Marco Polo – and the tradition has been kept up by all the rulers who followed them. Modern Beijing is a sprawling city that sometimes feels like one vast building site, with extensive construction under way and a confusing maze of roads, all packed with traffic, and crowds of people in every nook and cranny.

We start our first morning in the city by walking from our hotel to the infamous Tian'anmen Square, about 20 minutes away. As we approach, I spot an enormous queue of people and ask our guide what they are all waiting for.

'That's for Mao's mausoleum – 2000 people line up each day for up to four hours to walk past his coffin.'

I am absolutely stunned. I have grown up with such a negative view of Mao, especially for unleashing the havoc of the Cultural Revolution, which strangled the country for ten years and led to the death of millions before Mao himself died in 1976. How could any devotion still be given to such a person? In China, however, I discover that opinions are not so clear-cut. For a start, when he took power in 1950 Mao also ended a century of civil conflict that had seen the emperor kicked off his throne and the country humiliated by foreign invasions, so people here admire him for that. And, whatever use he might have put it to, there is no denying that he was an incredibly powerful figure – perhaps many of the people filing past his tomb are simply hoping a little bit of this will rub off on them.

In reality, Mao's influence on contemporary China seems relatively minor, as the government has long since abandoned his policies. Also, most older people don't willingly talk about the Cultural Revolution, and the younger ones who didn't experience it and have never really known times when opportunities didn't seem to get better by the day, know about it but don't see it as relating to their lives. Apparently, the official view on Mao is that his policies were 70 per cent right and 30 per cent wrong . . .

We follow the queue into Tian'anmen Square, which opens up in front of us and is incredibly intimidating: a 400,000-square-metre expanse of grey paving stretching to the distant walls of the Forbidden City. We all turn around slowly on the spot, struggling to

An imposing portrait of Mao hangs over the entrance to the Forbidden City

PREVIOUS PAGE: Rickshaw drivers take a well-earned break in a quiet *hutong*

take everything in. I find the experience somewhat haunting, remembering the terrible events that took place here in June 1989, when tanks were deployed against unarmed student demonstrators who had gathered in this public space seeking democratic reforms.

We spend about half an hour just standing in Tian'anmen Square, transfixed as tourists swarm around its various memorials and civic buildings. Our guide points to the soldiers guarding one monument who are not allowed to move at all for three hours at a time. But perhaps the most stunning thing here is simply the number of people: Beijing's population is over 15 million, and most of them seem to be in Tian'anmen Square with us! And overlooking them all, from the back of the square, is the famous and rather formidable portrait of Chairman Mao, with his unmistakable receding hairline, round face and distinguishing mole under his bottom lip. Mao was actually responsible for having Tian'anmen Square built in the 1950s, and I now understand why: his portrait presiding over this surging mass of humanity makes the power that he wielded in China almost tangible. At the same time, you're left in no doubt as to the collective strength of the Chinese people either.

Under Mao's watchful gaze, we walk up to the studded doors of the Forbidden City.

Once again, we feel dwarfed by the sheer scale of its red walls towering above us. Beyond them lies a vast complex of palaces that was founded in the fifteenth century by the Ming emperors. They and their successors lived lives of unimaginable privilege, completely segregated from their subjects. The last emperor, who lost the throne in 1911, was overthrown by warlords a decade later and, having been looted, the Forbidden City fell into disrepair until restoration began in the 1970s.

Inside the confines of the Forbidden City, we marvel at the sheer enormity of the space, the magnificent architecture, the gilded bronze statues of mythical creatures, and the exquisite towers and courtrooms. Red and gold colour schemes are everywhere; red is considered a lucky colour in China, while gold or yellow represents heaven and was once reserved for the emperor's use alone. Interestingly, the modern Chinese flag of gold stars on a red background, which is also flown all over the place, symbolically uses the same colour scheme. So do all the massive wooden doors guarding the entrance to each set of courtyards, their red-lacquered wood studded with an auspicious 81 burnished brass domes. Showy statues and carvings of dragons – another symbol of imperial power – protect the temples, and elegant carvings cover all the stone pillars and pavilions.

乾清門

Behind the imposing walls of the Forbidden City, vast courtyards surround a series of halls, including the Hall of Supreme Harmony with the emperor's golden throne at its centre

A succession of ornate gateways leads into ever-larger open courtyards, one of which is so big that the entire court, comprising tens of thousands of people, could assemble there. We really have to watch our step here to avoid twisting an ankle on the ancient, uneven cobblestones, beautiful as they are. Climbing a broad staircase either side of a marble ramp exquisitely carved with dragons weaving in and out of clouds, we reach the magnificent Hall of Supreme Harmony, where the emperor sat on a golden throne to receive important visitors. Dazzling red pillars support the beamed ceiling, which is covered with elaborate designs painted in bright shades of aqua, cobalt blue, red, gold, mustard and burnt orange. Every gateway, doorway, window frame, roof tile, corridor and corner adds a new texture, with a different motif, pattern, material or colour, all overlain with the patina of age. It's just incredible to think that this whole complex represented the empire in miniature, a smooth bureaucratic machine with the emperor at its centre.

As we wander through the labyrinth of palaces, halls and gardens, I notice many elderly people and am reminded of my own grandparents. It is wonderful to see how many of these older people are agile, healthy and sprightly, practising tai chi, ballroom dancing, opera singing, tree hugging, all types of martial arts, card playing and mah-jong. One woman must have been an acrobat when she was younger – she is so flexible that she seems to be made of rubber. Most of the women are dressed in simply cut blouses and trousers with an elastic waist; the men are similarly attired, but their trousers have zips and they wear belts. Thongs or plastic slipper-shoes seem to be the norm, both entirely comfortable and appropriate for the humid summer weather. It makes me proud of my heritage and upbringing when I see that there is still a place in Chinese society for the aged; both my grandmothers lived with us at different times, and my parents raised me to respect my elders. I notice a middle-aged woman dutifully pushing her elderly mother in a wheelchair. Her mother, with her white hair pinned back to the side, has bound feet, and I find myself thinking of the changes she must have seen in her lifetime. With a big smile, I spontaneously reach out to hold her hand. She is tentative at first, but soon her face softens into a smile. I am demonstrative, like my father, and I think reaching out to someone is a beautiful and profound way to communicate your feelings; I love the 'directness' of it.

We walk out of the Forbidden City in a complete daze – this is only our first morning in Beijing and already there has been so much to take in. Now, for some respite from the monumental scale of Tian'anmen Square and the Forbidden City, we're heading to Beijing's *hutongs*, the intricate maze of lanes and courtyard houses that once criss-crossed the whole city centre. I've been looking forward to this moment, the chance to glimpse an older, more traditional side of the city. Sadly, it turns out that there are now only a handful of *hutong* areas left: our guide informs us that many are being demolished to make way for huge property developments, in an attempt to 'clean up' and 'modernise' the city in time for the 2008 Olympics. As with all cities that win the honour of holding the Olympic Games, the event is making its mark on Beijing, and everywhere we turn there is work in progress.

吊便

We jump into a brightly coloured rickshaw, and its sinewy driver pedals us into one of the main *hutongs*, in the Houhai area.

We wind though charming, narrow alleyways, and there are signs of street-life everywhere: men selling watermelons off the back of their blue trucks, young children wrestling with one another in the street, rows of bikes leaning against ancient-looking brick walls, workmen taking an afternoon nap on pieces of cardboard. After a while, though, we begin to notice how many other foreigners in rickshaws have passed us, and how clean, orderly and, well, characterless this *hutong* is, and we begin to wonder if it has been somewhat sanitised for the sake of tourists. We were hoping to see something a little grittier, and we mention this to our guide. Sometimes in China, there is a reluctance to show visitors places that are considered to be less attractive or even shabby, as they feel that the country 'loses face' if it is shown to be anything less than modern and progressive. To get off the beaten track, you need to persist until you find what you are looking for.

For the time being we drop the matter and stop for lunch at the *hutong* home of Mr Ding. He and his family are cooking us lunch as part of our Beijing experience and, as we are welcomed into his tiny dining room, we are all looking forward to tasting authentic local food. Images of Beijing dumplings float across my mind's eye . . . walking around the Forbidden City all morning has really given me an appetite.

On a previous trip, I had lunched at a Manchurian family home and been served a splendid meal: braised soy beans with garlic and vinegar, delectable braised gelatinous beef tendons, a fine salad of tofu and sesame oil, a hearty dish of braised brisket with white radish and carrot, some crispy homemade spring onion pancakes, pork dumplings, roasted peanuts and a plate of dried apricots.

Imagine our disappointment, then, with the appetisers Mr Ding brings us – crackers, processed ham and cherry tomatoes. We go into a huddle with our guide, Chris (who I suspect is having a difficult morning with us) and, through him, tell Mr Ding that we have come to Beijing for a genuine experience and would like to try the local specialities, so could we please eat traditional Chinese food for lunch? Mr Ding understands, and returns in 10 minutes with a selection of dumplings, a plate of braised soy beans with star anise, and a smoky hot chicken stir-fry with dried red chilli and green garlic chives. There are sighs of relief all round.

Settling in, we chat to Mr Ding about his daily life. A very kind man, he proudly shows us a picture of his teenage daughter, his only child, and it is quite evident that he and his wife are devoted to her well-being and education. It is heart-warming to see how much affection the Chinese generally lavish on their children; you almost never come across a parent screaming at or scolding a child.

Red-Braised Chickpeas with Star Anise and Vinegar

1 cup dried chickpeas (garbanzo beans)

Red-Braise Sauce

½ cup shao hsing wine
5 cm (2 in) piece ginger, finely sliced
1 spring onion (scallion), trimmed and cut into 5 cm (2 in) lengths
3 star anise
⅓ cup brown sugar
⅓ cup light soy sauce
1 teaspoon sesame oil
½ cup water
2 tablespoons brown rice vinegar

Soak chickpeas overnight in cold water, then drain and transfer to a heavy-based pan or stockpot. Cover generously with cold water, bring to the boil, then turn down to a gentle simmer and cook for 1–1½ hours or until tender, adding more water as necessary. Drain and set aside.

Next, make the red-braise sauce. Place shao hsing wine, ginger, spring onion and star anise in a wok, then bring to the boil and simmer for 2 minutes. Add sugar, soy sauce and sesame oil and simmer for a further minute. Add chickpeas and water, then simmer briskly for 10 minutes. Stir in vinegar and serve.

Serves 4–6 as part of a shared meal

I've used dried chickpeas here, as they are generally easier to obtain than dried soy beans, but if you do come across dried soy beans, they can be cooked in the same way for a slightly more authentic result.

Coriander Salad with Five-Spice Tofu and Sesame Oil

2 bunches coriander (cilantro), leaves and stems only, roughly chopped
100 g (3½ oz) five-spice firm tofu, finely sliced
1 tablespoon light soy sauce
1 tablespoon brown rice vinegar
2 teaspoons sesame oil

Gently toss all ingredients in a large bowl and serve.

Serves 4–6 as part of a shared meal

Braised Beef Brisket with Carrot, White Radish and Liquorice Root

1 kg (2 lb) beef brisket, cut into
 5 cm (2 inch) slices
2 medium carrots, peeled
2 medium white radish (daikon), peeled
2 tablespoons brown rice vinegar

Stock
3 litres (3 quarts) cold water
1½ cups shao hsing wine
1 cup light soy sauce
1 cup brown sugar
6 garlic cloves, crushed
½ cup ginger slices
4 spring onions (scallions), trimmed
 and cut in half
½ teaspoon sesame oil
2 cinnamon quills
1 tablespoon dried Chinese liquorice root
4 star anise

To remove any impurities from meat, place brisket in a large pan or stockpot, cover with cold water and bring to the boil. Simmer for 20 minutes, then drain, discarding water. Rinse brisket thoroughly under cold water and drain well.

Cut carrots in half lengthways, and then into pieces about 6 × 2 cm (2½ × ¾ in). Cut white radish in half lengthways and then into pieces approximately 3 × 2 cm (1¼ × ¾ in).

Place all stock ingredients in a large pan or stockpot, then bring to the boil and simmer gently for 30 minutes. Add brisket, carrot and radish to simmering stock, ensuring they are all fully submerged. Braise very gently for 2 hours, or until brisket is soft and gelatinous, regularly skimming any scum from the surface of the stock using a ladle.

Remove from stove, stir through vinegar, and carefully transfer brisket and vegetables to serving bowl. Ladle over stock and serve.

Serves 4–6 as part of a shared meal

Dried liquorice root is available from Chinese supermarkets.

Smoky Hot Chicken Stir-Fried with Dried Red Chillies and Green Garlic Chives

600 g (1 lb 4 oz) chicken thigh fillets, cut into 1 cm (½ in) cubes
2 tablespoons cornflour (cornstarch)
2 tablespoons shao hsing wine
2 tablespoons peanut oil
10 small dried red chillies
2 tablespoons peanut oil, extra
5 cm (2 in) piece ginger, cut into thin strips
1 tablespoon brown sugar
2 tablespoons light soy sauce
1 tablespoon brown rice vinegar
1 small handful green garlic chives, cut into 5 cm (2 in) lengths

Combine chicken with cornflour and shao hsing wine in a bowl. Cover, place in refrigerator and leave to marinate for 1 hour.

Place oil and chillies in a cold wok and *then* turn heat to low. Cook for about 1½ minutes or until chillies begin to darken slightly. Using a slotted spoon, immediately remove chillies and drain on kitchen paper.

Leaving chilli-infused oil in wok, turn heat up to high and stir-fry half the chicken cubes for 3 minutes. Remove with a slotted spoon. Add extra oil to wok with remaining chicken and stir-fry for 3 minutes. Return all chicken to wok, along with ginger and reserved chillies, and stir-fry for 1 minute.

Add sugar and stir-fry for 30 seconds. Add remaining ingredients and stir-fry for 30 seconds. Serve immediately.

Serves 4–6 as part of a shared meal

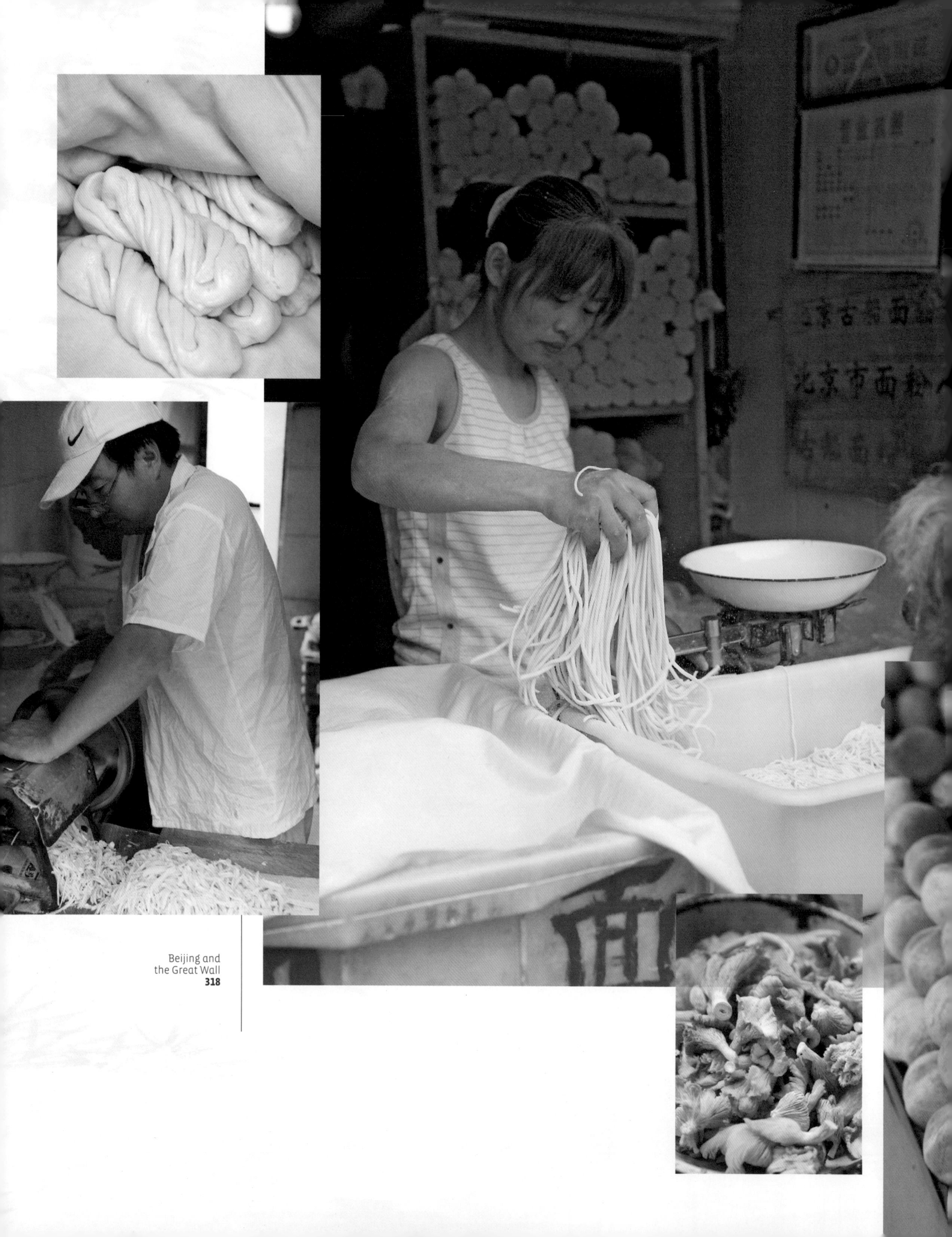

Knowing of my obsession with food markets, Chris takes us to one nearby, on Beijing's Second Ring Road, which turns out to be among the best I have been to in Asia.

It's an absolute hub of artistry and activity, with an expanse of open-sided sheds shading hundreds of stalls packed with every imaginable type of fresh and dried produce. An area of walled-in cubicles off to our left houses dozens of bakers, dough kneaders, noodle makers, pancake rollers, dumpling fillers and shapers, and spring onion pancake masters. We are drawn to one stall, where a whirring electric millstone grinds roasted sesame seeds into paste and oil. The rich, nutty aroma of sesame fills the air, and I buy several bottles of the dark golden oil to use in my cooking during the trip.

Barrows stacked with watermelons are being wheeled in and parked next to the stallholders, who hurl them around with abandon, cutting a few in half to show how fresh and juicy they are before arranging the rest in piles. There are also mounds of plump, ripe peaches (apparently Beijing is renowned for its peaches), carrots with dirt still clinging to them, shiny purple eggplants, black fungus, every type of Chinese cabbage imaginable, fresh soy beans, dried bean curd skins, tubs of oyster mushrooms and square tins of dried spices and chillies, star anise, fennel seeds, five-spice powder and cumin. One stand we all hover around sells an impressive selection of dried strawberries, figs, prunes, red dates and the most delicious dried apricots – a beautiful deep orangey-red in colour, they are luscious and have an incredibly intense flavour. Half a kilo is swiftly purchased to nibble on during our bus rides.

This evening, we plan to eat Beijing duck at the highly recommended Li Qun Roast Duck Restaurant. But on the way, we stop off to check out the night market in Xiagongfu Street, near Wangfujing Avenue, which sells street food from all over China. What a place. Pulsating masses of people gather around the hundreds of stalls that line

the street, eager to sample the sizzling-hot snacks. This is far and away the most amazing night market I have experienced: well laid out, clean, varied and with an ambience like no other, as the smell of the food wafts through the humid evening air. There are the usual snacks and stir-fries, but my attention is caught by the extraordinary range of food sold on skewers: all kinds of seafood, meat and vegetables, quail's eggs, frogs, grasshoppers, silk-worm cocoons, snakes, crabs, fish balls, cubes of solidified pig's blood, and vegetables. One stall sells a Beijing speciality, skewers of fruit with a toffee glaze. I stare at some crunchy-looking starfish, then at the stinging tails of the black scorpions perfectly skewered, three per stick, and wonder how on earth the Chinese can eat such sinister, devilish-looking creatures.

Even though we have a huge meal in front of us, we still can't resist trying the food. I buy a delicious savoury parcel made by wrapping a thin pancake around stir-fried green garlic chives and mushrooms; fried on a hot-plate, it's crunchy on one side and soft on the other. Another version has a filling of freshly stir-fried pork, bean sprouts, garlic and ginger: absolutely *scrumptious*. There are shucked oysters overflowing with soy sauce, chilli and ginger, and small bowls of a salad made from crunchy fresh black cloud ear fungus. On a nearby stall, a man with a red apron and matching red sun visor deftly rotates dumplings on a scorching-hot cast-iron plate.

Next I am intrigued by a large cooker filled with translucent cubes of a jelly-like substance. I don't know what it is, but I am desperate to try it. The cubes are doused with soy sauce and topped with a thatch of coriander and chopped spring onion. My guide points to it and cheerfully says, 'This is pork fat – a local snack.' Wobbling, glistening cubes of pork fat. Errr . . . no, thanks! Most Chinese people have a weakness for animal fat, associating it with abundance, since meat is scarce in many rural Chinese communities and is only eaten on special occasions like weddings and festivals. Really fatty meat signifies a good year in which there was surplus food to fatten up the livestock.

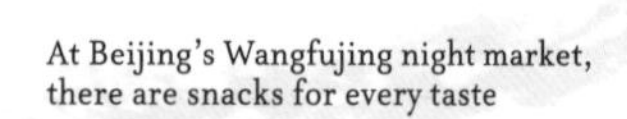

At Beijing's Wangfujing night market, there are snacks for every taste

Steamed Oysters with Ginger, Chilli and Soy Dressing

6 oysters, shucked but left on the half shell
2 tablespoons shao hsing wine
2.5 cm (1 in) piece ginger, finely chopped
1 large red chilli, finely sliced
¼ teaspoon brown sugar
1 tablespoon light soy sauce
¼ teaspoon sesame oil
2 tablespoons peanut oil
small pinch ground white pepper

Place oysters in a shallow heatproof bowl that will fit inside a steamer basket. Pour wine over oysters, then sprinkle with half the ginger. Place bowl inside steamer and position over a deep saucepan or wok of boiling water and steam, covered, for 2 minutes.

Carefully remove bowl from steamer and transfer oysters to a serving platter, with their juices. Combine chilli, sugar, soy sauce, sesame oil and remaining ginger in a bowl and distribute evenly between the oysters.

Meanwhile heat peanut oil in a small heavy-based pan until surface shimmers slightly. Carefully pout hot oil over the oysters to 'scald' the chilli and ginger. Sprinkle with pepper and serve immediately.

Serves 1–2 as a starter

Instead of steaming the oysters, you could briefly cook them on the barbecue before adding the dressing: just be careful not to overcook them.

Fresh Black Cloud Ear Fungus Salad

400 g (13 oz) fresh black cloud ear fungus

Dressing

4 garlic cloves, finely chopped
5 cm (2 in) piece ginger, finely chopped
2 tablespoons brown sugar
3 tablespoons light soy sauce
2 tablespoons brown rice vinegar
1 teaspoon sesame oil

Place cloud ear fungus in a bowl.

Combine all dressing ingredients in a saucepan, then bring to a gentle simmer and cook, stirring, for 3 minutes to dissolve sugar.

Pour hot dressing over cloud ear fungus, mix well and serve.

Serves 4–6 as part of a shared meal

With our heads still spinning from the night market, we waddle to our waiting bus, which delivers us to the mouth of a rather downmarket-looking *hutong*.

Situated to the southeast of Tian'anmen Square, this district is obviously one of the *hutong* areas being cleared to 'modernise' the city, and has none of the easy atmosphere we experienced earlier in the day. Grey concrete slabs and drab brick walls are graffitied with red spray paint and faded bill posters. Sadness is everywhere, the street full of people sitting glumly on their steps, staring listlessly ahead or scavenging among garbage and rubble as their homes are bulldozed before their eyes. It's a stark reality-check after the excitement of the night market.

Ten minutes' walk down the alley we come to the Li Qun Roast Duck Restaurant, its entrance crowded by parked rickshaws, their drivers bantering with each other while they smoke. The scent of roasting duck lures us through to an open wood fire, where a chef is busy bringing out five whole prepared ducks on a large metal hook. He feeds them through the wood fire and hangs them on another hook, just above the glowing embers. What is unique about this restaurant is that they roast their ducks over an open fruit-wood fire, rather than using gas-heated cylindrical ovens as most places do nowadays.

We order Beijing duck (often still called Peking duck, after the capital city's old name), plus side-dishes of jellyfish, cucumber salad and some stir-fried greens with garlic. The chef soon appears at our table, showing off a freshly roasted duck for our approval, and we are engulfed by subtle, smoky scents. In a flash it is carved into separate plates of moist, tender sliced meat and crispy, mahogany-coloured skin. To accompany it we are given raw strips of cucumber, crunchy spring onions, steaming hot pancakes so fine you can almost see your hand through them – and a brown bean sauce, which I find rather harsh and rough compared to the softer, sweeter tastes of hoisin or plum sauce.

As I chomp, I look around me and take note of the restaurant's unusual layout: the central room is sunken, and it is decked out with simple wooden tables with glass tops, large matte grey tiles on the floor, and red hanging lanterns; a series of doorways lead off it into smaller dining rooms, each with a unique atmosphere. I can't quite put my finger on what I find so intriguing, but I love how it feels – almost like a family home.

The owners are Mr and Mrs Lin, and as I pose for photographs with them I tell them that theirs is the best Beijing duck I have ever eaten. I just hope the restaurant is here the next time I visit – with so much reconstruction going on nearby, it's hard to know.

Back in the dilapidated alley again, we pass a little room that is someone's kitchen. Inquisitive as ever, I stick my head in and say hello to the man inside. He is about 60, and is braising a fish in

Inside the Li Qun Roast Duck Restaurant

TOP LEFT: A photo opportunity with the owner

OPPOSITE: The makings of a duck dinner at Li Qun, one of Beijing's most famous roast duck restaurants

QUN ROAST
Restaurant
统挂炉 货真价实
话订餐 果木烧烤

小新开胡同
7
五福臨門
福門財門幸福門
金宅玉宅吉祥宅

a wok over a gas flame. Through Chris I ask him how long he has lived in this *hutong*. 'All my life,' he replies – but now the government wants everyone out. He is distraught and does not know where to go. The government has offered each resident 400,000 yuan as compensation for their homes – an astronomical figure elsewhere in China but, as this man explains, it will never be enough to allow him to buy property so close to the city centre. He and his family will be forced to live way out of town.

As little as he has and as modestly as he lives, this man still has the generosity of heart to offer me a taste of his fish. I accept and take a mouthful of his dinner. It reminds me of the braised flathead with preserved radish and cabbage my mum used to make.

We get back on our bus with elated bellies and subdued hearts. This has been quite a confronting first day in Beijing, and it has brought home to me both the complexity of China and the way that, here in the capital, the government seems to have the final say about everything and everybody.

This particular story has a happy sequel, however.

Two months later I return to the Li Qun Restaurant and on the way, I stop at the old man's home again. His wife comes to the front door, looking rather anxious – no doubt wondering why a group of foreigners are knocking on her door at 8.30 p.m. Chris explains to her that I am the Australian woman who spoke to her husband several weeks before, and that I have a gift for him. Her anxiety fades and she yells for her husband, who tentatively comes to the door before recognising me and smiling. We have a wonderful reunion and I give him a copy of my first cookbook, pointing out to him the family portraits inside and getting Chris to tell him that I am a chef from Australia. He is so happy and invites us all into his kitchen, with its naked light bulb swaying above the plastic tablecloth spread with a platter of freshly boiled dumplings, a side dish of vinegar, and a pot of Chinese tea. Later, when we bid each other farewell, we leave with warmth in our hearts.

Beijing's premier yum cha restaurant is Jing Ding, located in Dongzhimen.

After the slightly sombre postscript to our first day in Beijing, we are determined to get our second day off to a good start. It can be difficult in China to find restaurants that serve regional cuisine, but Beijing, as the national capital, is an exception and, despite being a long way from Guangzhou and Hong Kong, at Jing Ding we breakfast on excellent, fresh-tasting yum cha. A two-tiered trolley filled with colourful appetisers swings past our table: hard-boiled salty duck eggs, blanched green beans tossed in sesame oil and dried chilli, fermented bean curd, and fresh small cucumbers with a hoisin-style dipping sauce.

I pounce on a hot dish, one of my mother's favourites: a bowl of offal, tenderly slow-braised in soy sauce, shao hsing wine, yellow rock sugar, ginger and star anise. It's full of warming tastes, colour and texture, and we all agree that the dish is a winner. A waitress slides past with a trolley laden with steaming vats of congee, and Chris waves his hand in the air, 'One bowl, please!' A typical Chinese breakfast, congee is a supremely comforting meal. It is simply rice boiled for a long time in stock until it becomes porridge-like in consistency, then flavoured at the table with crispy wonton skins, finely sliced spring onions, slivers of salty duck egg and a splash of soy sauce.

The dumplings at Jing Ding are heavenly. Perfectly shaped, translucent *har gow*, filled with stir-fried green and yellow garlic chives, are slippery and silky; dipped into a dish of soy sauce, they are swiftly devoured. The *shao mai* (minced marinated prawn meat gathered in a wonton wrapper) come steamed, and are completely delicious – fresh and slightly salty. I grab one of my favourites, steamed beef balls – the beef mince is flavoured with fragrant dried tangerine peel and has been blended with egg yolk to give it a fluffy, light, mousse-like texture.

Rice Congee with Salty Duck Egg

2 litres (2 quarts) boiling water
½ cup jasmine rice
1 teaspoon sea salt
1 teaspoon vegetable oil

Accompaniments

⅓ cup light soy sauce, mixed with
1 tablespoon sesame oil
1 salty duck egg, peeled and cut into eighths
2 spring onions (scallions), finely sliced
1 large red chilli, finely sliced
½ bunch coriander (cilantro), leaves only

Place boiling water, rice, salt and oil in a large heavy-based pan or stockpot and bring to the boil. Reduce heat and simmer for approximately 1½ hours or until volume has reduced by half, stirring regularly with a wooden spoon to prevent sticking and adjusting heat as required to prevent burning.

When it is ready, the congee should be off-white in colour with a slightly translucent appearance. Its texture should be thick and creamy, almost gluggy, yet runny. Taste the congee for flavour: it should be ever so slightly salty. Turn off heat and leave pot on stove, covered tightly, while you place all the accompaniments in separate side dishes.

With lid off, bring congee back to the boil and serve piping hot. Diners add accompaniments to their bowl as they wish – in any quantity, in any combination, and at any time.

Serves 4

Salty duck eggs can be found in Chinese supermarkets, and they come already cooked.

Built by the Ming emperors, the Temple of Heaven is a matchless example of architectural purity.

The halls and terraces that make up the temple complex are laid out along a north–south axis, in perfect alignment for the main ceremony of the year, when the emperor prayed for a bountiful harvest at the winter solstice. Unlike the usual rectangular, blocky Chinese temple buildings, the two main halls here are circular, with conical roofs. We walk up to the largest, the Good Harvest Hall, where the emperors used to come to pray to the gods for a bountiful harvest across the land – it's absolutely breathtaking! Its three tiered roofs are covered in exquisite deep-blue tiles and topped by a golden finial. Inside, the main supporting pillars are painted with gleaming golden floral patterns on a rich red background. Like the buildings in the Forbidden City, every square inch of the walls and ceiling is decorated with intricate designs in blue, red, gold, yellow and green. It's all so opulent that I find it a bit overpowering, preferring a morning wander in the lovely, green gardens outside, full of ancient-looking trees and elderly folk doing tai chi, ballroom dancing, folk and opera singing, flying kites, or simply playing card games and dominoes. It is truly inspirational to see how the old are provided for in China, and the way this engenders a spirit of healthy fun and camaraderie, as well as a sense of deep friendship and connectedness. For me, this is a real lesson in how we should all live our lives.

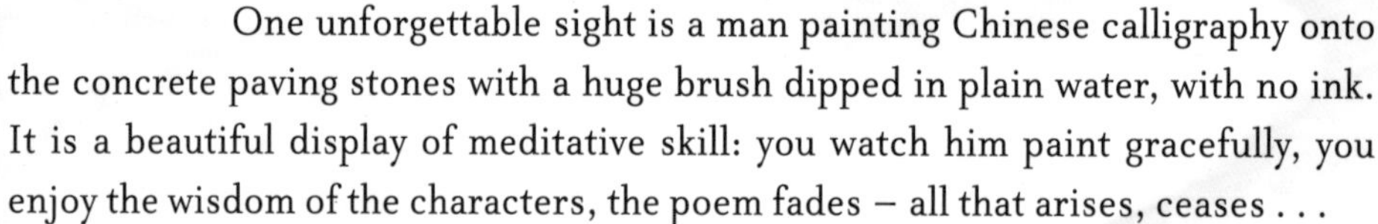

One unforgettable sight is a man painting Chinese calligraphy onto the concrete paving stones with a huge brush dipped in plain water, with no ink. It is a beautiful display of meditative skill: you watch him paint gracefully, you enjoy the wisdom of the characters, the poem fades – all that arises, ceases . . .

The extensive grounds and colonnades of the Temple of Heaven are popular with early-morning exercisers

Our appetite for art whetted, we decide on a detour to the Chaoyang area of northeastern Beijing to visit the Dashanzi 798 Art District, a Bauhaus-style factory complex that has in recent years become the focal point for much of Beijing's innovative contemporary art scene and the site of an annual international art festival.

Unfortunately we only have an hour to spare, but you could easily spend several days here, exploring all the fabulous art galleries, studios and workshops. There are enormous warehouse-style spaces and small, pokey dens, clothes shops, fabric stores, and plenty of funky cafes and bars when you're ready for a rest. We home in on the XYZ Art Gallery, which is owned by a charming, intelligent and well-spoken Chinese woman called Catherine. As I walk into her gallery a young artist is holding his artwork – beautiful female figures, painted with ink on paper – while another man takes digital shots. I soon learn that the artist is Shi Jianguo. I am also drawn to some haunting still-life and landscape oil paintings, the work of Xiao Gang.

We are all struck by the buzz and energy here. Modern Chinese art is going through a boom period, with a huge number of artists experimenting in

everything from traditional Chinese to Western techniques, many of them fusing elements of both to create completely new styles. The diversity and radical nature of the art being produced is such that it's a bit hard at the moment to see where it all might be heading, but many artists are nonetheless being acclaimed worldwide for their cutting-edge works. This sense of freedom and self-expression is so beautiful and moving to witness, representing as it does a powerful re-emergence of creativity and zest for life after the crushing of the nascent democracy movement in Tian'anmen Square and the suffocating times that followed. I feel intoxicated with the energy that exudes from every pore of the 798 Art District, reflecting China's new-found and hard-won freedom of personal expression through art.

For lunch, we have a date at the Huang Ting restaurant, in the Peninsula Hotel.

As always, I can't believe the multitude of Chinese variations on cucumber salad: here it comes as a great stack of raw, fresh cucumber batons, drizzled with an incredibly tasty and interesting sauce of horseradish, vinegar and soy sauce. The stir-fried king prawns with XO sauce are sensational and the cold platter of barbecued pork, duck and octopus is mouth-watering. But perhaps the most outstanding dish of the day is the utterly indulgent abalone fried rice: a bowl of piping-hot fried rice dotted with shreds of fluffy egg, spring onion and ginger, and laced with delicate slivers of glistening abalone and abalone sauce. The rice is so hot you have to negotiate just a few grains at a time with your chopsticks and lips, so as not to burn yourself. I serve a wonderful fried rice in my restaurant, based on one of my mother's recipes – with plenty of onion, ginger, salted radish, duck sausage, spring onions and egg – which has always got the thumbs-up from friends. But even I have to admit that Huang Ting's version wins hands down!

Our next port of call is the Beijing branch of the Hong Kong–based China Club. This occupies a stunning, 400-year-old Beijing mansion in the Xidan district, with four main courtyards surrounded by a series of interconnected pavilions. These courtyard houses or *siheyuan* used to be a defining feature of Beijing architecture, but now, like the *hutongs*, there are very few left, so we feel honoured to have the chance to visit one.

The whole place is elegance personified, but the library is my room of choice, with its row of 1920s Art Deco-style windows looking out into one of the courtyards. It is Chinese in design but has a blend of antique European and Chinese furnishings, and walls lined with mahogany bookshelves piled high with rare volumes on Chinese history and politics. The furniture includes a pleasing mix of comfy Western-style armchairs and more formal Chinese high-backed chairs made from a lustrous, dark wood. It's all even more extraordinary at night, with lotus-bud-shaped fabric lampshades illuminating the long polished wooden bar which runs the length of one of the walls.

We feel as though we have stepped back in time; the club is a wonderful, living museum. We walk through several courtyards toward the dining room. Flowering lotuses fill the ornamental ponds, with their enormous vibrant-green

Lunch at Huang Ting restaurant

OPPOSITE: The august surroundings of Beijing's China Club

当代名人录
道藏子目引得
佛藏子目引得
现代汉语词林
杜诗引得
当代中国社会科学手册

leaves gently laid on the water creating an air of tranquillity. A sense of ceremony and tradition permeates the whole place: decorative screens and doors are silhouetted against the evening sky, where a full moon tries ever so hard to shine brightly amid the thick polluted air of Beijing.

The dining room is even more sumptuous than the library, if that is possible. There is the same elegant cultural mix of antique décor, all dimly lit by red fabric lanterns, perched on dark wooden Art Deco lamp stands. As always, I order far too much food: for cold starters, there is some delightful marinated cucumber with tangerine peel, thinly sliced pork belly with garlic and soy sauce, shredded cabbage marinated with aged vinegar, and a plate of jellyfish with sesame. For mains we try the hot and sour soup, e-fu egg noodles with enoki mushrooms and dried scallops, stir-fried freshwater shrimps, braised tomatoes with egg, and steamed chicken with Yunnan ham and black mushrooms – altogether an interesting and varied slice of Chinese regional cuisine.

A series of courtyards leads to the China Club's atmospheric dining room

Today the Great Wall is a source of great pride for the Chinese, but for much of its history the wall has been a symbol of tyranny.

The first large-scale version of the Great Wall was built around 220 BC, to keep out the marauding tribes to the north during the reign of China's first emperor, Qin Shi Huang (of Terracotta Army fame). He set a pattern for subsequent rulers by drafting millions of peasants to work on the wall, untold numbers of whom died during its construction. The wall was patched up, fortified and extended by many dynasties, but the truth is that this seven-metre-high barrier, which stretches thousands of kilometres into China's remote northwest, was useless for defence. China's last dynasty, the Qing, had no trouble invading from their Manchu homelands and later let the whole structure fall into ruin.

Many parts of the Great Wall near Beijing have now been restored and are open to the public. Today we are going to a well-preserved section northeast of the city at Huang Hua Cheng, which is less developed than most, with almost no tourists. It's a two-hour drive away, so we pile into our minibus at 6.30 a.m., planning to have breakfast en route. As our stomachs grumble away, Chris keeps his eyes peeled for any roadside bun sellers and finally spots a stall. Excellent. I run out of the bus and, with lots of pointing and smiling, 'ask' the stallholder what she has hidden inside her bamboo steamers. She lifts the lids to reveal fluffy steamed buns stuffed with luscious braised lamb, an absolutely delicious local take on the more familiar roast pork buns you get in southern China. I buy the whole lot and happily skip back to the bus, sharing them around.

The drive is beautiful. An hour out of Beijing finds us winding through hilly, rural scenery, a welcome sight after the clamour of Beijing. It is, however, a bit hot and unfortunately very hazy, so our views are somewhat limited. Even so, as we arrive I have to pinch myself. I cannot believe I am really here, at the Great Wall – somewhere I've dreamed of visiting all my life.

The Huang Hua Cheng section is renowned for its well-preserved watch-towers and incredible gradients. The builders just followed the line of the ridge on which the wall stands, and the ascent is unbelievably steep. What makes it worse is the shape of the bricks: they are longer and deeper than regular ones, which means that every step forward turns into a sort of small lunge to cover the extra distance. We puff and struggle upwards, already regretting that, in our excitement to climb the wall, we didn't do any warm-up exercises or stretches – and did we suffer later on . . . (With the benefit of hindsight, my advice would be to do the walk at a leisurely pace, not only to take in the breathtaking visual beauty and enormity of the whole experience, but also to ease the strain on your feet, leg and thigh muscles.)

A breakfast stop on the way to the Great Wall

OVERLEAF: The Great Wall follows the ridge-line, irrespective of gradient

When we reach the top, though, it's all worthwhile: this is truly one of the most magical moments of my life. The scale of the wall is so massive that you can't help but be in awe of the fact that this is a man-made structure. The wall is wide enough at the top for five horsemen to ride abreast, and snakes way off into the distance. I just want to quietly take it all in, to breathe the fresh country air, and really appreciate this experience.

After a couple of hours' walking along the top, it's time to leave. I'm not sure which is worse though, going up or coming down. The path is so narrow and treacherous at times that you have to watch every step, and by the time we reach the bottom my hamstrings and thigh muscles are screaming and my legs are wobbling like jelly. My guide (who is not terribly sympathetic) keeps saying to me, 'Kylie, we call it the birth of new muscles, don't worry, three days and it's over!' Mind you, for the next three days I can hardly walk . . .

Physically exhausted but mentally and emotionally exhilarated, we climb back into the bus and triumphantly head for Beijing airport and our next destination, the glitzy and glamorous city of Shanghai.

Punctuated by fortified watchtowers, the Great Wall stretches as far as the eye can see

Shanghai: East Meets West

SHANGHAI: EAST MEETS WEST

宫廷
茶砖

ZHEJIANG
王開
Wang Kai Photo Company
住 5F 宿
上海明牌银楼
上島咖啡
明牌首饰
MING JEWELRY
住宿

Shanghai is China's most populous city, with a population of more than 13 million.

Set about two-thirds of the way up the eastern coastline, near the mouth of the Yangtze River, Shanghai was the first place I ever visited in China. And I must admit that, at the time, I found it a challenging experience: the city's confusing, sprawling mass, the crowds, and the fact that I couldn't speak or read Mandarin, all contributed to my culture shock and sense of disorientation. But now, almost ten years later and with a lot more travelling under my belt, I'm back to find that I love the place.

There's such a varied blend of old streets and new, high-tech towers, chic bars and local street food, modern shopping malls and beautiful traditional gardens that you simply can't get bored exploring. Even the crowds, which I found so daunting before, now seem just to add to the city's sheer vibrant energy. And, like Hong Kong, Shanghai has an international, cosmopolitan atmosphere, with many adventurous foreigners setting up shop here, introducing businesses that include sophisticated, Western-style restaurants. In all honesty, this is something of a relief. While I love eating all the local food and regional specialities while travelling around China, the reality is that there comes a point where fatigue kicks in, and you need to sneak back into your comfort zone.

Shanghai isn't an especially old place for China. It didn't really get going until the sixteenth century, and its last boom was during the 1930s, when it became famous as the heart of China's international trade and – in the West, anyway – for its ramshackle slums, organised crime and sleaze. Mao brought those days to an end when the Communists took hold of the country in 1949, and the city was allowed to run down for forty years.

The futuristic skyline of Pudong, on the east bank of the Huangpu River

OPPOSITE: Neon-lit facades in Shanghai's main shopping district

PREVIOUS PAGE: A quiet corner of Yu Gardens, Shanghai

The change since my first visit has been simply mind-boggling: old streets are vanishing under the bulldozers, and gleaming business districts are springing up east of the Huangpu River where a decade ago there were fields. Shanghai is rapidly regaining its title as China's commercial capital, with an ultra-modern skyline and vast suburbs, much to the chagrin of Hong Kong. A few pockets of period architecture have survived in the Old City, and in the former French Concession district, where you could almost imagine you were in Europe among the tree-lined boulevards and throngs of bicycles. The city is such a huge, bustling place that you can't see all of it in one go, but fortunately there's plenty to discover within walking distance of the Bund (now known as Zhongshan Zhong Lu), the famous riverside shopping and entertainment district that had its heyday in the 1930s.

The pace at which this city grows is phenomenal, and one of the best ways to witness the awesome width and depth of Shanghai's pulsating modern economy is to take an evening cruise down the Huangpu River, which flows into the Yangtze. Skyscrapers engulf you, spotlights blind you, and scenes of the 21st century sail past your very eyes on barges specially designed as state-of-the-art advertising billboards. Flashing neon signs twist and turn all night, oscillating between English spellings and Chinese characters for global brand names. Although it's all visually astounding, I cannot help but think of how much damage those neon lights are doing to the planet . . .

For me, a perfect day in Shanghai would be spent sampling the many different faces of the city, exploring the rickety and rustic back streets before dressing up and spending the evening sipping cocktails in one of the fantastic bars overlooking the Bund. I put this plan into action right after arriving at our bland but well-located hotel on Nanjing Lu by heading straight off into the Old City, on the west bank of the Huangpu River. The buildings are low-rise downmarket rather than ancient, but what I really like about this area is that you can see people cooking and living their day-to-day existence right on the street. Everywhere you look there are watermelon sellers, pork butchers, old men playing cards or mah-jong, kids kicking a ball in the laneway, stray cats darting in and out of dark, musty corners, naked light bulbs swaying in the afternoon breeze, motorbikes constantly beeping you out of the way, and women on their haunches cleaning whole fish in the gutter. This particular street we are in is almost like a shanty town, with rickety roofs and crumbling walls holding each other up, and the residents' laundry hung out to dry alongside their bamboo bird cages.

Amid the encroaching skyscrapers, life is still lived on the street in Shanghai's Old City

As we stroll, I spot an interesting-looking street stall out of the corner of my eye.

I stop to watch the owner cooking vigorously over his high-powered gas wok. He pours in the oil, then he adds ginger, pork, shao hsing wine, MSG, chicken stock powder and so on. I eye off all the fresh produce he has around him, and I start to get 'itchy feet' for cooking – something that always happens when I find myself in the vicinity of a wok, a flame and fresh food!

I ask my guide to ask the stallholder if I can have a go at cooking. 'No!' the man grumpily replies.

'Chris, can you just ask him once again – please, please, pretty please?'

'No!' he grumpily replies a second time.

'Please tell him I am a chef and I think his wok is great, and I'd love to have a go.'

'No – too busy!!!!' the stallholder retorts.

RIGHT! I say to myself, *I am going to get on that bloody wok if it kills me!* I take out a 100 yuan note, stuff it into the man's top shirt pocket, and what do you know? Down go his cooking tools and he gladly hands the whole set-up to me. I know this is a ridiculous sum – perhaps half his weekly rent – but I just had to get behind that wok.

My friends are giggling in total embarrassment at my sheer bossiness. The man is smiling too now, seeing the humour of it all. Soon there is a bit of a crowd gathering around the stall. (The Chinese love a bit of a commotion, and an inkling of anything unusual or noisy always draws a captive audience.)

I excitedly roll up my sleeves and clean the wok. I fire up the flames and soon there are *oohs* and *ahhhs* from the crowd, as they realise that I can actually steer this beast! I am in my element – if I don't cook regularly I start getting edgy, but this is the perfect remedy. I allow the wok to heat to a burning-hot temperature over the dancing, naked flame. I add a swoosh of peanut oil and a little salt, stirring vigorously to create sizzles and swirls, then in goes some finely sliced pork fillet and dried red chillies. The flames are licking high, and the fumes from the smoking chilli flakes are causing everyone to sneeze and cough. The crowd is increasing by the minute and is now about three-deep at the front. Old men and women going about their daily afternoon stroll stop and look on, inquisitive and entertained. They all stare intensely at my wok technique. I just know they are desperate to taste my food, and are probably thinking to themselves, *Can this outsider really cook?*

In goes the sugar to caramelise and deepen the flavour; this is balanced out with a dash of soy sauce and softened with a splash of shao hsing wine, then a hint of sesame oil adds another dimension. Finally, it's off with the flame and onto a white plate as I serve the piping-hot pork and chilli stir-fry. I offer it around to all within reach – first of all to the stallholder. A hush descends on the crowd as we await his approval . . . or not.

YES! Thumbs up, the crowd cheers and claps . . . phew!

晚市夜排挡
另加素菜1元荤菜2元
晚市夜排挡家常小炒
供应盒饭
Fuchun St.

Stir-Fried Pork Fillets with Dried Red Chillies

2 tablespoons peanut oil
600 g (1 lb 4 oz) pork fillets, cut into 5 mm (¼ in) slices
2 garlic cloves, finely chopped
5 cm (2 in) piece ginger, cut into thin strips
2 tablespoons shao hsing wine
1 tablespoon Chinese black vinegar
1 teaspoon light soy sauce
1 teaspoon dried red chilli flakes
1 teaspoon Sichuan pepper and salt

Heat half the oil in a hot wok until surface seems to shimmer slightly. Add half the pork and stir-fry for 30 seconds. Remove pork from wok with a slotted spoon and set aside on kitchen paper to drain. Add remaining oil and pork to wok and stir-fry for 30 seconds. Return all pork to wok, along with garlic and ginger, and stir-fry for 30 seconds.

Add remaining ingredients and stir-fry for about 2 minutes or until pork is just tender. Serve immediately.

Serves 4 as part of a shared meal

You can also add a small handful of bok choy or other Chinese greens to this stir-fry.

We head off again, laughing like a bunch of school kids – hot, tired, over-stimulated and very, very hungry. We are aiming for the traditional Chinese Yu Gardens, but first we need to find some dumplings. On a previous visit, I found a brilliant place in the Yu Gardens Bazaar, adjacent to the gardens, specialising in Shanghainese *xiaolong bao*, bite-sized steamed pork dumplings. I can't remember the name, though, so instead we settle into the nearby Lakeside Restaurant – it's packed to the rafters, which is always a good sign. We go upstairs and I see something very unusual: small bamboo steamers, each containing a single large Chinese bun with a plastic drinking straw coming out of the top. I am absolutely fascinated by them. *Why on earth do they have a plastic straw in the top?* I wonder. *Why are they sipping on them as if they were drinks?* My guide informs me that these are 'soup buns' (*dong bao*), stuffed with a fatty, jellied stock that melts when the buns are steamed. I ask him to order one immediately, so I can try this outrageous delicacy for myself.

I sip on the straw, and a hot, savoury, rich liquid burns my lips – it's mostly rendered pork fat peppered with crab roe. *Oh my goodness*, I think to myself, *only the Chinese could deal with turning this into a drink!* And what is even more astounding is that they drink this while chomping on equally rich *xiaolong bao* filled with fatty minced pork, ginger, shao hsing wine and spring onions. The dumplings are all expertly handmade and couldn't be any fresher. Just like the soup buns, when they are steamed, the pork fat softens and turns into this delectable, tasty, oozing liquid – as gross as it may sound, it's actually the secret, heavenly ingredient. The Chinese only ever use fatty pork mince in their cooking, as the fat contributes to the flavour and keeps the whole dish or dumpling moist and juicy.

We order several steamers full of pork dumplings and prawn dumplings, which come topped with a perfect carrot square. We also order three cold dishes: a plate of wonderfully fresh soy beans tossed in garlic, some pickled Chinese cabbage with chilli, and a plate of hot and sour cucumber salad. Altogether, a very welcome and delicious meal after all our walking.

Following our dumpling feast, we stroll across the zig-zag bridge to the famous Huxingting tea house, right in the middle of the lake, where they have an excellent range of green teas. Keen for something cleansing to wash down my meal, I try a delicate tea served in a glass teapot and made with chrysanthemum flowers and Chinese wolfberries. According to Traditional Chinese Medicine, this should cool me down and help to counteract all that pork fat – just what I need.

Cold Soy Beans Tossed in Garlic

400 g (13 oz) fresh or frozen soy beans, shelled

Dressing

4 garlic cloves, finely chopped
2 teaspoons sea salt
2 tablespoons brown rice vinegar
2 teaspoons sesame oil

Add soy beans to a saucepan or wok of boiling water and simmer for 5 minutes or until tender. Drain, refresh with cold water, then drain thoroughly.

Combine all dressing ingredients in a bowl and mix well.

Pour dressing over soy beans, then gently toss together and serve.

Serves 4–6 as part of shared meal

Hot and Sour Cucumber Salad

4 small cucumbers – about 875 g (1 lb 12 oz) in total, peeled
1 large green chilli, de-seeded and finely sliced
1 large red chilli, de-seeded and finely sliced
2 spring onions (scallions), trimmed and finely sliced

Dressing
4 garlic cloves, finely chopped
5 cm (2 in) piece ginger, finely chopped
1 tablespoon brown sugar
3 tablespoons brown rice vinegar
3 tablespoons light soy sauce
2 teaspoons sesame oil

Cut cucumbers in half lengthways and then into 5 mm (¼ in) slices on the diagonal. In a bowl, combine cucumber with chillies and spring onions.

To make the dressing, combine ingredients in a small bowl. Spoon dressing over salad, toss gently and serve.

Serves 4–6 as part of a shared meal

Pickled Chinese Cabbage with Chilli

1 medium Chinese cabbage – about 750 g (1 lb 8 oz) – cut into 2.5 cm (1 in) squares
3 tablespoons sea salt
2 tablespoons brown sugar
⅓ cup peanut oil
1 tablespoon Sichuan peppercorns
6 small dried red chillies
2 tablespoons brown rice vinegar
1 large red chilli, finely sliced

Combine cabbage in a bowl with salt and sugar, mix well and leave to stand for 2 hours.

Place oil, Sichuan peppercorns and dried chillies in a cold wok and *then* turn heat to high. Cook for about 30 seconds or until peppercorns and chillies begin to darken. Remove wok from stove and carefully strain flavoured oil through a metal sieve into a large bowl. Discard peppercorns and chillies, and set oil aside to cool.

Drain cabbage and, using your hands, gently squeeze out any excess liquid. Place cabbage in bowl containing flavoured oil, then add vinegar and fresh chilli and mix well.

Serves 4–6 as part of shared meal

Founded by a court official along classical principles back in the sixteenth century, the Yu Gardens consist of a maze of pavilions, courtyards, ponds and rockeries.

The Yu Gardens are very refreshing after the crowds and bustling street-life outside. We marvel at an exquisite bonsai-style garden in one pavilion, then watch as a gardener patiently lowers an old tin pail dangling from a piece of rope in and out of the pond – there are no hoses, so all day he waters the extensive gardens with this pail. The gardens are divided into six distinct areas by walls, their connecting doorways each fashioned in a different shape: one is a perfect circle, another traces the wavy outline of an urn, while a third is stepped. I love the way your eye is constantly entertained and teased by these contrasts in shapes and textures, and by tantalising glimpses of distant views.

Chinese Gardens

The Chinese tend to view nature as being a bit raw and wild. Although they appreciate that there are some good ideas there, the orthodoxy is that these need to be teased out from all the messy stuff and carefully rearranged, given the human touch. Garden design here is a real artform: the aim is not to try to faithfully copy natural landscapes, but rather – as with Chinese painting – to take elements from nature and use them to hint at a more complex whole.

Classical Chinese gardens were originally designed by scholars and officials as private retreats within their estates, where they could relax or entertain friends. Over the years, they became more public places, sometimes built in competition with each other – the more beautiful or elaborate the garden, the more its owner's reputation was enhanced. Archaeologists have found garden remains dating right back to the Qin dynasty (around 200 BC), but the surviving classically designed gardens in China today are far more recent, most of them founded within the last few centuries.

Like many other aspects of Chinese life, the best gardens create a harmonious sense of balance through contrasts: small spaces with large, smooth textures with rough, trees and flowers with buildings, shadows with light, and so on. Another element of the design is that these gardens always seem much more expansive than they really are, due to clever arrangements of walls, rocks, galleries, shrubs and buildings that block wide views. At the same time, these obstacles never quite stop you from seeing a little of what lies outside the space they enclose: an open doorway or a strategically placed window in a wall, for instance, that affords a glimpse of what lies beyond and thereby creates the illusion of space.

Calming ponds provide relief from the tangle of claustrophobic lanes linking courtyards and bamboo groves; in winter water reflects the sky, while in summer ponds are usually planted with lotus lillies, adding splashes of colour. Wavy or zig-zag bridges – intended to stop evil spirits from crossing, since they can only move in straight lines – lead over the water to pavilions or more complicated galleried buildings, which add yet another element of visual interest.

Classical gardens can be found all over China, often in temple grounds or connected with imperial buildings, but the largest collection is in the city of Suzhou, just to the west of Shanghai.

We leave the gardens and plunge back into the streets of surrounding bazaar. I come across a queue of people and, when I see what they are lining up for, there it is – the long-lost Nan Xiang Steamed Bun Restaurant, just as I remembered it. 'Here it is! Here it is!' I exclaim, dragging my friends over to a window that runs the length of the restaurant and lets you look right into the white-tiled kitchens, where an army of chefs is churning out amazing pork dumplings. It's all action, movement and work, everybody going flat out but looking relaxed and never getting in each other's way. One boy rolls the dough and tears it mechanically into identically sized lumps, the girl next to him rolls these into dumpling skins, the boy next to her speedily fills and seals the dumplings, and the last person in the line places the morsels in steamer baskets ready to be cooked. There are towers of steamers everywhere, but the cooks can barely keep up with demand – as soon as a basket is filled, it's whipped away to be steamed and served. The whole process reminds me of the Chinese woman who makes dumplings for my restaurant on special occasions, and the skill and craftsmanship that goes into them. Like these chefs, she does it so quickly and makes it look so easy.

My mouth is salivating as I watch school children buying take-aways and happily devouring their dumplings as they walk. Even though I am still bursting at the seams from lunch, I just have to go in for a quick look. I intercept a waitress carrying dumplings to a table; along with a small bowl of egg-drop soup, her order consists of some *xiaolong bao*, plus an open-topped dumpling stuffed with sticky rice, and another parcel of sticky rice steamed in bamboo leaves. They all look and smell so good that I almost steal one, but fortunately I restrain myself just in time!

Back in the Old City, we venture down a small street known as Dong Tai Lu, where there's a wonderful market selling all sorts of trinkets, jewellery, beads, leather bags, lamp shades, glass snuff bottles, carpets and rugs, porcelain, plastic, kitsch Mao objets d'art, old 1920s mirrors and assorted bric-a-brac. We all go a bit wild in a great antique store: I purchase a celadon-green statue of Mao as a present, and my friend buys an elegant porcelain statue of a young girl's upper torso and face, along with a beautifully hand-woven floor mat. Our purchases entail an hour of haggling, involving numerous phone calls by the store manager to his 'boss' to gauge how far the price can be dropped.

I just love haggling like this. For me, the key is to keep a sense of fun and treat it like a game. I also find that you have to keep a straight face, and can gain the upper hand by waving a few notes of Chinese currency around when you start bargaining – a whiff of cold hard cash often proves just too much, and the stallholder will sooner or later give in to your demands. It's important never to seem *too* interested, though; as soon as they know you really want something, you're lost. You also need to be prepared to walk away from the deal as a bargaining ploy, since the price often drops if

Shanghai's Dong Tai Lu is *the* place to find revolutionary memorabilia

ShiJie
静
毛主席指引我们向前进!

上海大不同天山茶城有限公司
Shanghai Dabutong Tian Shan Tea City Co.,Ltd
明码实价标价签
300.00
七子饼茶
120.00
茶之功用
SOPERVISION BY SING KEE
一品
宫廷茶砖

the stallholder thinks they're about to lose a sale. But even if I have really set my heart on something and am going to buy it whatever happens, I never give in without putting up a good-natured fight!

As we walk down the street, I notice a skinny doorway to my right, with a wonderfully patterned staircase leading to who knows where. I climb up the stairs and stumble upon a charming shop adorned with fabulous faded black-and-white photos of yesteryear, a solid silver Art Deco-style penguin teapot, framed posters from the Communist revolutionary years, and hand-tinted prints of Chinese movie idols.

Back down in the street again, we pass rows and rows of tea shops, which I adore for the beautifully designed packaging of their wares: round cakes, square blocks and flat rectangular packets of tea, and ornate gift-boxed tea sets. Surrounded by distinctive graphics and strong, bold colours, I could browse in these shops for hours, touching the different papers, smelling the packets and just admiring them all lined up in a row.

By now, it is 5.30 p.m., the temperature is in the low thirties, and we're desperate for a sit down and a good stiff drink!

Our hotel is a good 20 minutes' away if we factor in the peak-hour traffic, so we decide to make for the Xintiandi complex, centred around Tai Cang Street. This block of renovated *shikumen* – Shanghai-style shophouses – is full of high-end retail stores and chic modern eateries and bars. We head to a slick place called T8, which is all mood lighting, with designer chairs and artworks strategically dotted around. In the middle, a glass wall surrounds a spectacular open kitchen where six smartly dressed chefs work away, while the staff glide around as cool as can be, one waitress sporting an amazing Mohawk hair-cut and looking as if she has just stepped off the set of *Blade Runner* – I love it.

T8 is so appealing that, refreshed and cooled by air-conditioning and margaritas, it's an easy decision for us to stay and have dinner here. The menu showcases modern fusion-style cuisine, so we order a bottle of cool, crisp Sancerre while we wait. Just as we did at the Nan Xiang Steamed Bun Restaurant, we watch the chefs preparing and cooking in the kitchen, so beautifully disciplined and restrained. It is not easy cooking when you have strangers gawping at you, but these chefs are well trained, and do not allow onlookers to disrupt their flow.

I enjoy a pungent, sweet, sour, hot and salty green mango salad, then I devour a delectable piece of imported Australian beef rib-eye, grilled rare, which I have been craving. Having seen the way most markets and restaurants in China store their meat, I must admit I usually avoid eating it except at high-end places. But I can't feel guilty about coming all the way to Shanghai to eat Western food – we've certainly done the local cuisine proud today. For me, the way you can switch between Chinese and Western culture on a whim is one of Shanghai's great pleasures.

By 9 p.m. we are all well fed, well watered and feeling pretty good. But I'm secretly dying to get into that beautiful kitchen. I have been eyeing off the fiercely hot wok and smoking grill all night and, when T8's general manager, Walter Zahner, comes over to chat, I tell him about my inner urge. He looks at me as if I am mad, before succumbing to my nagging – secretly delighted, I think, that I want to cook in his kitchen. My friends are laughing at me again, half embarrassed and half amused at my determination.

The chefs are all a bit bemused. I don't think they really know what to do with this strange, bossy person who has just landed in their kitchen, and they watch my every move. I pounce on a spectacular piece of Angus beef fillet and plonk it in a bowl to marinate with garlic, ginger, brown sugar, shao hsing wine, soy sauce and sesame oil. Next I dart across the kitchen to raid the salad section for baby rocket, watercress, baby spinach, mint, coriander and Vietnamese mint. Then it's out with some juicy, fat king prawns, which I ask the chef to peel and de-vein. Meanwhile, I'm back with the beef: I ask the chef to grill it rare, giving it about four minutes on one side and two minutes on the other, and then to let it rest for five minutes. He nods confidently, and cooks it to perfection.

Another chef, who has been crafting fine tuna sashimi salads all night, expertly sears the prawns in a sauté pan. I make the dressing for the salad: brown sugar, soy sauce, vinegar, extra virgin olive oil and sesame oil. I instruct the chef to cut the beef into fine slices while I toss the lettuce leaves and herbs with some of the dressing. I arrange the salad on a large white platter, with the succulent slivers of pink beef and the juicy, caramelised prawns on top, all finished off with a drizzle of the remaining dressing. I garnish the dish with some peeled soft-boiled eggs, cut in half so that the yolks ooze over everything.

Voilà! The chefs clap and I invite them to dive in and try the new dish. I am even more charged up now; my hunger to cook is sated and I feel pretty satisfied. I chat to the head chef, who has worked in some of the world's top hotels, and I mention that I only use organic ingredients in my restaurant. He informs me that there's an organic farm and shop in Shanghai. Excitedly, I take down all the details and ask my guide if he can take us to the organic farm the next day. No problem – it's not too far outside the city and everyone agrees it will be a worthwhile trip.

Colonial buildings line the Bund, on Shanghai's waterfront

Rare Beef and King Prawn Salad with Soft-Boiled Eggs

300 g (10 oz) best-quality beef fillet
1 handful watercress
1 handful baby spinach
1 handful mint leaves
1 handful coriander (cilantro) leaves
1 handful Vietnamese mint leaves
2 tablespoons peanut oil
8 uncooked king prawns (jumbo shrimp), peeled and de-veined but with tails left intact
2 free-range eggs, soft-boiled and peeled

Marinade

2 garlic cloves, finely chopped
2.5 cm (1 in) piece ginger, finely chopped
2 tablespoons brown sugar
¼ cup shao hsing wine
1 tablespoon light soy sauce
1 teaspoon sesame oil

Dressing

1 tablespoon brown sugar
2 tablespoons light soy sauce
1 tablespoon brown rice vinegar
½ teaspoon sesame oil
⅓ cup best-quality extra virgin olive oil

Combine all marinade ingredients in a bowl, then add beef and mix well. Cover, place in refrigerator and leave to marinate for 1 hour.

Remove beef from marinade and sear on a hot chargrill plate or in a heavy-based frying pan for 4 minutes, then turn over and cook for 2 minutes on other side. Transfer to a plate, cover loosely with foil, and allow to rest for 5 minutes.

Meanwhile, combine all salad and herb leaves in a bowl. Next, combine all dressing ingredients in another bowl and mix well.

Heat oil in a hot frying pan or wok and sear prawns for 2–3 minutes on each side, or until golden and cooked. Remove and drain on kitchen paper.

Toss salad with a third of the dressing and transfer to a serving platter. Cut beef into 5 mm (¼ in) slices and arrange over salad, along with prawns. Carefully cut eggs in half and place on top of salad, then drizzle with remaining dressing and serve immediately.

Serves 4 as a starter

Vietnamese mint, also known as laksa leaf, can be found at Asian supermarkets; if it is unavailable, just add a little more coriander and mint to the salad.

Continuing our quest for the perfect dumpling, our first stop next day is for breakfast at Yang's Fried Dumplings.

This famous dumpling house on Wujing Lu has a queue morning, noon and night for the best seared and steamed pork dumplings in the world. We stand in the queue and peer into the tiny kitchen area, where six or so chefs are standing around a small stainless-steel work bench, busily rolling, stuffing and shaping dumplings – they belt out literally hundreds and hundreds of dumplings each day. These dumplings are slightly bigger than Beijing-style pork dumplings, and are slightly squarish in shape instead of being round, but they share the same pleated and gathered topknot. The crafting of the pleats in a dumpling is considered to be a reflection of the skill of the dumpling maker, and these ones are articulate and refined.

The filling consists of fatty pork mince, spring onions, salt and shao hsing wine. The secret ingredient is, of course, the rendered pork fat. When the dumplings are made, they are placed on a huge round, black, cast-iron tray that is red hot and covered in vegetable oil. When the raw dumplings hit the surface, there's an awesome sizzle as the base of the dumplings is seared. The dumpling-laden tray is then placed over a volcanic gas flame and the dumplings are covered with a lid, so that they steam. After 10 minutes or so, the lid is removed and the dumplings are ready: the dough is fried a crunchy, golden brown on the underside and steamed to velvety, silky and luscious perfection on top. Take one bite and piping-hot juices fill your mouth as you chew on tender, moist pork mince. It is a truly revelatory experience, and a must-do when in Shanghai.

Anxious to learn some of the secrets of Shanghainese cuisine, we set off for our next destination, Shanghai Cooking School. Shanghai-style cooking – *benbang* – dates back to the Ming

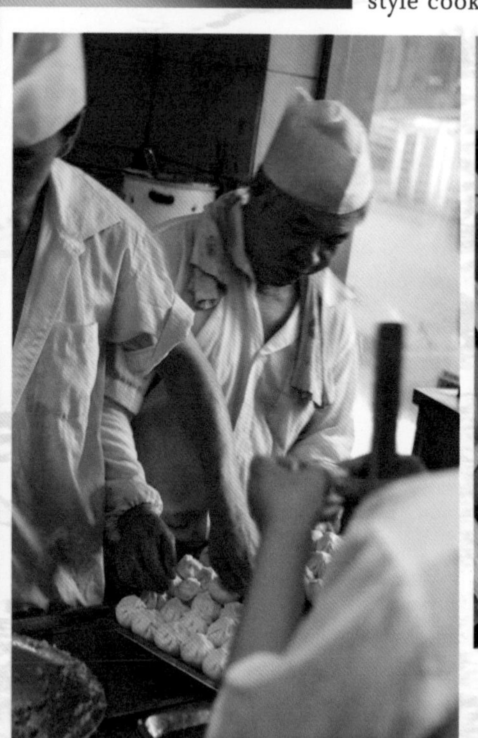

dynasty, but was first recognised through dishes specially created for a visit by Qing dynasty emperor Qianlong in 1737. It's a seasonal cuisine, based on using fresh seafood and fish from the river, including the famous hairy crab, and vegetables as they become plentiful through the year. The emphasis is on bringing out the intrinsic qualities of the ingredients, but climate also has an influence: Shanghai's cold winters demand heavier, richer meals than the steamy hot summers. Seasoning tends towards the sweet and slightly salty, often using locally produced shao hsing wine to mellow and round out the flavours. *Benbang* also uses far more oil than, say, Cantonese cuisine.

Mr John is our teacher for this morning's session, a senior chef with more than forty years' experience. In his white chef's uniform and hat, he looks very dignified as he stands confidently over his thick wooden tree-trunk of a chopping board, wielding a very sharp cleaver. His white-tiled kitchen classroom has a central stainless-steel cooking bench and the customary wok stalls. A big blackboard covers one wall, a large freestanding fan cools us down, and the whole space looks immaculately clean and very 1950s. Mr John does not speak English, so our guide Chris interprets.

The three dishes Mr John is cooking today are 'squirrel' mandarin fish, soy-braised pork and 'flying dragon' silk squash, which together serve to demonstrate different Chinese cooking techniques and methods. 'Squirrel' mandarin fish get its intriguing name from the story of a visit to Suzhou by Qianlong. The emperor ordered fish at a local restaurant, but the only fish they had was meant for altar offerings at the restaurant's shrine. The cook cut and twisted the fish so that when fried it resembled a squirrel, thereby both pleasing the emperor and averting the wrath of the kitchen gods. So the fish is all about cutting skills, colour, and the texture achieved when food is deep-fried; the pork is about the gentle yet powerful art of 'red cooking', a classic technique involving braising and reducing in soy sauce; and the silk squash also showcases knife skills in creating a certain look.

As Mr John lectures, I notice the ingredients he has at hand near the wok: peanut oil, vegetable oil, light and dark soy sauces, white sugar, MSG crystals, sesame oil, shao hsing wine and yellow chicken stock powder. Through Chris, I ask Mr John his opinion on MSG. Mr John says that it has a limited place in certain dishes, but that many inexperienced chefs over-use MSG because they don't know how to bring out and balance natural flavours, and that lazy chefs over-use it because it's easier than learning to cook properly. In general, he feels that the more expensive Chinese restaurants have better chefs and higher-quality ingredients, and so tend to be less reliant on MSG.

Between each demonstration we are invited to taste the results. While I appreciate the artistry of the fish dish, it is far too sweet and cloying for me – my preferred flavours are salty and savoury. It's also very much a restaurant dish, rather than something you'd cook at home. The pork is heavenly and just melts in your mouth (however one piece is enough, as I feel like I am still digesting the pork overload from the day before!), and the squash is really good – beautifully smooth, with a velvety texture and a refreshing taste.

Making dumplings at Yang's Fried Dumplings in Shanghai

Soy-Braised Pork Belly

750 g (1 lb 8 oz) pork belly, cut into 1 cm (½ in) cubes
4 tablespoons peanut oil
5 cm (2 in) piece ginger, finely sliced
½ cup shao hsing wine
3 tablespoons light soy sauce
2 tablespoons dark soy sauce
1 cup brown sugar
5 cups water
2 tablespoons brown rice vinegar

To remove any impurities from meat, place pork belly in a large pan or stockpot, cover with cold water and bring to the boil. Simmer for 5 minutes, then drain, discarding water. Rinse pork thoroughly under cold running water and drain well.

Heat oil in a hot wok until surface seems to shimmer slightly. Add pork and stir-fry for 3 minutes. Add all other ingredients except vinegar and simmer gently, covered, for 50 minutes or until pork is tender. Stir in vinegar and serve immediately.

Serves 4–6 as part of shared meal

Flying Dragon Silk Squash

750 g (1 lb 8 oz) silk squash or large zucchini (courgettes)
2 tablespoons peanut oil
6 fine slices ginger, cut into thin strips
2 garlic cloves, finely sliced
2 tablespoons shao hsing wine
2 tablespoons light soy sauce
½ cup chicken stock or water
1 teaspoon sesame oil

If using silk squash, peel away tough outer skin, then cut each squash in half crossways. If using zucchini, cut in half crossways. With a sharp knife, carefully score each piece of squash or zucchini at 5 mm (¼ in) intervals, taking care not to cut right through. These incisions create the characteristic 'flying dragon' look.

Heat peanut oil in a hot wok until surface seems to shimmer slightly. Add ginger, garlic and silk squash or zucchini and stir-fry for 3 minutes. Add shao hsing wine, soy sauce and stock or water and simmer gently, uncovered, for 5 minutes or until squash is tender. Drizzle with sesame oil and serve immediately.

Serves 4–6 as part of a shared meal

Silk squash (also known as angled loofa or Chinese okra) is a ridged cucumber-like gourd that is sometimes available at Asian markets. Zucchini makes a good substitute.

We wave Mr John farewell at about 11.30 a.m. and excitedly set off on our journey to the O Organic Farm.

A 45-minute drive west of the city, O Organic Farm is located near Jiading rural township. During the drive, I try to imagine what a Chinese organic farm might look like, but soon discover that the reality is completely different from the image I have conjured up in my mind. Rather than open fields and rustic wooden housing, I see rows and rows of neat hothouses and white cement farmers' dwellings.

The chief gardener is 25-year-old Song Yuan, a sweet man with a gentle nature and a wonderful, open face. He has the hands of an artist who works with the earth – long, creative fingers with dirt under the nails. He explains that the hothouses create a controlled environment, minimising attacks by pests and so removing the need for pesticides. The micro-climate inside the hothouses also allows farmers to grow a greater variety of fruit and vegetables all year round. The effects of pollution – always a worry in China – are reduced by the farm being located in the countryside, away from any factories. River water is filtered three times before it is used to irrigate the plants; apparently it's so pure that you could drink it. The soil is chemical-free, and the compost is a mixture of animal manure and a special blend of nutrients produced by a registered organic-quality supplier.

As we go through each hothouse, Song Yuan proudly shows us the thriving, beautiful, healthy crops: tomatoes, eggplants, peppers, water spinach, pumpkins, sugar beet, onions, carrots, lettuce, mint, basil, cucumber and an entire section devoted to spring onions – he pulls a bunch out of the dirt to show us just how vibrant and luscious they are. Up to one hundred different kinds of vegetable are grown here (including eighteen types of bean sprout), but at this

particular time of the year, there are only forty. Unfortunately, the high cost of organic produce in China – up to nine times more expensive than the regular equivalent – means that it is beyond the reach of most ordinary Chinese, and so the majority of the farm's customers are Western-style restaurants and wealthier Chinese people.

After talking with Song Yuan for an hour, we are all rather hungry. So, piling into our bus again, we head back to Shanghai and the O Store, which is also owned by this farm. Located on Zunyi Road, the store is a haven stocked with all manner of organic and biodynamic produce: fruit and vegetables, fresh tofu, Japanese shoyu and tamari, muesli, cereals, milk and yoghurt; there's even a shelf devoted to environmentally friendly cleaning products. Also attached to the store are a bistro, café and bakery. Starving as usual, we all make a dash for the café, desperate to sample their delicious spelt-bread sandwiches, which we wash down with refreshing beetroot and carrot juices.

Predictably, I end up buying a whole lot of fresh produce from the store. At a thriving market or in a great food store, I just cannot resist buying something so that I can surround myself with food and enjoy its rapturous scent, texture and visual beauty.

This afternoon I have a special mission to perform at the Jade Buddha Temple.

One of the few active Buddhist temples in Shanghai, this peaceful sanctuary is located in the northwest of the city on Anyuan Street. I have been here three times before, and I always appreciate its meditative atmosphere amid such a frenzied city.

My mission is on behalf of a friend in Sydney, who is a practising Buddhist and has asked me to run a special errand for her. Buddhist monks and nuns wear cloth sandals, and my friend acquired two pairs of these as a gift from a nun during her last visit to China. She was so delighted by the present that she fears she accepted them too hastily. After her return to Sydney, she felt she had not behaved very well, having taken the sandals in a greedy and ungracious way. Disappointed in herself, she has given them to me to return to any monk I find in China.

I step inside the main temple, which always blows my mind with its decorative art, large Buddha statues, and porcelain and bronze sculptures. There is a sweet-looking Buddhist monk fast asleep on a chair in the corner. *He is the one I will give the shoes to*, I think to myself. I gently tap him on the arm and he suddenly jolts awake. Although I must have frightened the living daylights out of him, he soon relaxes and gives me a huge, warm smile. I offer him the two pairs of sandals and he cannot believe his luck. He promptly slips off his old shoes and tries on the new ones, which fit him perfectly. He gets up and thanks me, bowing graciously, and I hug him and smile.

When I tell my friend later, she is thrilled to learn that the shoes have gone to such a good home.

中国电信
CHINA TELECOM

AURORA

Tonight my friend Michelle Garnaut, owner of M on the Bund restaurant, has invited us for dinner, and we're all looking forward to having a night out in style.

Michelle is one of a new breed of entrepreneurial expats seeking their fortunes in Shanghai, broadening China's horizons by bringing in foreign ideas and, perhaps, taking a little of their Chinese experience into the rest of the world. Originally from Melbourne, Michelle spent many years living in Hong Kong, where she established the highly successful M at the Fringe bar in 1989. A decade later, she opened her Shanghai restaurant, M on the Bund – the first of its kind in the city, and the first to make such imaginative use of the wonderful, old colonial buildings along the Bund.

I first met Michelle in 2005 when I was shooting my second TV series in Hong Kong and Shanghai. We wanted to include Michelle in the show, and so I was privileged to spend an entire day with her on location. She led me around the back streets of Shanghai: we meandered along rustic old alleyways, we haggled for exotic fruit from street stalls, we giggled with old people gambling in the street, and I made her laugh when I briefly took over a fried-rice stall from its bemused owner.

Michelle has spent years travelling and working around the world, and is one of these people who genuinely 'loves it all'. She has a real presence, such strength of spirit and endless amounts of positive energy, and is strikingly successful at what she does. In her, I feel as if I have finally found someone who is as straightforward and bossy as me!

As you can guess from the name, Michelle's restaurant overlooks the Bund, and is said to have the finest views in Shanghai, but before we head upstairs for dinner, we sneak downstairs to her latest venture, the classy Glamour Bar. With large wooden windows in the long back wall, this terrifically stylish space also looks out over the city, but what really catches my attention is the very 1920s blend of Chinese and Western décor: clever, restrained lighting around the long, oval-shaped bar is complemented by stunning glass chandeliers, mirrors and contemporary Chinese silk fabrics elsewhere, while wooden parquetry flooring and a beautiful black, sleek and shiny grand piano add a touch of old-world sophistication. We all clink champagne glasses just as Michelle arrives to take us all two floors up to M on the Bund for our meal and a guided tour of the kitchen.

The restaurant kitchen is huge and intense, seething with specialist chefs from around the globe who cook the restaurant's international menu. I find myself once more taking over, this time finishing off a stir-fry of Chinese cabbage with garlic, salt and stock being assembled by a young chef who gasps out 'staff dinner, staff dinner' as she wrestles with the largest cabbage I have ever seen. We go to the stove section, where I dip my finger in a big pot of fluffy potato mash – *yum.* Further along a chef stands proudly over a simmering pot of red-braised pork belly with preserved cabbage. *Mmm* . . . hints of ginger, the subtle yet intoxicating flavour and aroma of shao hsing wine, and the juicy pork fat that is so bad for you, but so irresistible.

Right from the start, M on the Bund has made the most of the view from its balcony, where we lounge in comfort over an aperitif while gazing out at all the activity along the Bund and the Huangpu River. Illuminated barges and tourist cruisers chug past; the Pudong Pearl TV Tower lights up the sky, stealing the show; and people crowd the banks of the river, staring at the line of skyscrapers that symbolise modern Shanghai. We sip crisp Italian white wine as we share stories about our travels through China – we are in heaven . . .

While I was in the kitchen, I spotted a piece of beef fillet that made my mouth water, so I ask Michelle if the chef could simply grill it for me and serve it with some salad. Indulging in another break from Chinese food and the endlessly fascinating but sometimes exhausting daily grind of travelling in China seems perfectly in keeping with the opulent mood – the Art Deco furnishings, crystal glasses and polished cutlery. Tonight is magical.

Our time in Shanghai has turned out so well: authentic Chinese experiences in the gardens, streets and cooking, with the added bonus of being pampered in Michelle's sumptuous restaurant. We spend a long time discussing our next destination, Hangzhou, home to West Lake, which has reputedly inspired generations of artists and, so Michelle tells us, is the source of Longjing or Dragon Well tea, among the most revered in China.

Inside the Glamour Bar, Shanghai
PREVIOUS PAGE: Shanghai at night

Hangzhou and Wuzhen

HANGZHOU AND WUZHEN

翰林客棧
龍井珍品
歲貢御茶
色翠香鬱
味甘形美

龍井珍品
歲貢御茶
色翠香鬱
味甘形美

There are many reasons to come to Hangzhou, a small, affluent city about 200 kilometres southwest of Shanghai.

And most of them have to do with its setting, right on the edge of West Lake. This expanse of water with verdant shores has been a famous beauty spot for well over a thousand years, praised by everyone from Chinese poets to Marco Polo, who visited during the late thirteenth century. The hills just beyond the lake are also home to Longjing tea, one of China's finest, and the bountiful local produce has given rise to a whole host of regional dishes and specialities. All in all, this is a great place for a break from Shanghai's hectic pace and pollution.

However, as soon as we arrive in Hangzhou, we embark on an unlikely excursion. One of my travelling companions is in search of a famous scissors shop. Her 90-year-old mother, who lives in the UK, is very taken with a particular type of nail scissors that apparently can only be purchased there. We duly ask our driver to take us to Zhang Xiaoquan Scissors, at 27 Daguan Lu.

Funny the things you find out about people when you are travelling closely with them day-in, day-out. We all go into a scissor frenzy – never knew there was such a thing! Not only does this extraordinary shop sell the scissors Ruth's mother has requested, but it also stocks all manner of wonderful Chinese cleavers: some with wooden handles and others with stainless-steel handles, heavy and light ones, curved and straight ones, long and short ones. I go a little crazy and buy three sets of them for my home and another for my head chef. I also buy a pair of incredibly comfortable and sturdy, sharp, black-handled scissors that prove to be invaluable in the kitchen.

After this diversion, we head straight to West Lake for a calming walk to stretch our legs and fill our lungs with fresh air. We pass many couples strolling romantically around the shore; old men in wooden boats offer to take us out to one of the small islands and try to sell us pearls; it's all very laid-back and, for China at least, unusually clean and tidy. One stretch of the shore is renowned for its mesmerising weeping willows, and the lake's shallows are a mass of magical lotus blossoms, gently swaying above their deep-green, elegantly shaped leaves. At the centre of the bloom, each petal is white but grades into a marvellous lollipop pink, and at the heart of each bloom is a vibrant, rich yellow pod full of lotus seeds. The whole plant is used in Chinese cooking: the crunchy, honeycombed rhizome (lotus 'root') from which it grows is sliced and cooked in soups, braises and stir-fries; the seeds are boiled with sugar and mashed to make a sweet filling for buns; and the leaves are used to wrap sticky rice for steaming – as the lotus-leaf parcel steams, the earthy, straw-like essence and scent of the leaves infuses the rice. The famous West Lake

Hangzhou's lakeside setting makes it a relaxing place to visit

PREVIOUS PAGE: A boat trip on the Grand Canal, which links Hangzhou with Beijing

dish of beggar's chicken uses lotus leaves to wrap a whole chicken that has been stuffed with herbs and vegetables before being encased in clay and baked.

We eat lunch in one of the many charming tea houses lining the lake, which luckily serves several of Hangzhou's specialities. The first one we order, Dongpo pork, is named in honour of famous Song dynasty poet and court official Su Dongpo. An endlessly patient man who accepted the many twists and turns of his life with calmness and serenity, he always put ordinary people first in his stints as governor of various remote districts. He even helped restore West Lake after it almost dried up in 1090. There are many variations of Dongpo pork, in which belly pork is gently braised to butter-like tenderness, but the essentials of the recipe appear in a poem by Dongpo himself:

Ode to Pork
Use a low flame
Add very little water
Cooked long enough, it becomes delicious

We also order West Lake fish, a whole steamed fish bathed in a sweet-and-sour sauce sharpened with black vinegar. The story behind this famous dish tells of the wife of a scholar whose husband is murdered by a corrupt official. Incensed by the senseless death of his brother, her brother-in-law decides to become an official himself so he can personally bring the killer to justice. Before he sets off to take the necessary exams, the widow cooks him West Lake fish, to remind him of life's 'sweet and sour' times. The tale ends, of course, with the man passing his exams, having the official arrested, and then being reunited with his sister-in-law.

Our last choice is steamed parcels of sticky rice stuffed with meat and bamboo shoots and wrapped in bamboo leaves – which, like lotus leaves, add a subtle fragrance to the contents. Aromatic rice bundles such as these were eaten as far back as 278 BC, when the patriotic poet and administrator Qu Yuan drowned himself in a river as a protest against corrupt government. People desperately rowed out to try and save him, but were too late – the origin of the dragon boat races now held around the world. Afterwards, they made these rice parcels as offerings to appease his spirit.

Dongpo Pork with Braised Potatoes

750 g (1 lb 8 oz) pork belly, cut into
 1 cm (½ in) cubes
5 cm (2 in) piece ginger, cut into thin strips
4 tablespoons shao hsing wine
4 tablespoons peanut oil
375 g (12 oz) potatoes, peeled and
 cut into 1 cm (½ in) slices
3 tablespoons shao hsing wine, extra
4 tablespoons light soy sauce
2 tablespoons dark soy sauce
2 tablespoons brown sugar
5 cups water

To remove any impurities from meat, place pork belly in a large pan or stockpot, cover with cold water and bring to the boil. Simmer for 5 minutes, then drain, discarding water. Rinse pork thoroughly under cold running water and drain well.

Combine pork with ginger and shao hsing wine in a bowl. Cover, place in and refrigerator and leave to marinate for 1 hour.

Heat half the peanut oil in a hot wok until surface seems to shimmer slightly. Add half the pork and stir-fry for 4 minutes. Remove pork with a slotted spoon and drain on kitchen paper. Add remaining oil to wok with rest of pork and stir-fry for 4 minutes.

Return all pork to wok, along with potatoes, and stir-fry for 2 minutes. Add remaining ingredients and simmer gently, covered, for 50 minutes or until pork is tender. Serve immediately.

Serves 4–6 as part of a shared meal

Longjing or Dragon Well tea has been grown in the hills surrounding Hangzhou for at least a thousand years.

As we head for the hills the next day, to sample some of this life-enhancing elixir, our bus follows the gently winding Hupao Road through lush, dense forest into the Dragon Well country. We wind down all the windows and delight in breathing in the clean fresh air. We are making our way to a particular tea plantation, owned by an extraordinary woman called Mrs Xu (pictured below left).

As we pull up, a short, stocky middle-aged woman greets us warmly, giving each of us a firm handshake and looking us straight in the eye. My guide explains to her that we are all food lovers from Australia, and that I have a restaurant in Sydney. She ushers us inside a beautiful old pavilion, her tea house. With its imposing wooden doors thrown open, it is airy and spacious, with traditional wood-carving everywhere, in that deep, rich mahogany-brownish red that I adore. Works of Chinese calligraphy adorn the walls, and the room is laid out with simple square wooden tables and chairs. To one side, a man sits alone, quietly sipping his tea and drawing on a cigarette. On the other side of the room is a glass counter holding a set of old-fashioned scales, a cash register, and behind this is a dark wooden shelf, proudly displaying the plantation's elegant, emerald-green tea tins.

We all sit down around a long, central table with our guide and Mrs Xu. We ask her all manner of questions about her life and the tea plantation. We learn that Mrs Xu owns and runs the business; her grandparents began the tea plantation, her parents then took it on after them, and they passed it on to her. She has two children: her son works in the finance business in Hangzhou city, while her daughter works with her at the tea plantation. Most of the people who live in this village are extremely wealthy by Chinese standards.

Mrs Xu proves to be quite a character. She cheekily says to our guide: 'I am 60 years old and I can carry a 150 kilo sack of tea leaves on my shoulder, because I drink this Longjing tea twice a day.'

'Wow!' we all exclaim.

At that, Mrs Xu immediately raises her right hand towards me, elbow on the table, and says: 'Come on then, let's have an arm wrestle!'

We all laugh and laugh. Never one to turn down a challenge, I reach my hand across the table to hers. And, I tell you what, she beats me hands-down . . .

Inside Mrs Xu's tea house
OPPOSITE: Tins of Longjing tea on display

獅峰山龍井
龍井珍品
歲貢御茶
色翠香鬱
味甘形美
獅峰山龍井

But Mrs Xu isn't just physically strong. When we arrived and she shook my hand and looked straight into my eyes, I sensed then that her real strength stemmed from her innermost being. We discover that Mrs Xu's path through life has taken many twists and turns and, as a result, she has real presence and charisma. I find myself attracted to women who are at this stage in their lives – they have such depth and substance of character, are stoic and strong, yet still deeply compassionate and kind-hearted.

Mrs Xu tells us a little about Longjing tea. The tea bush can live for more than a hundred years, yielding two harvests per year – 20 April to 10 May, then 20 September to 1 October – though the first crop produces by far the better brew, and the first young tips of the first harvest produce the most sought-after tea. Also, the higher up the hill, the finer the quality, with this high-grown tea fetching up to 40 per cent more than leaves grown lower down the slopes. Longjing village consists of five different hamlets: Lion Peak, Dragon, Cloud, Tiger and Plum. Mrs Xu's plantation is in the Lion Peak area, which has a reputation for producing the finest tea, although she concedes that even tea grown in the lowest hamlet, Plum, still makes an excellent drink.

Next she brings out three grades of Longjing tea, and explains the processing stages: after being picked from the bush, the leaves are dried for 3 days before they are dry-roasted three times in a large cast-iron pot. At the end of the process, 4.5 kilos of fresh leaves yield 1 kilo of dried tea leaves; from each tablespoon of this dried tea, 5–6 glasses of tea can be brewed. She adds that people here dry their used tea leaves and use them to stuff their pillows – this is said to promote a peaceful night's sleep.

Mrs Xu then shows us some of the processed Longjing leaves, all rolled and pressed into flattened green needles with a sheen of soft, silvery fuzz on them. She takes four glasses and fills them with boiling water, sprinkles a teaspoon of leaves on the surface, and then hands one to each of us. She explains that preparing it this way releases a finer aroma than pouring the water onto the leaves. Apparently, Longjing is always served in glasses, so you can see the leaves as they slowly sink vertically to the bottom of the cup, where they bob upright. We watch the tea leaves take on a new life in the glass as we smell and savour this refreshing tonic.

Three grades of Longjing tea

OPPOSITE: Relaxing in the tea house

hinese Tea

ea is made from the dried eaf of the Chinese camellia ree (*Camellia sinensis*), and ıas been drunk in China for ıround 2000 years.

Vhite, green, black and red ea all come from the same plant, and the differences are lue to processing: white tea s simply picked and dried; or green tea, the leaves ıre minimally fermented or a few days, before being dry-roasted; red or semi-ermented teas are left to erment for a little longer efore the drying process; ınd in black or fermented tea, he leaf is allowed to fully larken (about 2–4 weeks) efore being dried. When rewed, green teas produce ı clear green or pale yellow nfusion, while semi- or fully-ermented leaves give a dark vellow to deep red liquor.

Vhite and green teas are onsidered to have the most lelicate scent and flavour, though any one bush can produce different quality leaves depending on the time of year they are picked and the size of leaf – in general terms, the earlier and smaller, the better. The fragrance of inferior teas is often perked up by the addition of flower petals, as with jasmine tea.

Tea is grown all across central and southern China, with every tea-growing district producing tea with a slightly different taste, though most are only available at the local markets. Each region has a tea ceremony designed to bring out the best qualities of the local leaves so, depending on where you are, tea might be served in tiny cups, in tall glasses or in large mugs; in Tibet, it's even blended with yak butter and served like a soup.

Of the well-known teas, Longjing is the most famous green variety, followed by the semi-fermented ti kwan yin ('Iron Buddha') from Fujian province and Yunnan province's fully fermented pu-er, which is often served in yum cha restaurants as it's said to help digest fats.

According to Traditional Chinese Medicine, all teas are considered to have a 'cooling' effect on the body, and many are said to have other beneficial qualities.

Mrs Xu has really livened up now and her true, somewhat eccentric self is emerging. There is no stopping her, as she walks around her tea house demonstrating that she can still do high kicks at her age! I feel a deep connection with this incredibly strong woman who soldiers on in life, through thick and through thin – all in the name of honour and family. These are the sort of women that hold families together.

I ask Mrs Xu about the local food of the Hangzhou area, and she waxes lyrical about crystal prawns with Longjing tea, 'lion's head' meatballs, West Lake fish, pork wrapped in lotus leaf with sticky rice, beggar's chicken, rice noodle and braised beef soup, West Lake beef porridge and Dongpo pork.

My mouth is watering at this point and I start to get that *twitchy* feeling again! Mrs Xu obligingly offers her courtyard as a place where we can cook and eat some of her favourite local dishes, surrounded by lush tea plantations. Together we prepare her version of prawns with Longjing tea, as well as some simply poached asparagus dressed with soy sauce and chilli. She also gives me a recipe for 'lion's head' meatballs, but as these need long, slow cooking, we don't have enough time to make them today.

While we're sharing the food we've cooked, Mrs Xu gives us yet another interesting take on the use of MSG in Chinese cooking. According to her, China's tragic agricultural policies of the 1950s and 1960s led to crop failures across the nation, meaning that most people had very little to eat and, with no oil or soy sauce available, what there was tasted awful. Hence MSG was used in huge quantities to enliven drab food and render it edible. By force of habit, many people continue this practice to this day, even though a whole generation has passed since tasty, fresh ingredients became readily available again.

With Mrs Xu and her daughter

ABOVE & OPPOSITE: Terraced slopes of the Dragon Well tea plantations

Mrs Xu's Prawns with Longjing Tea

500 g (1 lb) uncooked prawns (shrimp), peeled and de-veined but with tails left intact
1 tablespoon cornflour (cornstarch)
2 tablespoons shao hsing wine
1 tablespoon Longjing tea leaves
½ cup boiling water
2 cups vegetable oil for deep-frying
1 tablespoon peanut oil
2.5 cm (1 in) piece ginger, finely chopped
2 garlic cloves, finely chopped
1 tablespoon shao hsing wine, extra
2 tablespoons light soy sauce
½ teaspoon sesame oil

Combine prawns with cornflour and shao hsing wine in a bowl. Cover, place in refrigerator and leave to marinate for 30 minutes.

Put tea leaves in a heatproof bowl, pour over boiling water and allow to steep for 2 minutes. Strain and reserve tea leaves, discarding liquid.

Heat vegetable oil in a hot wok until surface seems to shimmer slightly, then carefully add half the prawns and deep-fry for 3 minutes. Using a slotted spoon, remove prawns from wok and drain on kitchen paper. Repeat process with remaining prawns. Carefully pour oil out of wok and wipe clean with kitchen paper.

Heat peanut oil in cleaned wok until surface seems to shimmer slightly. Add ginger, garlic and prawns and stir-fry for 30 seconds. Add extra shao hsing wine, soy sauce and sesame oil and stir-fry for a further 1–2 minutes. Add reserved tea leaves, mix well and serve immediately.

Serves 4–6 as part of a shared meal

The distinctive elongated, needle-like leaves of Longjing tea add a delicate flavour to this dish. Any high-quality, long-leaf green tea can be substituted, but don't try to make this with the same quantity of tea made from shredded leaves, or with large-leafed tea, as these will spoil the texture of the sauce.

Poached Asparagus with Soy Sauce, Chilli and Peanut Oil

12 stems asparagus – about 400 g (13 oz) in total
2.5 cm (1 in) piece ginger, cut into thin strips
1 large red chilli, finely sliced
2 tablespoons light soy sauce
3 tablespoons peanut oil

Wash asparagus and trim, discarding woody ends. Peel lower parts of stems using a vegetable peeler.

Combine ginger, chilli and soy sauce in a heatproof bowl.

Bring a pan or wok of water to the boil, then add asparagus and simmer for 1 minute. Drain asparagus and arrange on a serving plate.

Heat oil in a small heavy-based pan until surface seems to shimmer slightly, then carefully pour into bowl with ginger, chilli and soy sauce. Stir to combine, drizzle over asparagus and serve immediately.

Serves 4–6 as part of shared meal

Lion's Head Meatballs

2 tablespoons cornflour (cornstarch)
2 large outer leaves and 4 smaller inner leaves Chinese cabbage
4 tablespoons peanut oil
½ cup shao hsing wine
2 cups chicken stock
1 tablespoon light soy sauce

Meatballs

500 g (1 lb) fatty pork mince
5 cm (2 in) piece ginger, finely chopped
2 garlic cloves, finely chopped
3 spring onions (scallions), finely chopped
1 tablespoon light soy sauce
2 tablespoons shao hsing wine
1 tablespoon brown sugar

To make the meatballs, place all ingredients in a large bowl and, using your hands, mix thoroughly, taking small handfuls and 'slapping' them against side of bowl to tenderise meat.

Spread cornflour over a large plate. Divide meatball mixture into four equal portions, shaping each one into a rough round cake – a 'lion's head'. Carefully roll each meatball in cornflour to coat.

Cut each of the large cabbage leaves crossways into four strips, then use these to line the base of a claypot or flameproof casserole dish.

Heat oil in a hot wok until surface seems to shimmer slightly. Reduce heat to medium–low, then carefully place two meatballs in wok and fry for 2 minutes each side, or until golden brown. Remove with a slotted spoon and transfer to cabbage-lined claypot. Repeat with remaining meatballs.

Cover each meatball with one of the smaller cabbage leaves, wrapping the cabbage leaf around so that it resembles a lion's mane. Add shao hsing wine, stock and soy sauce to claypot, then bring to the boil. Reduce heat to low and simmer gently, covered, for 2 hours.

Using a slotted spoon, carefully transfer lion's head meatballs to a serving platter, ladle over sauce and serve immediately.

Serves 4 as part of a shared meal

We finish our visit with a tour through Mrs Xu's beautiful, thriving tea plantation.

She plucks leaves left, right and centre, to show us the healthy quality of her tea bushes. I promise to return in the not too distant future, when we will cook 'lion's head' meatballs together. I ask Mrs Xu if there is a guesthouse in the area where we might stay, but she says absolutely not – it is an affluent village and people are very suspicious of foreigners. She is grinning now as she says that she would like to come and work in the kitchen of my restaurant in Australia, insisting that she would work very hard for me! When we say our goodbyes, I clasp her to me in a big hug and give her the string of Tibetan beads that I have around my neck as a sign of friendship and respect.

Back in Hangzhou, we indulge in an afternoon shopping spree in the market area of Xinhua Lu, which is famous for its silk. I buy some divine, pure silk pyjamas for my mother – she tells me later that they are like a second skin – and my friends return with shawls, scarves, cheong sams, stockings and camisoles.

For dinner, Mrs Xu recommended we go to Longjing No. 1 Restaurant, near Hangzhou. We enjoy an amazing meal of glass noodles with dark soy sauce and five-spice tofu, braised pork belly with bamboo, rich and caramelly braised potatoes with Chinese ham, another version of crystal prawns (this time with gingko nuts in addition to the Longjing tea), and an interesting type of Chinese melon – reminiscent of choko – finely sliced and lightly pickled.

The stand-out dish, however, is a fish fillet poached in hot oil, which I noticed at someone else's table and ordered in my usual way by grabbing a waitress and pointing. The dish arrives at the table in a charming wooden bucket-style pot, lined with metal. The pot is half-filled with clear, hot oil enclosing perfect, white slivers of fish. I smell it first of all: there is a lovely, clean aroma, but I can tell the oil is not peanut oil, since there is no nuttiness and smokiness. I carefully pick out a piece of the delectable-looking fish with my chopsticks. Hhhhmmmm – absolutely divine, refined, melt-in-your-mouth fish. A friend has also taken a mouthful, but she is stunned to find a decent-sized, smooth, round, hot pebble in her mouth. A hot pebble, hot oil . . . but the fish is poached, and shows no trace of the crunchy texture that would result from frying. *How does this dish work?*

Through our guide, the waitress explains. The stones are heated up and placed into the specially lined wooden bucket, then hot oil is poured in – the stones keep the oil hot. Fresh slivers of fish are lowered into the oil and a lid is placed over the whole bucket; there is no pre-cooking on a stove. The fish poaches in this way for 10 minutes, and so is cooked very gently. The result is heavenly . . . The more time I spend in China, the more I learn to expect the unexpected.

While we were at T8 restaurant and bar in Shanghai, Walter Zahner, the general manager there, told us about the last thing I expected to find in China: a glamorous resort.

Called the Fuchun Resort, and located just outside Hangzhou, in Fuyang district, it sounded so unusual that we were determined to have a look for ourselves. So the next day, after an hour's drive through depressingly ordinary suburbs, we arrive at the gates of an enormous property, and through them we enter a completely different world. As we wind our way down the white drive, we all marvel at the spectacular golfing range, the landscaped gardens and the lush forest. What a relief to be in the fresh air again – we just know we are going to have a great time here. We realise just how beautifully designed the resort is as we pile out of the bus and into the lobby. The exposed beams of the low ceiling rest on a wooden frame supported by columns, a method of construction based on traditional, Tang-style architecture. The space is lit by daylight, which streams in through one side, supplemented by minimalist, subdued lamps, and the walls are hung with masterful Tibetan-style paintings of gods and demons, with small Tang dynasty sculptures placed in niches at intervals. It's all so stylish but delightfully understated.

We are met by the managing director, Michael Fuchs, an utterly charming, immaculately presented man who treats us like royalty. He invites us to join him for a drink in the Lake Lounge, a wonderful room overlooking the resort's lake and terraced hillsides, and furnished with ever-so-comfortable leather lounges. In the centre is a large glass table covered with lavish books on art, and the setting is given substance by an old-fashioned

chess board, and softness by beautiful artwork and orchids. Michael talks about the resort's owner, a retiring businessman whose vision was to build one of the world's most elegant and beautiful resorts. Every element is a reflection of the taste and sophistication of this man, and his unrivalled attention to detail – even the music, which Michael says is programmed to create different moods and atmospheres at different times of day.

It is late afternoon by now – and I, of course, cut straight to the point and ask Michael if there is a kitchen where I can cook us all dinner. He is quite taken aback by my proposal, I suspect, but he soon comes around and introduces me to the head chef, who says that the kitchen is all mine once the resort's dinner service is finished, at about 7.45 p.m. I feel that familiar rush of energy, as I always do when I am about to launch into a cooking frenzy. I unpack my hoard of fresh organic produce from the O Store: fresh ginger, garlic, soy bean sprouts, mung bean sprouts, spring onions, eggplants, cucumbers, red and yellow baby tomatoes, eggs, bok choy, choy sum, carrots, red onion, baby spinach, peppers and Chinese cabbage. While I was there, I also raided their sauce shelf and purchased some exquisite Japanese organic tamari, shoyu and brown rice vinegar, as well as some shao hsing wine, sesame oil, chilli oil and brown sugar.

All the chefs are really sweet young boys – they watch my every move, and Michael tells me it is a big thrill for them to observe a foreign chef at work. I think through the menu I plan to cook and realise that there are no meat dishes, so I ask the head chef if he could spare us some beef, please. Of course. He disappears and returns with six magnificent pieces of beef fillet. Now the menu is complete in my mind, and I am ready to start cooking.

I decide to roast the beef rare and serve it with a ginger dressing. First, I marinate the meat in a mixture of garlic, ginger, shao hsing wine, tamari, brown sugar and sesame oil. Next, I prepare a refreshing cool salad: I peel and halve some cucumbers,

The stylish interiors of Fuchun Resort, near Hangzhou

OPPOSITE: Cooking at the resort

de-seed them and cut them into irregular shapes before sprinkling them lightly with brown sugar and setting them aside in the fridge.

I plan to make a luscious omelette with the beautiful organic eggs, and perhaps a sweet-and-sour fresh tomato sauce to dress it. *Aarrhhh, these eggs are so fresh* – they have taut, deep-yellow yolks that retain their shape as they are cracked into a bowl, and such viscous, clear whites. Using chopsticks I beat the eggs loosely, leaving the white and yolk still partially separate so that they will form silky strands as they cook. This is the same technique I use when adding the finishing touch to a classic Cantonese sweet corn soup: when the stream of lightly beaten egg is drizzled into the boiling-hot soup, it is immediately transformed into delicate, eggy ribbons.

For the accompanying sauce, I finely chop some garlic and slice some ginger and a handful of spring onions, then halve the tomatoes. Sweet, vibrant, organic tomatoes – there is nothing better! A dash of peanut oil goes into a hot wok, then the garlic and ginger are sizzled and swirled to release their aromas and seal in flavour. Some brown sugar adds depth and warmth. In go the tomatoes, along with a splash of shao hsing wine, some shoyu and brown rice vinegar and a dash of sesame oil. I taste to see if the flavours are a balance of salty (shoyu), sweet (sugar) and sour (vinegar), before setting the sauce aside to be reheated later. The omelette must be served as soon as it is ready, so I make sure all the other dishes are done first.

I finely slice the red, yellow and green peppers. I am drawn to their intensely beautiful colours and I want them to 'sing' from the plate, so I decide to stir-fry them very simply with some peanut oil, crushed garlic and tamari. I am absolutely bowled over by the exquisite mung bean sprouts and soy bean sprouts – they are so vibrantly fresh that they almost jump off the plate. To maintain their integrity, I lightly stir-fry the sprouts in some peanut oil with a little finely sliced ginger, sugar, shoyu and vinegar – barely cooked, the sprouts retain the most wonderful crunchy texture coupled with a subtle complexity of flavour.

I quickly sear the beef – the caramelly smell of the marinade is rich and intoxicating, dizzying and delectable – then whisk it into the oven and briefly roast it, before leaving it to rest in a warm place. Meanwhile, the head chef has put some rice on to cook. I put the finishing touches to my other dishes, including one of my favourites, which consists of the most divine, lightly pickled carrots and red onions, finely shredded Chinese cabbage, finely shredded Savoy cabbage, delicate strips of cucumber and spring onions, fresh mint and coriander leaves, sweet Thai basil and dill – like a Chinese 'coleslaw', if you will.

The last dish I need to cook is the omelette. I go to the other side of the kitchen, where the wok stalls are, and crank up the wok. With a volcanic roar, an intense flame leaps out, licking around the sides of the wok. I add a slosh of vegetable oil to the wok and wait patiently for the telltale shimmer and slight ripple across its surface that indicates it's ready. I swiftly pour the beaten eggs into the wok and *swoosh* – as if by magic, a big, fluffy omelette emerges, crackling and hissing in the hot oil.

'Quick! Quick!' I motion for a stainless-steel bowl to hold the hot, dirty oil. I drain the oil from the wok and am left with a beautiful, crispy, golden omelette, which I slide out onto a serving plate. I quickly reheat the sauce, pour it over the omelette and garnish with spring onion slices and a sprinkle of pepper – out she goes!

All the chefs clap enthusiastically. For me, there is nothing more inspirational than being around young people who are deeply excited and moved by what they are doing. Perhaps the most sustaining part of running my own restaurant is watching young chefs develop and rise up through the ranks – reminding them what their cooking skills were like on day one, and seeing how much progress they've made a year later, acknowledging all the lessons and techniques they have learnt.

And it's all done! The rare roast beef, refreshing cucumber salad, stir-fried vegetables and 'coleslaw' are laid out in the resort's sophisticated dining room. We enjoy the food and the atmosphere immensely, the soft lights and candles, the thoroughly charming and entertaining company of Michael – and a very welcome chilled white wine from the Margaret River region of Western Australia.

With Michael Fuchs, of Fuchun Resort, and his head chef

Marinated Rare Roast Beef with Ginger Dressing

600 g (1 lb 4 oz) beef fillet, in one piece

Marinade
2 garlic cloves, finely chopped
2.5 cm (1 in) piece ginger, finely chopped
3 tablespoons shao hsing wine
2 tablespoons tamari or light soy sauce
2 tablespoons brown sugar
1 teaspoon sesame oil

Dressing
1 spring onion (scallion), finely sliced
5 cm (2 in) piece ginger, finely chopped
2 tablespoons finely sliced coriander (cilantro) stems
1 tablespoon brown sugar
2 tablespoons brown rice vinegar
2 tablespoons tamari or light soy sauce
3 tablespoons extra virgin olive oil

Preheat oven to 180°C (350°F).

Combine all marinade ingredients in a bowl, then add beef and mix well. Cover, place in refrigerator and leave to marinate for 1 hour.

Remove beef from marinade and sear on a hot chargrill plate or in a heavy-based frying pan for 3 minutes on each side. Transfer beef to an oven tray and roast for approximately 12 minutes (for rare). Remove from oven, then loosely cover beef and oven tray with foil, and allow to rest for 15 minutes.

Meanwhile, make the dressing. Combine all ingredients in a bowl and mix thoroughly.

Cut beef into 1 cm (½ in) slices and arrange on a platter. Pour over dressing and serve while still warm, or at room temperature.

Serves 4–6 as part of a shared meal

Omelette with Sweet and Sour Tomato Sauce

¼ cup vegetable oil
6 free-range eggs, lightly beaten

Sauce
2 tablespoons peanut oil
3 garlic cloves, roughly chopped
6 fine slices ginger, cut into thin strips
1 teaspoon brown sugar
6 red cherry tomatoes, cut in half
6 yellow cherry tomatoes, cut in half
3 spring onions (scallions), trimmed and finely sliced
2 tablespoons shao hsing wine
1 teaspoon shoyu
1 tablespoon brown rice vinegar
½ teaspoon sesame oil

First, make the sauce. Heat peanut oil in a hot wok until surface seems to shimmer slightly. Add garlic and ginger and stir-fry for 2 minutes. Add sugar and allow to caramelise for 30 seconds. Add tomatoes and spring onions and stir-fry for 1 minute. Add shao hsing wine, shoyu and vinegar and stir-fry for 30 seconds. Stir through sesame oil and set sauce aside.

For the omelette, heat vegetable oil in a hot wok until the surface seems to shimmer slightly. Pour lightly beaten eggs into wok and leave to cook on base of wok for 30 seconds, without stirring. Using a spatula, fold omelette over onto itself and leave to cook for another 30 seconds. Fold over again and leave for 20 seconds or until almost set. Repeat once more before lifting omelette from wok onto a serving platter.

Meanwhile, gently reheat sauce, then spoon over omelette and serve immediately.

Serves 4–6 as part of shared meal

Stir-Fried Mung Bean Sprouts and Soy Bean Sprouts

2 tablespoons peanut oil
5 cm (2 in) piece ginger, cut into thin strips
100 g (3½ oz) mung bean sprouts
100 g (3½ oz) soy bean sprouts
1 tablespoon shao hsing wine
1 tablespoon shoyu
1 teaspoon sesame oil

Heat peanut oil in a hot wok until surface seems to shimmer slightly. Add ginger and sprouts and stir-fry for 2 minute. Add shao hsing wine and stir-fry for 30 seconds. Add shoyu and sesame oil and stir-fry for 1 minute, then serve immediately.

Serves 4–6 as part of a shared meal

If soy bean sprouts are unavailable, use a mixture of regular (mung) bean sprouts and snow pea sprouts.

Stir-Fried Red, Yellow and Green Peppers with Garlic and Tamari

½ red pepper, de-seeded
½ yellow pepper, de-seeded
½ green pepper, de-seeded
2 tablespoons peanut oil
4 garlic cloves, crushed
100 g (3½ oz) black cloud ear fungus – optional
2 tablespoons shao hsing wine
2 teaspoons brown sugar
2 tablespoons tamari or light soy sauce
1 tablespoon brown rice vinegar
½ teaspoon sesame oil
⅓ cup purple mint leaves – optional

Trim membranes from peppers, then cut into 1 cm (½ in) strips.

Heat peanut oil in a hot wok until surface seems to shimmer slightly. Add garlic and peppers and stir-fry for 2 minutes. Add cloud ear fungus, if using, and stir-fry for 30 seconds. Add shao hsing wine and stir-fry for 30 seconds, then add sugar and allow to caramelise for 30 seconds.

Add tamari or soy sauce and vinegar and stir-fry for a further 2 minutes. Stir in sesame oil and mint, if using, and serve immediately.

Serves 4–6 as part of a shared meal

Chinese Coleslaw

1 small carrot, peeled
1 small red onion, finely sliced
2 teaspoons sea salt
1 cup brown rice vinegar
¼ cup brown sugar
1 small cucumber, cut in half lengthways
½ cup finely shredded Savoy cabbage
3 spring onions (scallions), trimmed and cut into thin strips
⅓ cup mint leaves
⅓ cup coriander (cilantro) leaves
⅓ cup dill leaves
3 red cherry tomatoes, cut in half
3 yellow cherry tomatoes, cut in half

Dressing

1 tablespoon tamari or light soy sauce
½ teaspoon sesame oil
1 tablespoon brown rice vinegar

Using a vegetable peeler, peel carrot, then slice finely lengthways into ribbons. Cut carrot ribbons into thin strips and place in a bowl with half the salt, then mix well. Place onion slices in a separate bowl with remaining salt and mix well. Set carrot and onion aside for 1 hour.

Combine vinegar and sugar in a small heavy-based saucepan and stir over medium heat until sugar dissolves. Simmer, uncovered and without stirring, for about 10 minutes, or until reduced and slightly syrupy. Set aside to cool.

Drain carrot and onion and, using your hands, gently squeeze out any excess liquid. Place carrot and onion in the cooled syrup to pickle them lightly.

Using a vegetable peeler, finely slice cucumber lengthways into ribbons and then cut these into thin strips. In a large bowl, combine cucumber with pickled carrot, onion and all remaining ingredients, using your hands to mix thoroughly.

To make the dressing, combine all ingredients in a small bowl. Spoon dressing over salad and serve on a platter.

Serves 4–6 as a starter or as part of a shared meal

On our way back to Shanghai, from where we'll fly to Hong Kong, we decide to break our journey at one of a string of ancient villages that flank the Grand Canal between Hangzhou and Beijing.

At first Wuzhen seems like yet another overcrowded tourist attraction, as we pull into a massive car park crammed with tour buses. Once through the gates, though, we are transported back to another time and a gentler way of life. A small flat-roofed open boat, not unlike a gondola, carries us along the canals and waterways that weave their way though this ancient town, past weeping willows, stunningly ornate stone bridges, and compact, wooden-fronted houses with grey-tiled, mossy roofs. The houses have intricately carved window shutters, their black wood faded to brown and red tones by the elements and the passage of time. Everywhere we look there are countless scenes of ordinary life: old raggedy mops hanging out of windows to dry; women clad in floral polyester tops, rolled-up trousers and pink plastic slippers standing on the steps of their houses, nonchalantly doing their laundry in the canal; old black bicycles leaning up against faded white walls – and always, always, people eating.

We hop off the boat and wander around the narrow lanes for a couple of hours. My favourite part of Wuzhen is the area where indigo tie-dying is done. I love the rich moodiness of indigo and its intense depth of colour. I come across a sweet old man who spends all day making patterned Chinese slippers with a distinctive indigo hue. Another interesting place is the Gongsheng Grains Workshop distillery, which produces a pungent rice wine you can smell a mile off – just inhaling the fumes leaves me feeling vague and dizzy.

Walking past houses and discreetly peering through the windows, I find fragments of an old, old China. The houses are all so gloomy – there's bright sunlight outside but somehow none of it penetrates – yet they are full of life. In one house four people in slippers and well-worn clothes are playing mah jong and sipping tea; in another, a mother is feeding her children dumplings at the kitchen table.

The timeless scenes I witnessed in Wuzhen will linger in my memory forever.

Daily life in Wuzhen

PREVIOUS PAGE: Houses and gardens overhanging the Grand Canal

Hong Kong and Lamma Island

HONG KONG AND LAMMA ISLAND

Newsweek
Newsweek

SHARP
HITACHI
SIEMENS

SAMSUNG

One of the most amazing cities in the world, Hong Kong comprises a small peninsula and a handful of islands tacked onto the underside of the Chinese mainland.

With a population of 7 million, Hong Kong is an incredibly crowded, densely built-up place, but an exciting one, enlivened by a thriving blend of European and Chinese culture. The Hong Kong region was only sparsely settled when the British claimed it from China as a trophy during the nineteenth-century Opium Wars, subsequently transforming it into the trade and business hub that it remains today. When British rule ended in 1997, it left a strong colonial legacy in some of the older architecture, double-decker buses and trams, and the way many people speak English. Scratch the surface, though, and you'll find a surprisingly conservative Chinese streak: having avoided Mao's attempts to destroy China's past on the mainland during the 1960s and 1970s, people in Hong Kong look on themselves as guardians of authentic Chinese culture – and so it's here, in this seemingly futuristic city, that you may encounter some of the more traditional superstitions and beliefs.

Looking from the air like a giant electrical circuit board, the centre of town lies either side of a bustling harbour, split between the mainland peninsula of Kowloon and the facing north shore of Hong Kong Island. Heading away from the downtown area's hyper-modern skyline and its gorgeously blue harbour, large tracts of the territory are still rural, especially the outlying islands and in the so-called New Territories between Kowloon and the border with Guangdong.

We arrive at the height of summer, and it's 34 degrees outside and intensely humid. Fortunately, we're spirited from the airport by a stunning green Rolls Royce limo with golden stripes sent by The Peninsula, one of Hong Kong's most outstanding hotels. This city revels in unashamed exhibitions of wealth, good fortune and success, and The Peninsula is perhaps its ultimate symbol, a surviving memento of the British era and the epitome of taste and style.

After we've settled in, we head upstairs for pre-dinner drinks at Felix, the hotel's sumptuous Philippe Starck–designed restaurant and bar. Even if you're not staying here, Felix is worth a trip for its décor and staggering harbour and city views, not to mention its wonderful martinis. Catching the lift up to Felix is an experience in itself: the lift walls and ceiling are made from rich, dark wood fashioned into free-form, organic shapes and, as you near the twenty-eighth floor, the lights gently fade until it is almost completely dark, enhancing your mood and expectation. Witty, individualistic design is Starck's trademark, and each of the chairs is printed with photographs of faces – apparently, these are Monsieur Starck's 'nearest and dearest'.

Arriving at The Peninsula hotel

PREVIOUS PAGE: A stunning vista of Victoria Harbour, Hong Kong

As we sip our drinks, I recognise the face of Deanne, one of the previous head chefs at Felix. And the men's loos are just brilliant, with the entire city visible through the thick green glass walls. *Yes, I have secretly snuck in there on occasion to catch a glimpse of the outrageous view!*

Our appetites whetted, we are ready for Spring Moon, The Peninsula's chic Chinese restaurant. It's a ravishingly handsome room, with floors, tables and chairs all crafted from dark mahogany. Ornate Art Deco lamps illuminate every corner, golden lacquered walls feature panels of embossed goldfish, and there are antique Chinese porcelain vases, old-style black telephones and the most wonderfully rare, frosted mirrors. I take great delight in the delicate image of a violet-blue butterfly etched into the corner of one of these mirrors.

Felix restaurant and bar, designed by Philippe Starck

I order traditional dishes, including Peking duck, which is deftly dissected at our table by an immaculate waiter, in the most exacting and elegant manner. One by one, perfect pieces of duck skin and flesh are shaved from the carcass – there is silence at the table as we are mesmerised by this sophisticated display of precision and impeccable knife skills. The sound of his razor-sharp cleaver slicing through the shiny, mahogany-coloured duck skin is reminiscent of a blade cutting through parchment paper. We also devour intensely textural and tasty abalone with green vegetables, wonderfully crunchy yet tender jellyfish with sesame and vinegar, the intriguing delicacy of bird's nest soup, and a plate of sweet, succulent chicken braised with soy sauce and shao hsing wine.

Chicken Braised with Soy Sauce and Shao Hsing Wine

- 4 × chicken leg and thigh portions on the bone, with skin – about 1.5 kg (3 lb) in total
- 100 g (3½ oz) fresh shiitake mushrooms, stems discarded and caps halved

Stock

- 2 cups shao hsing wine
- 6 garlic cloves, crushed
- 8 cm (3 in) piece ginger, finely sliced
- 400 ml (13 fl oz) honey
- 2 cups light soy sauce
- 4 star anise
- 2 spring onions (scallions), trimmed and cut in half
- 4 cups water

Place all stock ingredients in a heavy-based pan or stockpot, then bring to the boil and simmer for 30 minutes.

Carefully lower chicken pieces into stock, skin-side down, and cover with a cartouche (see below) to keep them fully submerged. Poach chicken gently for 15 minutes. There should be no more than an occasional ripple breaking the surface; adjust temperature, if necessary, to ensure stock does not reach simmering point again. At the end of the poaching time, remove pan from stove and allow chicken to steep in stock for 5 minutes to complete the cooking process. Using tongs, gently remove chicken from stock, being careful not to tear skin. Place chicken on a tray to cool slightly.

Meanwhile place pan back on stove, then add mushrooms and bring stock back to the boil. Simmer until reduced by approximately half – this should take about 20 minutes.

Using a cleaver or heavy knife, separate chicken portions into legs and thighs, then chop into thick, even slices. Arrange chicken on a serving platter, then drizzle with hot stock, spoon on mushrooms and serve.

Serves 4–6 as part of a shared meal

To make a simple cartouche, just tear a piece of baking paper or greaseproof paper roughly the size and shape of your pan and press it down onto the surface of the liquid, covering all the ingredients.

Stir-Fried Snow Peas with Garlic

2 tablespoons vegetable oil
½ teaspoon sea salt
250 g (8 oz) snow peas (mange-tout), trimmed
4 garlic cloves, roughly crushed
½ teaspoon brown sugar
½ cup chicken stock or water
¼ teaspoon sesame oil

Heat vegetable oil in a hot wok until surface seems to shimmer slightly. Add salt and snow peas and stir-fry for 2 minutes. Add garlic and stir-fry for 1 minute, stirring constantly to ensure garlic does not burn. Add sugar and stir-fry for 10 seconds.

Pour in stock or water and simmer for 2 minutes or until snow peas are tender. Lastly, stir through sesame oil and serve immediately.

Serves 4–6 as part of a shared meal

One of The Peninsula's colonial credentials is that it still serves afternoon tea in its sumptuous, elegant lobby – a slightly anachronistic but wonderfully sedate experience, complete with cucumber sandwiches, dainty rye-bread sandwiches filled with smoked salmon, tiny quiches, petit fours, lemon tartlets, scones and jam. Right now, though, we're headed back to the Spring Moon restaurant, where one of the hotel's resident tea masters will take us through some of the finer points of Chinese tea appreciation.

A superb collection of centuries-old Chinese teapots takes pride of place in the main dining room: an effervescent amber light silhouettes hundreds of teapots, all displayed at their most flattering angle on tailor-made shelving. The tea master is tall and willowy, with an open, serene face and thin-rimmed spectacles. As he works, he displays a beautifully precise economy of movement. He trained in his profession for five years, and what strikes me most is the level of care and respect he shows, and the proud manner in which he speaks about his art.

We try two types of green tea, Longjing from Hangzhou in mainland China, and a flower-scented tea from Taiwan. First of all, the tea master shows us the leaves: they are this year's pickings, and very high quality. Then he rinses the cups with hot water before pouring the boiling water into a jug to cool it slightly – using boiling water can make green tea taste bitter. He checks the temperature first with a thermometer, then just by holding the jug in his hand until experience tells him that the water has reached the ideal 80–82°C. The tea is prepared in two ways to show us the difference: first adding the leaves to boiling water, which releases the tea's scent slowly and creates a more subtle flavour; then adding the water to the leaves, for a mellower, fuller taste. The 'teapot' is actually more like a large glass cup with a lid, so we can observe the leaves as they gradually sink upright to the bottom of the pot, releasing their aroma as they go. Skilfully lifting the pot with one hand, and using the lid to hold back the leaves, the tea master fills delicate little porcelain cups for us with the clear golden liquid.

Witnessing this ceremony has irrevocably changed the way I experience tea-making and drinking. Now, I am conscious of the temperature of the water, I am pedantic about the quality of the tea leaves I use, and I am mindful of the temperature of the teapot and cup before the tea is brewed. I am now aware that the way you make the tea, the order in which you do things, directly affects the resulting taste, as well as the weight, intensity and aroma of the tea.

Taking high tea at The Peninsula hotel

The iconic Star Ferry shuttles between Kowloon and Hong Kong Island every few minutes.

The Kowloon terminal is almost right outside The Peninsula, and we soon find that this is one of the few ways of getting around the city that is a sheer joy. The ferries themselves are painted green and white with wooden seats, and as they chug across the harbour, they offer unrestricted views of one of the most spectacular cityscapes in the world. Riding them at night is even better, with all the skyscrapers on Hong Kong Island lit up like Christmas trees.

Our first stop on Hong Kong Island is the Luk Yu Teahouse, one of the most famous places in the city to partake of that classic Cantonese breakfast, yum cha. In fact, Luk Yu's food isn't the greatest in the world, but I love the faintly sinister atmosphere: the 1930s interior with low ceilings, dark wooden panels, heavy tables and winding staircases – and the grumpy old waiters, who serve their selection of dumplings from metal trays hung around their necks. I order a few of my favourites: crunchy *har gau*, delicate prawn dumplings enclosed in a translucent wrapper; gelatinous, steamed chicken feet; *cheung fan*, folded rice noodle sheets stuffed with roast pork; and some superb beef balls, which are firm, juicy and silky smooth. All have that clean, clear, slightly savoury flavour so typical of Cantonese cooking; having grown up with such food, I find it utterly comforting and hard to resist. The other distinguishing characteristic of Cantonese food is its freshness. People here are obsessive about the quality of their ingredients, and might well go to the markets before every meal to ensure that they are only cooking the very best.

After yum cha, we decide that a walk might be a good idea. Bad move. The streets are packed full of people going to work, shopping, just filling up the space – very frustrating. We head east towards two of Hong Kong's most famous buildings: the Hong Kong and Shanghai Banking Corporation (HSBC), a big slab raised off the ground by an external 'skeleton', which means that you can walk right underneath and look up through the hollow centre; and the brilliant Bank of China (BOC), a bamboo-like spear of a tower fashioned of deep-blue glass encased in a framework of strong white steel. These two buildings are players in one of Hong Kong's real-life soap-operas, the struggle for symbolic superiority between the two great financial institutions. Both are designed by famous modernist architects (the HSBC by Sir Norman Foster, the BOC by I. M. Pei) and both use feng shui, the traditional Chinese art of positioning buildings harmoniously within a landscape, to try and attract the most 'luck'. The HSBC building is raised off the ground because feng shui dictates that there has to be an unobstructed flow of energy between Government House, on the hill behind the building, and the harbour. The BOC tower, however, has its sharp corners directed towards Government House and has a pointed top 'stabbing' upwards at the heavens (which supposedly acts like a lightning

Illuminated facades of the HSBC [TOP] and BOC buildings

OPPOSITE: White neon girds the BOC tower

conductor for good luck, drawing it straight down into the building) – both very threatening attributes in feng shui.

We'd originally planned to head to Hong Kong Park, just beside the BOC tower. Amid the crush of buildings and people in the centre of the city, there are three large parks full of flowers, trees and narrow paths, which make Hong Kong a much more bearable city. However, we soon decide it's too hot down here, and instead ride the Peak Tram up to the cooler climes of Victoria Peak, Hong Kong Island's 552-metre-high summit. This leafy enclave of shady woodland walkways and manicured gardens, far above the steamy streets below, was once home to wealthy Europeans; now most of the residents are Chinese businessmen and glitterati. I love catching the Peak Tram, sitting inside the wooden carriages as they're hauled uphill along an incredibly steep track. And the views from the top are amazing: not only can you see far across the harbour and into the patchwork fields of the New Territories, but you can also look *down* onto the city centre's skyscrapers.

We have arranged to meet my friend Chun Lau in his restaurant for lunch, so head back down into the hot, humid streets to keep our appointment.

Chun studied architecture in Melbourne for several years, until he decided to return to Hong Kong to take over the running of the family restaurant, the Yellow Door Kitchen, which was established in 2002 by Chun's father, Mr Kin Lau. Chun is multi-talented and, as well as writing articles for various food and art magazines, he speaks impeccable English and reads insatiably. For me, Chun represents the face of *modern* Hong Kong: he is not afraid to show his feelings, he has broad-minded views on politics and the state of the world, and he is well-read on many, many subjects and travels widely, yet he retains strong family values and the deep-rooted respect the Chinese have for the elderly. I always look forward to spending time in his company.

The Yellow Door Kitchen is one of the pioneering 'private' restaurants, small-scale ventures that have sprung up to circumvent the complex and expensive process required to run a business in Hong Kong. These places get around some of the paperwork by calling themselves clubs or kitchens, rather than restaurants.

The Yellow Door Kitchen is in Cochrane Street, Central, on Hong Kong Island: from the street, you climb a small flight of stairs in what appears to be a rather dull, nondescript block of apartments or business suites. You then take the lift to the sixth floor and, when the doors slide open, you are in another world, facing a brightly painted yellow door. It is F-A-N-T-A-S-T-I-C. Think small, think intimate, think home-cooking – this is my kind of place.

Chun Lau is not here yet, but we are seated and made very welcome, with Chinese tea in one hand and a delicious-looking menu in the other. The chef behind this restaurant is an adorable Sichuanese woman who is affectionately known as 'Big Sister Wah'.

Born and bred in rural Sichuan, she is a wonderfully talented, natural cook. She has an inherent feeling for food, teamed with a big, big heart and generous, all-encompassing spirit. She is also a young mother, and her nurturing qualities are reflected in every dish she turns her deft hand to. The first thing I do each time I eat at the Yellow Door is push my way into the shoebox-sized kitchen and give Big Sister a big hug. She is really sweet and cuddly – and such a mean cook! I am always reassured to see the fabulous huge pot of Sichuan chilli paste she has hiding under her kitchen bench – I suspect it is the secret ingredient in every dish.

Today Big Sister Wah serves up an unforgettable meal. We begin with pickled cucumber, wontons in chicken broth, mung bean noodle sheets and dumplings with chilli sauce. I have never eaten wonton-style dumplings as *fresh* and *silky* as these. Floating in a broth that has a distinct but subtle chicken flavour, they make perfect comfort food: warm, soft and delicate. In contrast, I just love the crunchy texture of cucumber: these particular ones are slightly prickly, like gherkins, and with their sweet and sour taste, they make a great palate-cleanser. As for the mung bean sheets, these seductively slippery, transparent noodle-like creations, which have no real flavour to call their own, come alive with Big Sister Wah's famous Sichuan chilli sauce made from dried red chillies lightly caramelised in oil and sugar, and infused with garlic, ginger and soy sauce – YUM! Next we have the restaurant's signature dish of 'mouth-watering chicken', a splendid dish with complex flavours – fresh whole chicken poached in a simple white master stock, chopped up Chinese-style, and served with a sensational dressing of pounded dried red chillies, chopped garlic, crushed roasted peanuts, caramelised sugar, soy sauce, vinegar, chilli oil, Sichuan pepper, finely sliced cucumber and sprigs of fresh coriander.

Chun Lau and his father, Mr Kin Lau, arrive, accompanied by Mrs Lau. A highly accomplished cellist, Mrs Lau is an intelligent and vibrant woman with a petite frame. And Mr Lau is quite a character. He is of medium height but has a rather slight build, and he wears his whitish-grey hair pulled back in a ponytail. I reckon he is probably in his mid-50s – he looks very cool. He used to be one of Hong Kong's most highly acclaimed art critics and has written about art and architecture for years.

Mr and Mrs Lau sit down to lunch at the table next to ours, but halfway through their meal Mr Lau abruptly turns to us and says: 'Let's go for a quick walk outside to buy some fish for your lunch.' We immediately follow his orders and, in the next breath, find ourselves out in the street, wrestling with that heat again and ducking down some back alleys to find the local fish market, where Mr Lau buys spankingly fresh fish for his lunch every day. Today, he points to a whole sole flapping in his hand and, with a big smile on his face, proudly exclaims, 'I buy this fish and take it back for Big Sister Wah to cook it for you, my Aussie friends!' Off we scamper, back to the air-conditioned restaurant, where Big Sister Wah perfectly steams the sole with ginger and spring onions – it is sublime.

After lunch Chun escorts us to the famous Wanchai markets, a short taxi ride from the restaurant. Since I last visited about a year ago, this area has become less lively and more bland, following local government crackdowns in the wake of the bird flu and SARS scares of 2002–2003. These measures have prompted the relocation of many local food markets inside large shopping malls – all much cleaner, of course, but I hanker for the labyrinthine quality of the outdoor markets and the colourful street-life they foster.

We stroll past many smelly, weird and wonderful stalls of dried this and shrivelled-up that before we all start to flag, and readily agree that the day has been rather long and it is time to head home to the soothing embrace of The Peninsula. The humidity really saps your energy, and could be quite distressing if you let it get to you – I find I have to train myself to mentally surrender to it and just 'go with the flow', otherwise I would fall into a hysterical heap within minutes. To make things worse, my glasses fog up each time I step into and out of the icily air-conditioned cabs. Hong Kong is definitely not a place for those sensitive to temperature fluctuations.

Shopping at Shanghai Tang's flagship store in Hong Kong

After its food, Hong Kong is most famous for its shopping, and the next morning we're back on the streets for a good session.

You can buy just about any consumer item in the world here, but Hong Kong is probably best known for its many markets, its electronic goods and clothing stores. Computers, cameras and other electronic equipment aren't such a good buy anymore, but the markets are still incredible, very Chinese and very specialised; one sells nothing but goldfish, another only songbirds and their bamboo cages, yet another just pieces of carved jade.

And then there are the clothes. Hong Kong has a reputation as somewhere to pick up anything from a cheap shirt to a good suit or stylish evening outfit, and the local obsession with up-to-the-minute fashion means you can often find inexpensive examples of the previous season's attire at warehouses and markets. For me, however, only one place will do: Shanghai Tang is my favourite shop in the world, and is where I buy many of my clothes. Originally established by the entrepreneurial David Tang, the flagship store is a sight to behold. Art Deco in style, it is all dark wood highlighted by terrazzo-tiled floors and brass fittings, its three floors linked by sweeping staircases.

I just can't get enough of Shanghai Tang's Mao-style jackets and shirts. They are square-cut, with big patch pockets and mandarin collars, and fastened down the front with frog clasps and Chinese knots. I love the unisex shape of these jackets, I love the fact that you can dress them up or wear them casually. My most prized Shanghai Tang outfit is a pure black velvet jacket with matching pants. The pants are simply lined with lime-green silk, but the jacket boasts a silk lining printed with the work of Chen Yu, a contemporary Chinese artist who explores the notion of individuality through his depiction of rows of seemingly identical human faces, one of which is subtly different from the rest.

SHANGHAI TANG

As usual, I leave the store weighed down with their brightly coloured bags, and we walk east to another David Tang brain child, the ritzy China Club. This is situated in the old Bank of China building – like The Peninsula hotel, it is a relic of the colonial era and is just as grand inside. The décor is a mix of colonial and modern European alongside antique Chinese, making this a unique and rather eccentric place, replete with the creativity of its founder and owner, and his love of art. In consultation with Johnson Chang (see page 460), David Tang personally chooses all the artwork that is displayed in the China Club across all its locations.

Even in the foyer, I am taken with the polished wooden flooring and furniture, gleaming in the soft lighting, its elegance offset by some quirkier touches. An old-fashioned antique hat rack and coat stand sits earnestly in one corner, and the maitre d' wears a white Mao suit with red stars on the jacket, symbolising the Chinese flag. Whole walls of the lobby and staircase are covered by David Tang's extensive collection of contemporary Chinese oil paintings; painting in oils is a recent innovation in China, though artists often pay homage to the great European masters. The object I love most in the foyer, though, is a large, shallow Chinese blue-and-white porcelain fish bowl where red and black goldfish happily swim around porcelain figurines. Dressed in patterned 1920s-style frocks, the figurines are simultaneously raunchy, flirtatious and coy.

The staircase, its wrought-iron bannister fashioned into longevity symbols, winds its way up through four of five levels, passing many more modern artworks on the way to the magical China Club Library. Pushing open two Art Deco glass doors, we enter a room lined with hand-carved wooden bookshelves full of precious volumes. I run my fingers along the shelves and shelves of beautiful books on Chinese food, politics, art, Buddhism. The library smells as a library should – old, dusty and musty. Even though it is only 11 a.m., the gloom is dispelled by pools of light from table lamps; it is as if the density and volume of literature is absorbing all the daylight.

Occupying pride of place is a venerable sofa, which sits nobly in front of the fire and is upholstered in a patchwork of nut-brown leather, the result of many repairs over the years. Like the lines on a person's face, these patches tell the sofa's life story. Deep, sagging armchairs are dotted around the room, covered in the most lavish embroidered velvet and brocade in various shades of carmine red, midnight blue and dark sea-green. An antique writing desk, with a globe precariously perched on a brass stand, adds to the effect of a scholarly yet comfortable, peaceful escape from the world.

Objets d'art and portraits adorn the foyer of the China Club in Hong Kong

OVERLEAF: The China Club Library

LEOS JANÁČEK

Our next port of call is The Long March Bar, an exquisite, narrow drinking den. The Long March is the name given to the gruelling trek across China undertaken by Mao's Chinese communist army in 1935, in order to escape the Chinese Nationalist forces that were trying to destroy them. And this bar is thronged with Mao memorabilia: matchboxes emblazoned with the Chinese flag, porcelain figures of the young Mao in every colour, black-and-white lithographs, brightly coloured orange and red etchings, linocuts and propaganda posters portraying triumphant Chinese peasants. The centrepiece is the beautifully carved wooden bar that runs down one side of the long, skinny room. The barman naturally looks the part, dressed in the China Club's signature white Mao suit.

But our last stop, the dining room, is the most impressive space in the China Club. There are easily thirty tables occupying the vast room, while rich-red leather banquettes partition off private dining areas around the sides. The chairs are Ming dynasty antiques, their distinctive lines softened by silk-upholstered seats in hues of peacock-blue, magenta-pink and lime-green. Every table has at its centre a different-shaped vase, in which is arranged a bunch of fresh flowers in a single colour, exuding effortless style, and filling the room with a vibrant and artistic aura. A spectacular black-and-white collage of portraits and prints of Mao occupies one cream-coloured wall, vying for attention with an enormous oil painting of mustardy-yellow Modigliani-style female images with elongated necks and almond eyes.

The atmospheric Long March Bar and glamorous dining room in Hong Kong's China Club

名茶

We leave the China Club artistically charged, and head around the corner to Hanart TZ Gallery, on the second floor of the Henley Building, where owner and curator Johnson Chang presides over one of the most reputable private galleries in Hong Kong. I first met Johnson on my second visit to Hong Kong several years ago, and he is one of the most charming, polite, sensitive and intelligent men I know. I always come away from my time with him feeling intellectually nourished and well-informed; I could listen to him talk about art for hours and hours. He represents many emerging contemporary Chinese artists, including the master of 'political pop art', Feng Mengbo, and the disturbing Liu Wei, whose monochrome landscape paintings turn out, on closer inspection, to be made up of body parts.

The exhibition showing at the time of our visit is by Caroline Chiu, a photographer who uses the world's second-largest camera, a Polaroid previously used by Andy Warhol and William Wegman, to produce rich sepia images that reveal what she calls the 'dark beauty' of everyday Chinese objects.

It has been another busy and stimulating day, and we are all starving, as usual!

We meet up with Chun Lau again, this time to visit his father's other restaurant, Kin's Kitchen, in Tin Hau. Our meal here comprises some of the best Chinese food I have ever eaten. The chef at the time of our visit (who has since moved on) specialised in imperial cuisine, which was invented at the behest of the emperors in Beijing – his cooking skill, knowledge and techniques were formidable.

We begin with his signature smoked soy chicken, which is to die for: beneath the golden-brown glazed skin that melts in your mouth lies succulent white flesh imbued with subtle hints of smokiness. What I find amazing is that it is never *too* smoky-tasting – a sure sign of the chef's expert restraint, since dishes prepared like this can all too easily be overpowering. We also indulge in some intensely flavoured stir-fried beef fillet with onions and an extraordinary dish called 'eight treasure' duck, a whole duck stuffed with sticky rice, gingko nuts, salted radish, ginger, shao hsing wine, soy sauce and sesame oil, then painstakingly basted for several hours in a large wok, using a mixture of shao hsing wine, dark and light soy sauces, star anise, dried orange peel, spring onions, yellow rock sugar, ginger and garlic. The result is a glistening dark-brown duck, with tasty, gooey, sticky rice within. As you can imagine, this is virtually a meal in itself.

Chun then tells us about the fresh fish tanks in the back alley, so we all lay down our chopsticks and set off to purchase our next dish. Sidestepping the fishmonger's gushing hose, I marvel at the beautiful coral trout and what appear to be vibrant-blue maori wrasse. I pounce on a tank filled with live prawns and promptly ask for half a kilo. We spend

10 minutes choosing a whole fish before settling on a beautiful orangey-red coral trout – simply steamed with ginger and spring onion, this will be transformed into one of the great classic dishes of Cantonese cuisine.

Back we go to the restaurant, taking our fish and prawns straight into the kitchen. Ten minutes later, a bowl of steamed prawns appears, accompanied by a soy and ginger dipping sauce. The shrimp are so sweet – peeling the shell off and sucking on the prawn heads is half the fun. Next comes the perfectly steamed coral trout: opaque pieces of flesh gently fall away from the bone, and there is just a suggestion of the best-quality light soy sauce, adding a subtle hint of salt to balance the sweet-tasting tender fish and the pungency of fine slivers of aromatic ginger and spring onion – a flavour profile I have grown up on, and one that I now cannot live without.

Choosing a fish for lunch with Chun Lau
ABOVE RIGHT: The chef at Kin's Kitchen

Stir-Fried Beef Fillet with Onions

2 tablespoons peanut oil
500 g (1 lb) best-quality beef fillet,
    cut into 2.5 cm (1 in) cubes
1 tablespoon peanut oil, extra
3 garlic cloves, crushed
1 white onion, finely sliced
1 teaspoon brown sugar
2 tablespoons light soy sauce
1 tablespoon Sichuan pepper and salt
juice 1 lemon

Heat oil in a hot wok until surface seems to shimmer slightly. Add half of the beef and stir-fry for 2 minutes. Remove beef from wok with a slotted spoon and drain on kitchen paper. Add extra oil to wok with remaining beef and stir-fry for 2 minutes.

Return all beef to wok, along with garlic and onion, and stir-fry for 2 minutes.

Add sugar and soy sauce and stir-fry for 3 minutes, or until beef is tender and just cooked. Serve immediately, sprinkled with Sichuan pepper and salt, and with a side dish of fresh lemon juice.

Serves 4–6 as part of a shared meal

Steamed Prawns with Soy, Ginger and Chilli Dipping Sauce

500 g (1 lb) small uncooked prawns (shrimp), unpeeled

Dipping sauce
6 spring onions (scallions), trimmed and cut into thin strips
5 cm (2 in) piece ginger, cut into thin strips
1 large red chilli, finely sliced
½ cup light soy sauce
1 teaspoon sesame oil
1 tablespoon brown sugar
2 tablespoons peanut oil

To make the dipping sauce, combine all ingredients except peanut oil in a heatproof bowl. Heat peanut oil in a small heavy-based pan until surface seems to shimmer slightly, then carefully pour into bowl to release flavours. Stir to combine and set aside.

Bring a large pan or stockpot of water to the boil. Add prawns and simmer for 2 minutes, then drain immediately.

Serve prawns while still warm, with a small bowl of dipping sauce alongside.

Serves 4–6 as a starter or as part of a shared meal

Try to find tiny harbour or school prawns (shrimp) for this dish – ideally about 7 g (¼ oz) each.

Lamma is the second largest of Hong Kong's 'outer islands', and is famous for its country walks and seafood restaurants.

For our lunchtime excursion to Lamma Island, we take a taxi to Aberdeen, a busy town on Hong Kong Island's south coast, fringing a harbour where traditional sampans and junks are still moored. From Aberdeen we catch a rickety wooden ferry to the tiny village of Sok Kwu Wan, at Lamma's north-eastern end. The leisurely 35-minute journey is an extremely welcome respite after several jam-packed days in the bustling city.

We arrive at the jetty, which leads directly into a covered but open-sided compound of around a half-dozen restaurants built over the water, all laden with tanks of live seafood, from which you can choose your fish and specify how you want it to be cooked. Our destination is the Rainbow Restaurant, and their famous dish is the unlikely sounding 'urinating shrimp', which are in fact small crayfish dry-fried with garlic, chilli, ginger, salt, pepper and coriander. Apparently, the dish gets its rather graphic name from the action of the shellfish as their juices spurt out when they are tossed vigorously in a hot wok. But it doesn't put us off stuffing these creatures from heaven into our mouths as quickly as possible!

We also suck contentedly on the tasty bones of red-roasted pigeon, which is served with piquant black vinegar and Sichuan pepper and salt; and slurp the scrumptious juices of steamed razor clams with black bean and chilli. And I can't resist some baby crabs steamed and then stir-fried with ginger and spring onions. We sip on chilled glasses of Sancerre and sit back contentedly, admiring the little fishing village around us and reflecting on how good life really is.

A9920
SKW 4
A9920
24438

Dry-Fried 'Urinating Shrimp'

2 × 750 g (1 lb 8 oz) live crayfish or lobster
4 tablespoons peanut oil
5 cm (2 in) piece ginger, finely chopped
4 garlic cloves, finely chopped
2 tablespoons finely chopped coriander (cilantro) stems
1 large red chilli, deseeded and finely chopped
1 lemon, cut in half
1 teaspoon roasted and ground Sichuan pepper
3 tablespoons sea salt

Cut crayfish or lobster in half lengthways, then cut each half into four sections.

Heat half the oil in a wok until surface seems to shimmer slightly. Carefully add crayfish and stir-fry for 2 minutes. Add remaining oil, along with ginger, garlic, coriander stems and chilli, and stir-fry for 3 minutes, constantly stirring to ensure ginger and garlic do not burn.

Squeeze juice from lemon halves over crayfish, then sprinkle with Sichuan pepper and sea salt, and serve immediately.

Serves 4–6 as part of a shared meal

These primeval-looking shellfish are hard to find outside Asia, so I use crayfish or lobster instead. If you don't feel confident about humanely dispatching live crustaceans with a sharp knife, ask the fishmonger to kill the crayfish or lobster for you when you buy it. Just make sure you cook it soon afterwards.

Steamed Baby Crabs Stir-Fried with Ginger and Spring Onions

6 × 150 g (5 oz) baby crabs
2 tablespoons peanut oil
5 cm (2 in) piece ginger, cut into thin strips
3 spring onions (scallions), trimmed and finely sliced
2 garlic cloves, roughly chopped
2 tablespoons light soy sauce
2 tablespoons finely chopped coriander (cilantro) roots and stems
1 teaspoon brown sugar
½ teaspoon sesame oil

Clean baby crabs by lifting up the top shell and removing the furry grey gills from each side.

Wash crabs well, cut in half widthways and place in a shallow heatproof bowl that will fit inside a steamer basket. Place bowl inside steamer and position over a deep saucepan or wok of boiling water and steam, covered, for 3 minutes. Remove crabs from steamer basket and drain well.

Heat peanut oil in a hot wok until surface seems to shimmer slightly. Add ginger, spring onions and garlic and stir-fry for 1 minute. Add crabs and stir-fry for 30 seconds. Add remaining ingredients and stir-fry for a further minute. Serve immediately.

Serves 4–6 as part of a shared meal

Stir-Fried Razor Clams with Black Bean and Chilli Sauce

1 kg (2 lb) live razor clams or mussels

Black bean and chilli sauce
3 tablespoons peanut oil
5 cm (2 in) piece ginger, cut into thin strips
2 garlic cloves, finely chopped
1 large red chilli, finely sliced
2 tablespoons salted black beans
3 tablespoons shao hsing wine
2 teaspoons brown sugar
2 tablespoons light soy sauce
½ teaspoon sesame oil
⅓ cup water
2 teaspoons brown rice vinegar
2 spring onions (scallions), trimmed and finely sliced

Scrub, de-beard, rinse and drain razor clams or mussels.

Next, make the black bean and chilli sauce. Heat peanut oil in a wok until surface seems to shimmer slightly. Add ginger, garlic, chilli and black beans and stir-fry for 2 minutes. Add shao hsing wine and stir-fry for 30 seconds. Add sugar and allow to caramelise for 10 seconds. Add soy sauce, sesame oil and water and cook for 10 seconds. Lastly, add vinegar and spring onions and stir-fry for a further 30 seconds, then set aside.

If using clams, place them in a shallow heatproof bowl that will fit inside a steamer basket. Place bowl inside steamer and position over a deep saucepan or wok of boiling water and steam, covered, for 3–4 minutes. Carefully remove clams and transfer to a serving platter.

If using mussels, place them in a pot or a wok with 1½ cups cold water. Place over high heat, cover, and steam until shells open – about 2 minutes. As the mussels begin to open, immediately remove from wok with tongs and place on a serving platter.

Drizzle sauce over clams or mussels and serve.

Serves 4–6 as part of a shared meal

Salad of Poached 'Urinating Shrimp'

1 × 750 g (1 lb 8 oz) live crayfish or lobster
1 small cucumber, cut in half lengthways and then into 5 mm (¼ in) slices on the diagonal
3 spring onions (scallions), trimmed and cut into thin strips
½ cup mung bean sprouts
½ cup soy bean sprouts
1 large red chilli, finely sliced
⅓ cup coriander (cilantro) leaves

Dressing
2 tablespoons brown sugar
4 tablespoons brown rice vinegar
2 tablespoons light soy sauce
1 teaspoon sesame oil

Bring a stockpot or large saucepan of water to the boil, then lower in crayfish or lobster and poach for 4 minutes. Remove, drain and allow to cool at room temperature for 1 hour. Cut each crayfish or lobster in half lengthways along its belly, ease meat from shells, then cut into 1 cm (½ in) slices and set aside.

To make the dressing, combine all ingredients in a large bowl. Add crayfish or lobster meat, along with remaining ingredients, toss gently and serve.

Serves 4–6 as part of a shared meal

These primeval-looking shellfish are hard to find outside Asia, so I use crayfish or lobster instead. If you don't feel confident about humanely dispatching live crustaceans with a sharp knife, ask the fishmonger to kill the crayfish or lobster for you when you buy it. Just make sure you cook it soon afterwards.

With our flight back to Australia leaving tomorrow, our attention naturally turns to all we have experienced in China.

When we embarked on the first photography and research trip for this book, each day felt more challenging and greater in scope than the day before. Confronted with so many new sights, sounds, smells, tastes, physical and emotional sensations, we experienced sensory overload. Arriving in southwestern China, I was sleepless with excitement at the prospect of visiting my ancestral village in Guangdong: the place where it all began, the place where my great-grandfather was born – and the place he left for Australia to begin the Kwong family tree, of which I am a part. After spending time there and getting to know my extended family, I came away with a new sense of belonging.

Journeying on, through the breathtaking limestone pinnacles around Yangshuo, I marvelled at the glass-like stillness and serenity of the Li River, and was buoyed by a tangible sense of continuity and community in the charming old town of Lijiang. But the dream-like days I spent in Lhasa were a life-changing experience for me. Aside from being enthralled by the geographical and cultural landscape, I was profoundly moved by the Tibetan people's spirituality and their enlightened views on life and death.

Travelling through the heartland of Chinese civilisation, I found myself overwhelmed by the sheer scale of the Terracotta Army, and awed by seeing such skilled craftsmanship at close quarters. Witnessing the modernisation at breakneck speed of the capital city of Beijing was both heart-wrenching and awe-inspiring. In Shanghai, the co-existence of the old and new was humbling and delightful as we wandered from the gritty, characterful streets of the old city to the chic bars and restaurants along the Bund that have been the salvation of weary travellers over the years.

During our travels we were lucky enough to encounter, and often befriend, many extraordinary people, but the person I learnt most from was Mrs Xu. After spending time at her tea plantation in the hills around Hangzhou, I was impressed by her hard-won inner strength and courage, gained from living through some of the toughest times in China's recent history. In Mrs Xu, I sensed the same pride and pain that I see in so many elderly Chinese people; she seemed to have an indomitable spirit, and a philosophy that no matter what happens to you in this lifetime, you just get up and get on with it.

Chun Lau, who I met in Hong Kong, could not be more different. For me, Chun, who is almost 40 years Mrs Xu's junior, represents the new face of modern China, embracing all that the Western world has to offer while simultaneously maintaining a deep respect for traditional Chinese values. I found his enthusiasm and open-mindedness invigorating.

One of the aspects of my journey I had been eagerly anticipating was the chance to explore authentic Chinese regional cuisine.

Returning to my Cantonese roots was something I had been looking forward to for many years. I was keen to discover whether the steamed fish with ginger and spring onions would taste like the one my mum cooks several times a week, and if the white-cooked chicken would be poached in the same stock. However, on several occasions, I was bitterly disappointed with the food we ate in China, and I found the liberal use of MSG disheartening. Yet, as is often the case here, when I dug below the surface to find out why this was so, my expectations were confounded, and I gained a renewed appreciation of the many factors that have influenced Chinese cuisine.

Although I savoured the freshest rice noodles I have ever eaten here, and was privileged to share some beautifully simple and rustic home-cooked meals using market-fresh vegetables, herbs and spices, I also became more aware of the extraordinary quality of produce I enjoy back home in Australia. The sad reality is that the choking pollution so prevalent in China inevitably affects every part of the food chain.

Much as I enjoyed the elegance and refinement of the Cantonese cuisine I grew up on, with its subtle balancing of sour, salty and sweet flavours, in Chengdu I soon became addicted to the fiery robustness of Sichuanese cuisine, which is all about chilli-heat and mouth-numbing spiciness. I also met my match in the rich, meaty delights of Shanghainese pork dumplings and Beijing's wood-oven roasted duck with pancakes. In Hangzhou, I loved the stories behind the regional specialities. In some respects, Hong Kong is a bastion of Chinese tradition, and the many fine meals I enjoyed there are testimony to this. But, for me, some of the most stimulating times were those spent at the local produce markets throughout China and Tibet, where time and time again I found myself surrounded by people shopping and bargaining, caught up in the zealousness and excitement of seeking out the best and freshest food for their families.

Looking back on everything I have experienced here, I realise that my journey has truly been a feast for all the senses.

Ingredients

Everywhere I go in China, I am always impressed by the capacity to make do with whatever is to hand – and nowhere is this more clearly demonstrated than in the kitchen. In this spirit, you should feel free to make substitutions, depending on what is available and in season.

Bean curd *see* Tofu

Bean sprouts Two varieties of bean sprout are commonly used in Chinese cooking: mung bean sprouts, the familiar cream-coloured bean sprouts grown from soaked dull-green mung beans; and the thicker soy bean sprouts, which are grown from large yellow soy beans. Bean sprouts should be used within a day or two of purchase and are best stored in a paper bag in the refrigerator.

Black cloud ear fungus The beautiful, black, velvety-smooth fungus is crunchy and refreshing in salads, and adds texture to stir-fries and braises. Black cloud ear fungus is also available dried, but I prefer fresh, which is becoming increasingly available.

Black beans *see* Salted black beans

Bok choy One of the most popular, versatile and well-known Chinese vegetables, bok choy has been grown in China for centuries, and is available year-round. It has white or light-green stalks and green leaves with a mild, refreshing, tangy flavour.

Brown rice vinegar Chinese cuisine uses a variety of rice vinegars, some of which can be quite harsh. I like to use naturally fermented brown rice vinegar for its depth of flavour and subtle astringency, but you can use any rice vinegar or even malt vinegar in these recipes – just add a little at a time and taste as you go, so its flavour doesn't dominate.

Brown sugar I like to use brown sugar in my recipes for its rich, caramelly flavour.

Chicken stock *see* Stock

Chillies I use long red and green chillies a lot in my cooking: they are sweet and have a medium heat.

In general the smaller a chilli, the hotter it is, and the seeds are the hottest part – so if you want less heat, de-seed chillies before using them. For my recipes, it's really up to you and your taste buds how many chillies you wish to add.

see also Dried chillies; Pickled red chillies

Chilli flakes These are simply fresh chillies that have been left in the sun to dry and then pounded into flakes. The drying process intensifies the flavour, making dried chilli flakes flavourful and sweet as well as fiery.

Chinese black vinegar Also called Chinkiang vinegar after the place in China where it is made, this dark-brown aromatic vinegar has a low acidity and a malty flavour.

Chinese cabbage Sometimes called Shanghai cabbage or wonga buk, this elongated cabbage has a light, delicate flavour and a crunchy texture.

Choy sum This green, leafy vegetable has narrow stems, oval leaves and tiny yellow flowers. It is slightly bitter, with a mustard-like tang.

Coriander Also known as cilantro or Chinese parsley, coriander looks like flat-leaf parsley but its flavour is unmistakably musky and citrussy.

Cornflour Cornflour or cornstarch gives deep-fried food that essential crunchy coating. In traditional Chinese cuisine, it is also often used to thicken sauces, but I prefer to serve dishes with just their natural juices.

Dark soy sauce *see* Soy sauces

Dried chillies Although less frequently used in other areas of China, these are considered an essential ingredient in many Sichuanese dishes, either whole or ground.

Enoki mushrooms These elegant, thin-stemmed mushrooms are increasingly available in supermarkets and greengrocers.

Extra virgin olive oil I know it is slightly unusual to add olive oil to Chinese food, but because I love the fruity flavour and limpid green colour of extra virgin olive oil so much I just can't resist sneaking it into salad dressings.

Five-spice tofu *see* Tofu

Gai choy Also known as mustard cabbage, this deep-green vegetable has a bulbous core and thick curved stems with coarse, wrinkly leaves. It has a tangy, slightly bitter flavour.

Garlic Always buy the firmest heads of garlic you can find – firmness is an indication of freshness. For many Chinese stir-fries, garlic is roughly crushed with the flat of a cleaver or large knife, rather than being finely chopped or crushed to a paste. Aside from giving the dish a pleasingly rustic appearance, this also reduces the risk of the garlic burning in the intense heat of the wok and turning bitter. Sometimes the cooking oil is simply flavoured by searing a halved garlic bulb in it before adding other ingredients – you may choose not to eat the halved garlic bulb in the finished dish.

Garlic chives Also known as Chinese chives, these look like a more robust version of regular chives, with flat, slender bright-green stems. They are sold in bunches, sometimes with edible flower buds. Yellow garlic chives have slightly thinner leaves, but the same garlicky flavour.

Ginger Always choose the firmest, heaviest ginger roots with smooth, taut skin and avoid any wrinkled-looking pieces, as they will be dry and fibrous. Except for young ginger, which is in season from late summer to early autumn and has very fine skin, ginger should be peeled before use.

Light soy sauce *see* Soy sauces

Lotus root Actually a rhizome, lotus 'root' is ivory coloured, with swellings along its length similar to sausage links and a beautiful honeycomb pattern when cut crossways. As it is grown in ponds, it requires thorough washing to remove any muddy residue. In season, fresh lotus root is available in Chinese supermarkets.

Lup cheong With its chewy texture and salty flavour, this delicious dried pork sausage lends a unique colour, sweetness and richness to a dish. Bacon is a good substitute – although very different in texture, it will still add the right smoky note to a dish.

Lup yook This dry-cured pork belly is available from Chinese butcher shops and Asian supermarkets. It has an earthy, smoky aroma and releases a mouth-watering caramelly, salty-sweet flavour during cooking. Bacon may be used to give a similar flavour.

Mung bean noodles Also known as cellophane noodles, glass noodles and bean thread noodles, these transparent vermicelli-like noodles are made from ground mung beans, and are usually sold dried and tied into small bundles. They need to be soaked in water and drained before use.

Mung bean sprouts *see* Bean sprouts

Mushrooms *see* Enoki mushrooms; Oyster mushrooms; Shiitake mushrooms

Noodles *see* Mung bean noodles; Rice noodle sheets

Oil *see* Extra virgin olive oil; Peanut oil; Sesame oil; Vegetable oil

Oyster mushrooms These cream-coloured, fan-shaped mushrooms have a subtle taste and a silky texture. They are readily available in most supermarkets and greengrocers.

Oyster sauce This thick, light-brown sauce is made from oyster extract, sugar, salt, caramel and flour. Traditionally it comes from fishing villages in southern China, and is used as a condiment as well as in cooking.

Peanut oil Because it can be heated to high temperatures without burning, peanut oil is perfect for stir-frying and scalding. The nutty and toasty flavour heated peanut oil imparts to a dish makes it is a must-have in the Chinese pantry. However, if you are allergic to peanuts, vegetable oil with a dash of sesame oil makes a good substitute.

Pickled red chillies These are whole red chillies that have been pickled in a sugar and vinegar syrup. They are available from Asian supermarkets.

Rice Many first-time visitors to China are surprised to find that rice is not automatically served in restaurants, but is more likely to be offered at the end of a meal. This is because rice is often thought of as a filler, to be consumed only if diners are still hungry after the main dishes have been eaten.

In most Chinese homes, however, rice is always on the table – except in some of the northern regions, where the cuisine centres on a wheat-based repertoire of noodle dishes, pancakes and flatbreads. For perfect steamed rice, I prefer the absorption method. Place 1$^1/_3$ cups jasmine rice in a sieve and rinse under running water until the water runs clear. Combine rice and 2$^2/_3$ cups water in a heavy-based saucepan. Bring to the boil, immediately cover with a tight-fitting lid and reduce heat to as low as possible. Cook, covered, for 10 minutes. Remove saucepan from heat and stand, covered, for 10 minutes. Fluff rice with a fork before serving.

Rice noodle sheets These are made from ground rice that has been mixed with water, starch and peanut oil then rolled into thin sheets and steamed. They are usually sold in 500 g (1 lb) or 1 kg (2 lb) blocks and are normally kept at room temperature in shops. Unless you are going to use them straightaway, they are best stored in the refrigerator, and should be used within 2 days. Although they will go hard in the fridge, they soften again when stir-fried, steamed or added to soups. For rice noodles, simply cut the sheets into strips and separate them carefully.

Salted black beans Also known as fermented black beans, these small soy beans are preserved by fermentation with salt and spices, which gives them their distinctive salty, rich taste and pungent smell. Some people insist on rinsing black beans before use, but I never do.

Sea salt Salt brings out the natural flavours in food and also draws out the moisture in food. I like to use sea salt – simply evaporated sea water – for its purity and natural flavour, as well as its flaky texture.

Sesame oil This amber-coloured oil is pressed from roasted sesame seeds. Used in small quantities, sesame oil adds an aromatic, nutty taste that enhances other flavours.

Shao hsing wine This is the staple cooking wine in China, where it has been made in the eastern province of Zhejiang for over 2000 years. A blend of glutinous rice, rice millet, yeast and water, it is aged in earthenware vessels in underground cellars. Shao hsing deepens, broadens, sweetens and softens dishes, adding complexity of flavour. Dry sherry may be substituted.

Shiitake mushrooms These rich-flavoured mushrooms have brown velvety caps and pale cream stems; they are increasingly available fresh in supermarkets and greengrocers. The stems can be quite tough and so are generally discarded, although they can be used to add depth of flavour to stocks.

Shoyu *see* Soy sauces

Sichuan pepper These hollow reddish-brown 'peppercorns' are actually the dried berries of the prickly ash tree. They are intensely aromatic with a charming woody fragrance, and should always be dry-roasted before use to bring out all their aromatic oils. When eaten they leave a pleasantly numbing, tingly sensation on your tongue, which some find addictive – I can't live without them!

Sichuan pepper and salt
I find this spicy salt irresistible, and use it extensively in my cooking. To make it, dry-roast 1 tablespoon Sichuan peppercorns and 3 tablespoons sea salt in a heavy-based pan and, when the peppercorns begin to 'pop' and become aromatic, take off the heat. Allow to cool, then grind to a powder in a mortar and pestle or spice grinder. This makes about 4 tablespoons; stored in an airtight container, Sichuan pepper and salt will keep for several months.

Soy beans Fresh green soy beans (sometimes called edamame) are hard to find outside Asia, although you might come across them in Chinese supermarkets. They are, however, widely available frozen, both shelled and still in their pods. If using frozen soy beans in their pods, they need to be thawed and shelled before being used in the recipes in this book, but there's no need to defrost ready-shelled soy beans.

see also Bean sprouts; Tofu

Soy sauces This naturally fermented product is made from roasted soy bean meal and usually wheat and then aged. Dark soy sauce is aged longer than light soy sauce and is mixed with molasses, which gives it that dark, caramel colour. Shoyu and tamari are Japanese soy sauces, with shoyu being more delicate and refined and tamari being heavier in weight and richer in flavour. Tamari is available in a wheat-free version, which makes it a great alternative to regular soy sauce for those who are gluten-intolerant. Some inferior soy sauces are full of chemicals, so make sure you buy only naturally fermented ones.

Star anise This beautiful, star-shaped seed pod has a robust, liquorice-like flavour and scent.

Stock Any light chicken or vegetable stock works well in Chinese cooking. In recipes where a small amount of stock is called for, it's fine to use water instead – just make sure you season to taste.

Sugar see Brown sugar; Yellow rock sugar

Tamari *see* Soy sauces

Tofu A very versatile ingredient, tofu has a rather neutral, bland taste, but is a wonderful vehicle for flavour. Silken tofu has a soft, velvety texture and is perfect for steaming or adding to soups, while firm tofu stands up better to stir-frying and braising.

Five-spice tofu is pressed into flat square cakes, and is flavoured with five-spice powder (a variable mixture of 5–7 spices – cinnamon, star anise, fennel seed, cloves, liquorice root, Sichuan peppercorns, ground ginger).

Vegetable oil Cottonseed, canola, soybean, safflower and sunflower oils are perfect for deep-frying as they have a neutral, unobtrusive flavour and odour.

Vinegar *see* Brown rice vinegar; Chinese black vinegar

White radish Also called daikon, white radish has a crisp texture and a mildly pungent, mustard-like flavour.

Yellow rock sugar This sugar tastes both richer and subtler than refined, granulated sugar; it also gives sauces a beautiful lustre.

Resources

Accommodation

Bell Tower Hotel, 110 Nan Dajie, Xi'an; tel +86 29 8760 0000
Fuchun Resort, Fuyang Section, Hangfu Yanjiang Road, Hangzhou, Zhejiang Province; www.fuchunresort.com
Garden Hotel, Nanmenxi Road West, Toishan City, Guangdong Province; tel +86 75 0550 0888
Jian Nan Chun Hotel, 8 Guanyi Street, Dayan, Lijiang; tel +86 88 8510 2222
Nanjing Hotel, 200 Shanxi Road (South), Shanghai; tel +86 21 6322 2888
Paradise Hotel, 116 West Street, Yangshuo; www.paradiseyangshuo.com
The Peninsula Beijing, 8 Goldfish Lane, Wangfujing, Beijing; www.beijing.peninsula.com
The Peninsula Hong Kong, Salisbury Road, Kowloon, Hong Kong; www.hongkong.peninsula.com

Eating and drinking

The China Club Beijing, 51 Xi Rong Xian Lane, Xidan, Beijing; tel +86 10 6603 8855
The China Club Hong Kong, 13th Floor, Old Bank of China Building, Bank Street, Central, Hong Kong; tel +852 2521 8888
Cloud 9 (Ju Fu) Restaurant, 1 West Street, Chengzhong Road, Yangshuo, Guangxi Province; tel +86 773 881 3686
Dafachang Fast Food Restaurant, Bell & Drum Tower Square, Xi'an; tel +86 29 8721 4060
Felix, 28th floor (elevator entrance adjacent to Hankow Road), The Peninsula, Salisbury Road, Kowloon, Hong Kong; tel +852 2315 3188
Fuchun Resort, Fuyang Section, Hangfu Yanjiang Lu, Hangzhou, Zhejiang Province; www.fuchunresort.com
The Glamour Bar, 6th Floor, 5 The Bund (corner of Guangdong Lu), Shanghai; www.m-theglamourbar.com
Huang Ting, The Peninsula Palace, 8 Goldfish Lane, Wangfujing, Beijing; tel +86 10 8516 2888
Huxinting tea house, 257 Yu Yuan Road, Shanghai; tel +86 21 6373 6950
Jing Ding restaurant, 39 Dhongzhimen Nei Avenue, Beijing; tel +86 10 6404 4338
Kin's Kitchen, 9 Tsing Fung Street, North Point, Hong Kong; tel +852 2571 0913
Li Qun Roast Duck Restaurant, 11 Bei Xiang Hutong, Beijing; tel +86 10 6702 5681
Longjing No. 1 Restaurant, 1 Longjing Village, Hangzhou, Zhejiang Province; tel +86 571 8796 4286
Luk Yu Teahouse, 24–26 Stanley Street, Central, Hong Kong; tel +852 2523 1970
M on the Bund, 7th Floor, 5 The Bund (corner of Guangdong Lu), Shanghai; www.m-onthebund.com
The Mill restaurant, 23 Guangyijie Xinyuanxiang, Dayan, Lijiang, Yunnan Province; tel +86 888 511 2722
Nan Xiang Steamed Bun Restaurant, 85 Yu Yuan Road, Shanghai; tel +86 21 6355 4206
O Store Organic Food Market, Aetna Tower, 107 Zunyi Road, Shanghai; tel +86 21 6237 5140
Old Hong Kong Restaurant, 2 Yongninggong Plaza, South Street, Beilin, Xi'an; tel +86 29 8763 3798
Pavilion Restaurant, Liu Gong, Yangshuo, Guangxi Province; tel +86 773 892 2988
Rainbow Restaurant, 1A–1B, 16–20 First Street, Sok Kwu Wan, Lamma Island, Hong Kong; www.rainbowrest.com.hk
Spring Moon, 1st Floor, The Peninsula, Salisbury Road, Kowloon, Hong Kong; tel +852 2920 2888
T8 restaurant & bar, 8 Xintiandi North Part, Lane 181, Tai Cang Road, Shanghai; www.t8shanghai.com
Well Bistro, 32 Xinyijie Mishixiang, Dayan, Lijiang, Yunnan Province; tel +86 888 518 6431
Yang's Fried Dumplings, 54 & 60 Wujiang Road, Shanghai
Yangshuo Cooking School, Chao Long, Yangshuo, Guangxi Province; www.yangshuocookingschool.com
Yellow Door Kitchen, 6th Floor, Cheung Hing Building, 37 Cochrane Street, Central, Hong Kong; www.yellowdoorkitchen.com.hk

Health

For guidelines on travelling at high altitudes, refer to www.familydoctor.org/247.xml, or www.ismmed.org/np_altitude_tutorial.htm for more detailed information.
TCM practitioner: Dr Lily Li, 40 Gui Hua Road, West Street, Yangshuo, Guangxi Province; tel +86 773 881 4625

Art

Hanart TZ Gallery, 202 Henley Building, 5 Queen's Road, Central, Hong Kong; www.hanart.com
XYZ Art Gallery, 4 Jiuxianqiao Lu, Dashanzi 798 Art District, Beijing; www.xyzartgallery.com

Shopping

Old Shanghai Teahouse, 385 Fangbang Middle Road, Shanghai; tel +86 21 5382 1202
Shanghai Tang, Pedder Building, 12 Pedder Street, Central, Hong Kong; www.shanghaitang.com
Zhang Xiaoquan Scissors, 27 Daguan Lu, Hangzhou; tel +86 571 882 3065

Chinese dynasties

Shang: 1600–1050 BC
Western Zhou: 1066–771 BC
Eastern Zhou: 770–221 BC
Qin: 221–206 BC
Western Han: 206 BC– AD 9
Eastern Han: AD 25–220
Period of Disunity: 220–589
Sui: 581–618
Tang: 618–907
Five Dynasties & Ten Kingdoms: 907–960
Northern Song: 960–1126
Southern Song: 1127–1279
Yuan: 1279–1368
Ming: 1368–1644
Qing: 1644–1911

Bibliography

Barzaghi, Subhana, *Wild Grasses and Falling Wattle: Dharma poetry by Subhana* (2006)
Eyewitness Travel Guide to China (Dorling Kindersley, London, 2005)
Kwong, Kylie, *Kylie Kwong: Recipes and Stories* (Viking Penguin, Melbourne, 2003)
Kwong, Kylie, *Kylie Kwong: Heart and Soul* (Viking Penguin, Melbourne, 2003)
Kwong, Kylie, *Simple Chinese Cooking* (Lantern Penguin, Melbourne, 2006)
Leffman, David, Lewis, Simon, and Atiyah, Jeremy, *The Rough Guide to China* (Rough Guides, London, 2005)
Li Po and Tu Fu, *Poems*, translated by Arthur Cooper (Penguin, Harmondsworth, 1973)
Rinpoche, Sogyal, *The Tibetan Book of Living and Dying* (Rider Random House, London, 2002)
Wu Cheng'en (Xuan Zang), *Monkey* (Penguin, Harmondsworth, 1973)

Acknowledgements

This book has been a major undertaking, and I want to thank the many people who have made it possible:

Thank you to my publisher, Julie Gibbs, for your friendship, your creative energy and for helping me and my family through our darkest hour. To my editor, Alison Cowan – your patience, stillness and intuition are sage-like. To my graphic designer Sandy Cull – your artwork is masterful, and I am so privileged to have your veins running through every inch of this book. To Elizabeth Dias and Deborah Brash, for helping to make Sandy's design a reality. To my photographer, Simon Griffiths, for capturing the spirit of China and Tibet through your warm, rich and moving images. To David Leffman, for your expansive knowledge, research and generous assistance.

To Jo Lusby, of Penguin China, for casting her expert eye over the proofs, and to proofreader Caroline Pizzey, indexer Fay Donlevy and senior production controller Sue Van Velsen. Thanks also to Bob Sessions, Daniel Ruffino, Sally Bateman, Frances Bruce and everyone at Penguin.

To Fran Moore, my great friend and wonderful literary agent, and to Jodie Thompson, for assisting with the recipe writing.

Thanks also to Subhana Barzaghi, for generously allowing me to reproduce her beautiful poem, 'Sacred Mountain Home'.

At World Expeditions, thank you to Nick Kostos, Kathy Kostos, Sue Badyari and Rachel Imber. In China, thanks to Su and Helena Pan (Guangzhou), Linda (Cloud 9, Yangshuo), Lily Li (TCM practitioner, Yangshuo), Mei (tai chi teacher, Yangshuo), Pam Dimond (Yangshuo Cooking School), Malcolm (Pavilion, Liu Gong), Cecilia Lu (Peninsula Hotel, Beijing), Laura Lu (China Club, Beijing), Mr & Mrs Lin (Li Qun, Beijing), Walter Zahner and Richard Miller (T8, Shanghai), Mr John (Shanghai Cooking School), Song Yuan (O Organic Farm), Michelle Garnaut (M on the Bund, Shanghai), Mrs Xu (Longjing, Hangzhou), Michael Fuchs (Fuchun Resort, Hangzhou), Sian Griffiths (Peninsula Hotels worldwide), Lamey Chang (Peninsula Hotel, Kowloon), David Tang (Shanghai Tang, Hong Kong), Johnson Chang (Hanart TZ Gallery, Hong Kong), Kin Lau (Kin's Kitchen, Hong Kong), Chun Lau and Big Sister Wah (Yellow Door, Hong Kong). Thanks also to my guides, Arnie (Yangshuo), Joanne (Lijiang), Lily (Chengdu), Rintsen (Lhasa), and especially to Chris Che (Guangzhou, Xi'an, Beijing, Shanghai, Hangzhou and Hong Kong).

To Nell, for your deep friendship, and for being so constantly inspiring.

To all of my staff at Billy Kwong, for your beautiful hard work, energy and support. With special thanks to Kin Chen, for your mindfulness and compassion, and to Hamish Ingham and O'Tama Carey, for caring so much and for your superb cooking skills.

And thank you always to my precious family – Mum, Dad, Paul, Jamie, Ing, Indy, Jyesy and Finny – you mean *everything* to me.

Index

VIKING STUDIO

Published by the Penguin Group
Penguin Group (USA) Inc.
375 Hudson Street, New York, New York 10014, USA
Penguin Group (Canada)
90 Eglinton Avenue East, Suite 700, Toronto, Canada ON M4P 2Y3
(a division of Pearson Penguin Canada Inc.)
Penguin Books Ltd
80 Strand, London WC2R 0RL England
Penguin Ireland
25 St Stephen's Green, Dublin 2, Ireland
(a division of Penguin Books Ltd)
Penguin Group (Australia)
250 Camberwell Road, Camberwell, Victoria 3124, Australia
(a division of Pearson Australia Group Pty Ltd)
Penguin Books India Pvt Ltd
11 Community Centre, Panchsheel Park, New Delhi – 110 017, India
Penguin Group (NZ)
67 Apollo Drive, Rosedale, North Shore 0632, New Zealand
(a division of Pearson New Zealand Ltd)
Penguin Books (South Africa) (Pty) Ltd
24 Sturdee Avenue, Rosebank, Johannesburg 2196, South Africa

Penguin Books Ltd, Registered Offices: 80 Strand, London,
WC2R 0RL, England

First American edition
Published in 2007 by Viking Studio,
a member of Penguin Group (USA) Inc.

1 2 3 4 5 6 7 8 9 10

ISBN 978-0-670-01879-6

Printed in China
Set in Atma by Post Pre-press Group, Brisbane, Queensland
Designed by Sandy Cull, gogoGingko © Penguin Group (Australia)